GW01451469

SUSPENDED EDUCATION

Suspended Education

School Punishment and the
Legacy of Racial Injustice

Aaron Kupchik

NEW YORK UNIVERSITY PRESS

New York

NEW YORK UNIVERSITY PRESS
New York
www.nyupress.org

© 2025 by New York University
All rights reserved

Please contact the Library of Congress for Cataloging-in-Publication data.

ISBN: 9781479821143 (hardback)
ISBN: 9781479821136 (library ebook)
ISBN: 9781479821112 (consumer ebook)

This book is printed on acid-free paper, and its binding materials are chosen for strength and durability. We strive to use environmentally responsible suppliers and materials to the greatest extent possible in publishing our books.

Manufactured in the United States of America

10 9 8 7 6 5 4 3 2 1

Also available as an ebook

In loving memory of I. Leona Kupchik, 1943–2022. I miss you, Mom.

CONTENTS

FIGURES AND TABLES

TABLES

Introduction

Racial Inequality and School Punishment

Marcus is a senior at Benjamin Franklin High School. He is tall, Black, and seventeen years old. He is a good student academically, and he has never been in trouble in school. He is sitting in the second row of his math class doing work at his desk and needs to sharpen his pencil. He stands up to use the pencil sharpener, as students are allowed to do when needed; however, as he approaches the front of the classroom, his teacher, Ms. Stevens, a white woman in her forties, is startled as she sees him standing suddenly so near her. She feels threatened by his presence, even though he explains he is just trying to sharpen his pencil. She gives him an office disciplinary referral, meaning that she sends him to the principal's office for punishment. Marcus objects, telling her that he only wanted to sharpen his pencil, but as he raises his voice to object, he only reinforces Ms. Stevens's perception of him as threatening. The school's interventionist, the staff member designated to respond to disciplinary referrals and assign punishments to students, relies on the teacher's reporting to understand what happened. Knowing that she felt threatened by Marcus as he stood in class and then responded to her with anger, he recommended that Marcus be suspended for two days. The school principal approved the suspension.

This story was told to me a few years ago by Marcus's mother, who is an educator herself.[1] I met her because I was using her classroom to conduct a teacher training session on implicit bias and school punishment on behalf of the American Civil Liberties Union (ACLU) of Delaware. During my presentation, I was summarizing the results of research that shows how students of color, particularly Black male students, are often seen as more threatening or disorderly than white students and, as a result, are at greater risk of school punishment.[2] A white male high school principal in his forties who was attending the session became defensive. He interrupted me, saying, "It's not like we walk around with pitchforks looking for Black students to kick out of school!" He continued to talk about the unfairness of focusing on racial bias in school punishment. He claimed that educators—at least those in his school—approach discipline fairly, and if they give out more punishments to Black students, it is only because those students misbehave more, not because of any racial bias. After listening to his concerns, I tried to explain more about implicit bias and specifically that the concept does not assume anyone carries a pitchfork around, to use his expression. Which is to say that implicit bias is different from explicit bias, when one holds and expresses racist views, since it is unintended and can occur despite efforts to treat students fairly. Implicit bias is nearly universal among people and often hidden, and it is important for well-intentioned educators to be aware of it so that they can recognize it and try to limit its influence. As far as I could tell, it was a productive moment, since it gave me the chance to explain how racial bias seeps into school punishment in subtle ways even when "good" people—people who earnestly wish to avoid racial bias—are deciding on school punishments.

After the session ended, I lingered to chat and debrief with the ACLU staff member who had organized the session and Marcus's mother, who had attended the session. Both of them are Black women and mothers, and each expressed their frustration that school administrators in the session we just finished had tried to deny the fact that race matters in school punishment. Marcus's mother told me about this incident because Marcus was a student in the school run by the principal who had interrupted my presentation in protest. In other words, the very same principal who was adamant that school administrators do not perceive Black students as threatening or unfairly punish them had suspended Marcus for appearing threatening as he stood to sharpen his pencil so he could continue his schoolwork. She shook her head in disbelief as she told the story. Her son was seen as threatening because he was tall and Black, and yet the man who had approved the suspension of her son had fiercely denied that implicit bias exists in his school.

I begin with this illustration for two reasons. One is that it perfectly highlights how racial bias can shape school punishment in ways that are overlooked by those who are doing the punishing. The principal who approved this suspension was adamant that he and his staff would not judge Black male students as threatening because of racial bias—he was offended at my discussion of evidence that this happens in general, without any mention of his school. And yet that is exactly what seems to have happened here.

The second reason is that this incident captures several characteristics typical of school discipline cases. The only aspect of this story that makes it stand out is the hypocrisy of the principal's complaint: the fact that the principal who approved the out-of-school suspension of a student for pencil sharpening while being Black, tall, and male was also adamant that it was unfair to think of school discipline as being shaped by implicit racial bias. Otherwise, the incident is sadly normal. Students are not typically suspended from school for violence, theft, drugs or alcohol, or other serious offenses. They are usually suspended because of disrupting class, disrespecting teachers, violating dress codes, cursing, or other forms of disorderly behavior that are nuisances but put no one in danger.[3] Disciplinary incidents typically begin with a student bothered by something and a teacher without the time, energy, or inclination to work through the problem with the student, and the situation usually escalates from there.

Suspending students from school because of minor misbehavior does not help anyone. Suspensions do not improve the student's behavior, nor do they help the other students in their classes or even their teachers. Instead, suspensions result in students losing instructional time and probably falling behind their peers. Suspensions also mean students go without the care and attention of adults who might be able to help them address the causes of their challenging behaviors. In short, there is a large volume of research that clearly shows that in the majority of cases in which a student is suspended from school, the suspension is harmful; it hurts the student suspended as well as their school, their family, and their community.

From a practical perspective, suspending children for minor misbehavior (which, again, is the most common reason for a school suspension) makes no sense. Minor disorderly behavior is an indicator that a child is having trouble; the trouble could be with other students, it could be a mental health issue, it could be difficulty learning, or it could be something else. Keeping them *in* school, so that caring adults could help address the trouble, would make much more sense if our goal is to foster the learning and well-being of children. Imagine that Marcus was standing up because he was frustrated that he did not understand the work he was trying to do at his desk, and standing up was his way of expressing his frustration. If that were the case, and he was in fact acting aggressively by standing up, it still would not make sense to suspend him from school. Instead, a better response would be to talk to Marcus and try to resolve the issue, such as by providing him some extra help with his math work. In no other context do we say, "Oh, you are having difficulty here, so we will give you *less* of the support you need."[4] We do not respond to seriously ill people by removing medical care or force severely depressed individuals to end psychotherapy, for example.

School suspension also makes no sense if we think about how we respond to children in other institutions, like the family. I have two teenage daughters. They are amazing (I could go on here . . .), but sometimes they can be challenging. Imagine one of my daughters does something wrong; let us say she violates our rules by having a friend over and drinking alcohol while my wife and I are out for the evening. Would it make sense for me to kick my daughter out of the house for a few days? Obviously not. In fact, it might result in a visit from Child Protective Services. So why is it acceptable to temporarily exclude a child from one environment (school) and not another (family)? Both are intended to be sites of caring, teaching, and support. Both schools and parents are required by law to care for children. Obviously the two institutions are very different in many ways. Families are private, whereas schools are public institutions. But the very idea of removing a child from their family because they violate family rules seems ridiculous, whereas it is a daily practice in schools, the public institutions with legal responsibilities to care for children. At school, challenging students are seen as problems to be managed, often by excluding them for periods of time; at home, challenging children are members of the family whom we need to help support.

And yet out-of-school suspensions are very common. The Department of Education's Office of Civil Rights estimates that in 2017–2018, over 2.6 million public school students—more than 5 percent of the student population—were suspended from school one or more times.[5] This figure does not include other punishments, such as in-school suspension, after-school detention, or Saturday school, nor does it include even more severe responses such as expulsion or arrests made at school. One analysis estimates that more than one in ten students born between 1998 and 2000 in large US cities was suspended out of school at least once by age *nine*.[6] Suspensions have declined in recent years, and some jurisdictions have implemented reforms that seek to reduce the use of suspension.[7] But these are reforms of degree, seeking to reduce a harmful practice, not challenge its very use. Furthermore, we still see millions of students suspended each year. While reductions in suspensions are indeed good news, modest improvements in the frequency of the problem do not reduce its importance as a social problem that needs to be understood.

Overall, school suspensions do not make schools safer or more orderly. Students who are suspended are *more*, not *less*, likely to misbehave after their suspensions.[8] And schools with higher suspension rates are no safer than schools with lower suspension rates (but that are similar in other ways).[9] Rather than being a punishment that helps improve student behaviors or prevent others from misbehaving, suspension means a day off. Think of the irony of suspending a student for truancy, which happens frequently! What is worse, research shows that suspensions can be destructive. When used too frequently, they harm school communities and pose many deep and long-term harms to the students who suffer them. And yet schools across the US rely on suspension on a daily basis as a primary response to frustrating (sometimes maddening), but developmentally normal, behavior.

On its face, suspending 2.6 million students in the US in a single year makes no sense. Doing so is ineffective and harmful. In this book, I argue that at its core, the frequent use of exclusionary school punishments—punishments like suspension that remove or exclude students from schools—only make sense if we see these students as *unwanted* in schools. If students were all wanted, we would not remove them from sites of learning and caring when they demonstrate the need for *more* learning and caring, just like we would not exclude a patient from a hospital if the patient's health worsened. In order to understand why students are unwanted, why schools punish students the way they do, and why exclusionary school punishments like suspension are used so commonly across the US, we need to consider our nation's history of racial oppression.[10]

Race and School Punishment

Students of color, particularly Black students, are more likely than white students to be punished at school. Results for Latino/a students tend to show that they are at significantly greater risk of punishment than white students as well, though substantially lower than that of Black students.[11] Study after study has now echoed the consistent finding that Black students are at the highest risk of punishments such as suspension—far higher than the risk faced by white students.

Black and Latino/a students are not the only groups that face increased risk of school suspension. Students who are LGBTQ+, are low income, and have disabilities are also more likely than others to be suspended out of school.[12] While boys are more likely than girls to be suspended, scholars find that the intersection of race and sex is particularly relevant; the gap between Black girls' suspension rates and white girls' suspension rates is much greater than the gap between Black boys' and white boys' suspension rates.[13] Thus, a full picture of the harms of exclusionary school punishment includes the problems faced by multiple groups of students, as several prior studies have shown. In this book, I sacrifice breadth for depth, focusing on the experiences of Black students as they first entered previously white schools and today, in an effort to better understand the roots of exclusionary school punishment. Rather than denying the importance of other students' experiences, my goal is to help explain how a practice that at first was used primarily for Black students has spread to be used for other groups as well.

Much of the research on school discipline looks at and compares the overall rates of punishments faced by Black and white students. Yet some studies go even further by statistically controlling for student behavior and find the same results. This means that even when comparing students with similar rates of misbehaviors, Black students are still more likely to be punished than white students.[14] The evidence is clear and consistent that student behavior does not explain the racial gap in school punishment. Instead, Black students' greater risk of school punishment is because of what schools do. When I discuss this problem with school administrators, they often respond by saying that they have to punish the students who misbehave and unfortunately the Black students in their schools tend to misbehave more frequently. But several carefully designed research studies demonstrate that this is not the case in general. It might seem that way to administrators who do not want to think of themselves as part of a racially biased system, but research clearly shows this assumption to be untrue. The greater rate of suspension among Black students is about how schools respond to them, not just because of any differences in behaviors between Black and white students.

The research on this subject is clear and consistent, with one exception that I can name. In stark contrast to the rest of the research on this topic, a single study found that differences in behaviors among Black and white students explain their different rate of punishment.[15] When the Trump administration's Commission on School Safety studied the issue of school discipline, it relied on this one outlier in its report rather than the overall body of work that consistently presents different findings.[16] Soon after the commission's report was published in 2018, the education scholar Francis Huang reanalyzed the same data used and found that the results were due to a methodological error, and when this error (a sample selection bias) was corrected, these data showed that student behavior does not account for the gap in suspension rates.[17] By relying on the sole outlier study and rejecting what the rest of the research on this topic showed, the commission's findings on this issue were flawed.

The discipline gap between Black students and white students has deep and long-term impacts on students. Students who are punished are at greater risk than others of academic failure, dropping out, and future arrest or incarceration.[18] The fact that Black students are more likely to experience these harms means that their future social and economic opportunities are limited and they fall further behind their white peers. In addition to these direct harms, Black students are also indirectly harmed by high rates of school punishment, since punitive school environments weaken the supports that might otherwise help them. Research shows that school punishment adversely affects academic performance within entire schools, that it creates toxic stress and financial burdens for families of students who are punished, and that it can actually increase levels of student misbehavior and criminal offending.[19]

Yet it is less clear *why* Black students are disproportionately punished in schools. Scholars have offered a few different explanations, though each has important limitations. One argument is that schools serving more Black students are more punitive, in that they dole out punishments like suspension more frequently and for less serious misbehaviors. Schools with larger percentages of Black students are indeed more likely than other schools to use punitive behavior-modification strategies rather than restorative-justice strategies and tend to have higher rates of suspensions than do other schools.[20] These results seem clear and help explain how more Black students come to be punished than white students. But they do not explain why schools serving Black students are more punitive or why we see that Black students are more likely than white students in the same school to be punished.

The idea of implicit racial bias helps us here. "Implicit bias" refers to subconscious stereotypes and racialized views that can affect how teachers and other school staff interpret the behaviors of youth and respond to them differently. Implicit bias is common among even those who view themselves as harboring no racial prejudice, like the school principal who suspended Marcus. School staff may be unaware of their subconscious views, but these views are impactful; often they result in staff viewing the behaviors of Black youth as threatening and defiant and seeing Black youth as potential threats that need to be contained. An excellent study by the psychologists Jason Okonofua and Jennifer Eberhardt illustrates this effect well.[21] The researchers had a sample of teachers read vignettes that described a student who misbehaved in class multiple times and then asked these teachers questions about how troubled they were by the misbehavior and what consequence they felt were appropriate. The researchers randomly varied the name given to the student, alternating between stereotypically white names (Greg or Jake) and stereotypically Black names (Darnell or Deshawn). Everything else about the vignette was the same for each respondent. The results showed that teachers were more troubled by the misbehavior and more strongly preferred disciplinary action when given a Black-sounding name.

Understanding implicit racial bias is indeed helpful in explaining racially disproportionate school discipline. But it does not fully answer the question. Implicit bias may help explain why one student is more likely than another student to be punished, but it does not explain why entire schools (with more Black students) can be subjected to more punitive policies and practices than other schools (with more white students). It also does not explain how or why punitive school punishment practices emerged to begin with—why suspension became so common as the punishment of choice in schools despite being ineffective and even harmful, or why suspension rates of white students are as high as they are, too (even if considerably lower than rates of Black students). Another limitation of implicit racial bias as an explanation for racially disproportionate school discipline is that it assumes that racial bias is implicit, giving a pass to explicitly racist educators. As a white, middle-class male who has had overwhelmingly positive experiences with teachers my entire life, both as a student and as a parent, I tend to view teachers as kind people doing important public service in the face of high stress, high workload, and low pay. But when I have discussed implicit racial bias with parents of those who are most impacted by high suspension rates, low-income students of color, these parents often push back on the concept, telling me that the racism their children face is not all implicit. I appreciate their correction.

Racial threat theory has also been used to help explain the disproportionate school punishment of youth of color. This theory stems from the work of the sociologist Hubert M. Blalock Jr.[22] Blalock argued that as the size of racial/ethnic minority populations grow, white majorities feel more threatened and respond punitively in an effort to maintain political and economic control. Scholars have applied this theory to schools by testing whether schools with larger populations of students of color are more punitive than others.[23] This explanation helps to explain why schools with more youth of color punish students more severely, but it is limited in a few important ways. One is that its predictions have to do with policies or school-level practices, not case-by-case variation in how policies are applied, so it does not help us understand how students within the same schools are more or less at risk of punishment on the basis of their race or ethnicity. A second is that it predicts a curvilinear relationship, meaning that it assumes that punishments would be harsher as the population of Black students increases to a point, but that increasing the population of Black students beyond that point would mean less punitive treatment (i.e., a tipping point, after which larger Black populations mean less punishment). In other words, fully integrated schools would be most punitive, and segregated schools with all or almost all Black students would be less punitive. Yet most studies do not test for a curvilinear relationship, finding only that more Black students equates to harsher punishments.[24]

School suspension has become normative. It is a commonly accepted, rarely questioned response to student misbehavior—a practice that would seem harmful, irresponsible, and neglectful in some contexts but is accepted as an everyday necessity in school. A more complete explanation of racially disproportionate school punishment should take into account how suspensions have become normative—how it came to be that kicking kids out of school is a common response to real and perceived (like Marcus's) student misbehavior, despite the fact that it is harmful to students and schools and contradicts the school's very mission (i.e., to educate). But neither of the current common explanations, implicit bias or racial threat, do so.

Explaining School Punishment

Perhaps part of the reason why we do not have a good explanation for why students of color are punished more frequently and severely than white students is that we do not really know why schools punish the way they do in general. We know a lot about the ineffectiveness, harmfulness, and racially disproportionate application of school punishment, but not why schools across the US suspend so many students. Criminologists who study this issue tend to agree that school punishment has become more intense and more common since the early 1990s or so, but offer few details on either the timing or cause of these changes. The most compelling analyses are those that identify other changes in society, primarily to the criminal justice system and macroeconomic changes, and argue that these broad social shifts also result in harsher school punishments. This kind of *add on* explanation (i.e., where we add on school punishment as another outcome explained by these broader social shifts) does not do justice to the important and unique position of public education in contemporary society.

The legal scholar Jonathon Simon's book *Governing through Crime* is an excellent example. Simon's goal is to explain the rise of contemporary security and criminal justice policies and practices, most notably mass incarceration. He argues that the collapse of a New Deal style of government occurred in the 1960s, marked by decreasing trust in government. Politicians needed new ways to garner public support for their positions, so they turned to the War on Crime. By highlighting citizens' potential for being victims, politicians could mobilize fear and garner public support for a range of policy agendas. This new style of governance resulted in a massive expansion of incarceration rates, private security (e.g., gated communities and home security alarms), concerns about drug use, and so on. One chapter of Simon's book addresses schools and how increasingly tight security and harsh punishment in schools are an illustration of how these social and political processes (the same ones that caused mass incarceration) have broad impacts on society. He describes exclusionary school punishments as part of the range of "technologies of exile" that remove offenders from communities; prison is the hard end of this range of technologies.[25]

In my 2010 book *Homeroom Security*, I borrow from and extend Simon's analysis to think more about the changes specifically to school security and punishment since the 1990s. I argue that people feel insecure and anxious about schools, generally. They fear problems like declining test scores and our children losing an educational battle to children from other nations, as well as concerns about teachers' unions perceived to be greedy and inflexible and fears over school shootings, among others. Strategies like stationing police officers in schools and zero-tolerance policies promise to help "right the ship," to provide structure and discipline to school environments perceived as unstable and failing. Thus, like Simon, I have suggested that policy makers responded to public insecurity and fear with more police control and punishment in schools.[26]

In these accounts, schools serve as an example of how criminal legal system trends regarding policing and punishment are also seen in other institutions. Several scholars have tried to explain the late twentieth-century trend toward mass incarceration.[27] Simon's and my prior work suggest that school punishment has also changed because the same crime-control logics that gave rise to mass incarceration are also found in schools.[28]

Others have focused more on macroeconomic or political economy trends. These accounts suggest that contemporary school security and punishment are part of a shift toward neoliberalism in society broadly. Here, neoliberalism refers to ways that a market-based logic has come to govern all sorts of institutions, resulting in increasing accountability for people with relatively little power in organizations, increasing demand for standardized performance measures, and bureaucratic rules and procedures that limit discretion of individual sites. These trends are perfectly captured by the landmark 2000 education bill No Child Left Behind, which mandated high-stakes standardized testing for all schools and tied funding (and even a school's continued existence) to test scores.[29] But they are also seen in zero-tolerance policies, which require standard punishment (without a principal's discretion) for any violation of a broad rule.[30]

In other words, prior explanations by criminologists for why contemporary schools punish students the way they do look to broader criminal justice and economic trends and argue that schools have responded in parallel ways to the same pressures and ideas. Yet schools are unique institutions that have an enormously important role in society. While they certainly are shaped by criminal justice and macroeconomic trends, they have unique pressures and norms shaping them. At the risk of being overly dramatic, I would argue that schools are the central, most direct location where most residents interact with government. School boards are elected by the public, and those elections are often the most local elections with the most public input. Education is required by law, meaning that residents are required to participate in public schooling unless they find an alternative (private schools, home school). Schools are where we send our children every day and whom we entrust with our children's safety and enrichment. They are where our children learn future social roles or where they are socialized into being community members, workers, and citizens. They are where our children learn how to manage and conform (or not) to expectations of authorities. Schools also have a central role in the American ideal of self-reliance, given that most "pick yourself up by the bootstraps" notions of individuals' potential for success start with an education. Schools are impactful on our lives and in the public sphere in ways that are entirely unique from the criminal legal system or other institutions. If school punishments have changed in ways that have enormous consequences for schools, students, and communities as many observers have argued, should we not be able to explain this in a way that does not just piggyback on explanations for changes in other, very different, areas like incarceration?[31]

If we look beyond criminological research, we still see a similar limitation, in that exclusionary school punishments are not adequately explained. In a recent and excellent account of changing school punishment over time, the education scholars Campbell F. Scribner and Bryan R. Warnick describe the evolution of school punishment from early American schoolhouses to today. Their focus is on the philosophy of punishment, or meanings of school punishment, and how schools shifted from enforcing moral standards (what they call punishment) to behavior-management strategies (what they call discipline).[32] As the field of education became professionalized in the twentieth century, it also became specialized.[33] Scribner and Warnick describe how suspensions arose because teachers began to specialize only in teaching, outsourcing discipline to school administrators, who then excluded students. This account is important, for it explains how the context of education resulted in changing practices; but it still does not explain why students were excluded from schools rather than punished (or disciplined) in other ways that might also have fit within an increasingly professional educational sphere. Again, we are left with the question,

Why use suspensions as an everyday response, given that they fail to improve students' behaviors, while causing so many other problems?

Existing explanations of school punishment also do not focus sufficiently on the problem of racial inequity. The increase in school punishments has not affected all students equally—far from it. But when we focus on broader social trends toward punitive control or neoliberalism, we invoke general ideas that, in this case, are applied to all members of society and move away from explanations centered around racial control. One of my biggest regrets of my earlier work, particularly my book *Homeroom Security*, is the use of a race-neutral framework for understanding why we punish students the way we do, which is a very racialized problem.

In this book, I take a different approach by relying on a structural race perspective, as it helps explain contemporary school punishment. The authors of the article "The New Jim Crow in School" define structural racism as "the interlocking constellation of institutional policies and practices and individual beliefs and behaviors, developed over at least 400 years that fabricated, and continues to fabricate, a racialized hierarchy that maintains the social and economic dominance of those with lighter skin color over those with darker skin color."[34]

The sociologist Eduardo Bonilla-Silva's theory of racialized social systems is an excellent example of a structural race perspective. Bonilla-Silva and other scholars use this perspective to describe how race is a fundamental organizing principle of US society.[35] Historical racist beliefs and practices have shaped institutions in ways that privilege white populations' interests and maintain a racial hierarchy, with these historical effects shaping present social configurations as well. As a result, racism is baked into entire social systems in ways that may be hidden or appear race neutral; it is embedded in how institutions like schools work and in commonsense understandings of how they operate.

Critical race theory (CRT) is another illustration of a structural race perspective. Critical race theory became a political football in 2020, eliciting anger mostly among people who have little understanding of what it is.[36] It is a collection of ideas and writing that describes and explains the impact of racialized processes and racism in society. It began in the 1970s out of concern that progress toward racial equality via the civil rights movement had stalled. The central idea behind CRT is that racism is normal—that it is embedded throughout society and is often unseen or accepted without critical reflection. Further, racism is permanent, since social progress that appears to support racial equity occurs only in ways that benefit the interests of dominant groups (i.e., white people) and maintain a racial hierarchy.[37]

As I illustrate throughout this book, a structural race perspective is helpful because it can explain how schools today are shaped by the enduring legacy of historical racial inequity in education and how racial inequity still thrives in schools despite apparent progress such as school desegregation. It does so by paying attention to how laws, policies, and institutions like schools are structured in ways that maintain an unlevel playing field and how the current state of unequal education is informed by historical inequality. A structural race perspective acknowledges the role of individual agency, such as how individual teachers might be biased in how they evaluate or punish students. But it focuses primarily on the social systems in which these individuals work and how broadly experienced social norms and institutional processes teach and can encourage bias.[38]

School Segregation

The denial of educational opportunities to Black children is hardly a new problem. It dates as far back as do African Americans, since enslaved people were typically forbidden from learning to read or from any other formal education—unless such skills were required for the work demanded of them.[39] Daring to learn to read would often be punishable with violence, even death, as slave owners sought to keep enslaved people illiterate as a way to facilitate violent oppression and prevent organized rebellion.[40]

After emancipation, Jim Crow segregation meant that many schools would not accept Black students, limiting their educational opportunities to learning in segregated and inferior schools. As W. E. B. DuBois and many others have described, the education that Black children were provided under Jim Crow included inferior facilities, watered-down curricula, out-of-date and inferior materials, and teachers paid far less than white teachers teaching in white schools.[41] Black children might have had to travel many miles to attend a one- or two-room schoolhouse, when a modern and large school dedicated to white children might be nearer their homes. In Delaware, the state where I live, for example, before 1950 there was only a single public four-year high school, in its largest city, Wilmington, to serve Black students in the entire state.

The landmark 1954 *Brown v. Board of Education* Supreme Court decision offered hope of better educational opportunities for Black youth. *Brown* was a part of a coordinated strategy—it was a key piece of the multidecade strategy of the National Association for the Advancement of Colored People (NAACP) to end racial segregation. When the NAACP Legal Defense Fund, with lead attorney Thurgood Marshall, won in *Brown*, the Court ruled that schools must desegregate but delayed ruling on how schools should do so. In a subsequent decision known as *Brown II*, the Court required that desegregation must occur with "all deliberate speed."

This vague, subjective timeline provided opportunity for school districts to delay and resist desegregation, which they did.[42] Several states passed laws that maintained segregation, such as forbidding local school boards from desegregating or prohibiting use of state funds for desegregated schools, while district court judges were often reluctant to override the barriers to desegregation erected by state legislatures. In 1965, more than ten years after the *Brown* verdict, less than 1 percent of Black students in Alabama, Arkansas, Georgia, Michigan, and South Carolina attended a school with any white students.[43] Resistance to implementing *Brown* should probably be unsurprising, given that almost all southern members of Congress signed onto a "Southern Manifesto" in 1956 denouncing the *Brown* decision. Formally known as the "Declaration of Constitutional Principles," the manifesto was signed by nineteen US senators and eighty-two representatives, all from former Confederate states. It called on citizens to push back against what it called "judicial overreach" and a "violation of states' rights" by resisting school desegregation.

In the 1968 *Green v. New Kent County* decision, a full fourteen years after *Brown*, the Supreme Court demanded an end to delays in desegregation by requiring that school boards affirmatively eliminate all traces of school segregation.[44] The Office for Civil Rights within the Department of Housing, Education, and Welfare put some teeth behind the mandate by suing school districts and/or eliminating their state funding if they maintained policies of segregated schools. Though formal, legal educational segregation was dismantled, critical scholars have demonstrated continued segregation since, both within and between schools. Much has been written about this continued segregation between schools, as school catchment-area boundaries and residential segregation combine to limit true racial integration in schools. While it is often referred to as "de facto" segregation, meaning that it is not the result of laws that require segregated schools, scholars have criticized this term for portraying it as by chance or by individuals' decisions, when in reality it is the product of educational, residential, banking, and other practices and policies.[45] One recent analysis finds that schools today are more segregated than in the previous decades; the typical white student goes to a school that is 69 percent white, and more than 40 percent of Black and Latino/a students attend a school in which eight of ten students are students of color.[46] According to the writer Jonathan Kozol, educational segregation is so extreme that as of 2005, we had "apartheid schooling in America."[47]

Racial segregation occurs within schools as well. Researchers have consistently noted how academic tracking, the process of separating students into academic groups according to their perceived ability levels, tends to result in white students and students of color being separated into different classes within the same school.[48] A recent analysis in North Carolina that spans twenty years of data shows that as segregation across schools declined over time, segregation within schools increased. The report authors estimate that 40 percent of all racial segregation that occurs within the state of North Carolina is within schools, not between schools.[49] Like the problem of racial oppression broadly, the problem of racially segregated schools has not gone away.

School Punishment and the Legacy of Segregation

My central argument in this book is that these two areas of concern—school punishment and racial segregation—are closely related. School punishments are shaped by a legacy of battles over racial segregation fought decades ago and that, in different form, continue today. School suspension, the most common exclusionary school punishment, became common in large part because it was a legal way to exclude unwanted Black students from previously white schools.[50] In the decades since desegregation was first contested, school suspension became institutionalized as schools' primary response to student misbehavior. It still has the effect of continuing racial oppression and denying educational and life opportunities for Black Americans, even if it affects some white students as well. In making this argument, I follow a structural race perspective and scholars who illustrate ways in which racial oppression finds new forms when old practices are dismantled. As Bryan Stevenson says, "Slavery didn't end. It evolved."[51]

Certainly, racial conflict and resistance to desegregation were not the only forces that shaped school punishment. As Scribner and Warnick demonstrate, long-term trends in the professionalization and growing bureaucratization of school systems encouraged exclusionary responses to student behavior rather than the use of corporal punishment.[52] Other forces were at work as well, such as whites' reactions to the migration of Black Americans northward in search of jobs, the civil rights era (including its victories and resulting conflicts and violence), opposition to the Vietnam conflict, government-assisted white flight from urban areas, Watergate, and many others.[53] The 1960s and '70s were certainly a time of great upheaval and change in US society, and many of these events altered how Americans understood the limits, trustworthiness, and responsibilities of government.[54] They may have shaped how we both punish and educate children as well.

Further, the entire terrain of school punishment was redrawn by a nationwide shift in the 1990s toward the use of exclusion. The 1994 Gun Free Schools Act in particular has been discussed extensively in prior analyses. This legislation required a "zero tolerance" approach to students who bring weapons or drugs to schools, with a mandatory one-year expulsion of any student who brings a gun to school. While the act was limited with regard to the scope of student behaviors it addressed, it was important for providing a template for using exclusion as a solution to student behavior problems. Schools across the US received the message and created zero-tolerance policies that resulted in suspensions for a wide range of student behaviors.[55]

These many and varied forces working simultaneously make it impossible to make definitive causal claims about any single cause of trends in school punishment—such a claim is not my goal in this book. Instead, I demonstrate how exclusionary school punishments fit perfectly as a tool for those who resisted racial desegregation and how this resistance still shapes school punishments today. Resistance to desegregation may not be the only force that shaped school punishment, but it was an important one, for it catalyzed the growth of suspension rates that began decades ago and still affects students. Structural racism thus fueled the problem of school suspensions that we see today, though it is not the only influence on suspension rates. Complex social processes, including punishments, are never reducible to a single cause, particularly since the aggregate outcomes we typically see are the result of so many local battles and histories and individual decision-makers' perspectives. Despite this variation, school suspension came to be seen as a good idea and used frequently because of the hostile response by segregationist whites to the unwanted presence of Black students.[56] Over time, its use grew and spread, in part because of racist responses to Black students' presence in schools and in part because of many other factors, including growing fear and anxiety as well as investment in punishment as a response to a wide array of social problems.

Michelle Alexander's influential 2010 book *The New Jim Crow* is probably the best-known example of work connecting the legacy of systemic racial oppression to contemporary punishment. In it, Alexander describes the changes that occurred in the midcentury US. After the victories of the civil rights era, Jim Crow–style segregation was no longer allowed. It became illegal to discriminate overtly against Black Americans in employment practices, real estate transactions, access to financial capital, and in other ways. New methods were needed to preserve the existing racial hierarchy and protect whites from losing political and economic power at the hands of Black Americans. The response, Alexander argues, was mass incarceration. She describes how a legacy of centuries of racial oppression shaped the criminal legal system to police and punish Black Americans more harshly than whites, resulting in preservation of white supremacy and Black oppression. In other words, racial oppression evolved—once the old Jim Crow practices were prohibited, society evolved to find new ways (i.e., mass incarceration) to oppress Black Americans and maintain advantages for whites.[57]

In the chapters that follow, I describe analyses of nationally representative data on school punishments and historical case studies of two sites: New Castle County, Delaware; and Boston, Massachusetts. Considered alongside what prior scholars have found, particularly with regard to school punishment in the southern US, I conclude that a narrative similar to Michelle Alexander's helps explain the state of school punishment today.[58] After schools across the US were forced to desegregate, they found new ways to exclude Black students with the "discovery" of exclusionary school punishment. The law required that schools must accept Black students, but it allowed schools to kick them out via suspension, which is exactly what started to occur. In this way, white children maintained educational advantages over Black children, whose exclusion from school reflected the fact that they were unwanted to begin with in those schools. Today, suspensions are both frequent and disproportionately given to Black students because of the legacy of racial oppression in the US.

Importantly, I am not arguing that suspensions are always part of an intentional strategy to maintain advantages. Racial oppression occurs not just because of explicit racism—actively believing in white supremacy and acting on this belief—but also because of racialized social systems. Bonilla-Silva explains how racial hierarchies, stereotypes, and racial categorization subtly inform economic, political, and social institutions. As he describes in a recent summary,

> The basis of my theory was that racialization forms a real structure—that racialized groups are hierarchically ordered and "social relations" and "practices" emerge that fit the position of the groups in the racial regime. Those at the top of the order develop views and practices that support the racial status quo and those at the bottom develop views and practices that challenge it. Although "prejudice" is part of the structure of any racialized society, I argued then and still believe today that the analytical crux for understanding racism is uncovering the mechanisms and practices (behaviors, styles, cultural affectations, traditions, and organizational procedures) at the social, economic, ideological, and political levels responsible for the reproduction of racial domination.[59]

One need not knowingly hold explicitly racist views in order to benefit from and help reproduce racial domination. Racism works in subtle, often hidden ways because it is embedded in how social systems, like schools, operate. Schools may be color-blind, in that their policy makers may earnestly wish to produce racially equitable outcomes, but the policies that they roll out tend to rely on racial schemas, or racially biased understandings of students and educational goals, that, in the end, tilt the playing field to give white students an advantage over Black students.[60]

The sociologist Victor Ray provides a theory of racialized organizations that helps us understand how organizations like schools incorporate and further racial social systems. In his article "A Theory of Racialized Organizations," Ray bridges the gap between scholarship that seeks to understand how complex organizations work and scholarship on race and ethnicity. He demonstrates the complex ways in which racial hierarchies guide organizational actions and how the ways that organizations are structured produce and reproduce racial hierarchies. He uses schools' responses to the Supreme Court *Brown* decision to illustrate:

> It is helpful to recall how the schema of segregation was reapplied following the landmark Supreme Court decision outlawing state-sponsored segregation in *Brown v. Board of Education*. Legalized school segregation coupled the racial schema of segregation with school resources to create meso-level structures that entrenched racial inequality. Following *Brown*, segregation did not disappear; rather, the schema of segregation was expressed via organizational resources in new ways, such as tracking programs that internally segregated students and the development of "segregation academies," as White parents enrolled their children in private schools. In the post-*Brown* era, organizational forms shifted as underlying schemas of racial inclusion were paired with emergent organizational resources. Segregation via exclusion was replaced by segregation through unequal incorporation.[61]

Schools, like other organizations, pursue ostensibly race-neutral goals, such as student learning and maintaining order—but they do so in ways that incorporate "racial schemas," or broader scripts about racial hierarchies, that legitimate unequal opportunities for success within the organization and create new opportunities for racial subordination.

In *Despite the Best Intentions*, the sociologists Amanda E. Lewis and John B. Diamond consider how schools reproduce racial inequality in subtle, often hidden ways. They dissect how a "good school"—one that is high performing and values racial integration—still produces racially disparate results. Their analyses demonstrate how a racial hierarchy influences the ways that students are categorized and evaluated, resulting in white students reaping the benefits that the school has to offer. The school's racial sorting mechanisms appear to be nonracial but are influenced by structural inequality, institutional practices and racial ideologies that prioritize the well-being of white students. For example, white parents tend to send their children to this school in part because they value racial diversity, but these same parents then leverage their political power to obtain educational advantages for their children (e.g., placement into advanced academic programs); Black parents tend to have less political power, and as a result, their children, who may be as academically gifted, tend to occupy the lower academic courses.[62]

Recent research by Jessica Dunning-Lozano also illustrates the power of racism in shaping school punishment. Studying a disciplinary alternative school in Texas for students removed from traditional schools, she finds that the school's disciplinary focus is oriented around racist, classist, and sexist tropes. School staff voice these tropes, showing their belief that students of color are lazy and deviant. She states that "the embodiment and internalization of power is structured into a punitive schooling space through the construction of students of color, and secondarily their families, as culturally deficient and therefore in need of punishment and rehabilitation."[63] In the chapters that follow, I show that this not only is true in a school (like the one she studied) for students removed from traditional schools in the present day but has, to some extent, been true in mainstream schools since students of color were admitted into previously all-white schools.[64]

Again, school suspensions may not be an intentional response to school desegregation, but racism need not be intentional to be impactful. It is no longer socially acceptable, as it was in the 1950s, for white parents to voice concern about their children going to school alongside

Black children. They may instead worry about how children from "bad" or "high-crime" neighborhoods will impact their children's schools or voice concern that low-income students will import into their children's schools the problems they see as stemming from poverty. These and other concerns are probably common, given that parents today are more anxious than ever about their children's academic opportunities.[65] Parents with the means to do so tend to make sure that their children receive all academic advantages they can. College admission and eventual job placements are competitive, meaning that the academic advantage received by one child results in relative loss for another child. Thus, white parents' fear of "other" students, and how these other students might erode their children's learning environment, translates into advantages for middle-class white children, even if nobody ever mentions race or ethnicity in the process.

Seeing suspensions as a legacy of racial oppression helps explain why the practice is so widespread. By any objective measure, the frequent use of suspension is bad policy. It fails to improve student behavior, while damaging students, families, and entire school communities. Some students probably see suspensions as a reward or a day off. Further, as I have noted elsewhere, teachers tend to explain student misbehavior as a result of students not understanding academic content of classes; students who are confused by the academic material might act up to escape the classroom, express frustration, or replace their frustration with positive peer attention.[66] The fact that our common response to this problematic behavior is to remove students from school, thus ensuring that they fall further behind academically, simply does not make any sense from a pedagogical or behavior-management perspective. It only makes sense if the students who are suspended are unwanted and unwelcome.

Writing in the 1980s, the political scientist Kenneth J. Meier and colleagues identified the effect of the legacy of resistance to desegregation, calling it "second-generation discrimination."[67] They describe how, in the aftermath of mandatory racial desegregation of schools, schools turned instead to racial sorting practices. By sorting Black students into lower academic tracks and subjecting them to school punishment more frequently and severely than white students, schools were able to make integrated schools more palatable to white families and stem white flight from public schools. They argue that while "second generation discrimination can be viewed as a racist response to desegregation pressures," this discrimination is institutionalized through taken-for-granted practices and norms rather than being a product of explicit bigotry.[68]

The work of Meier and colleagues is extraordinarily helpful, as they raise the very idea that I argue here: as one system of racial oppression ended, another took its place. They state, "The history of black education reveals that each time educational policies are changed, efforts are made to limit the access of blacks to equal educational opportunity. . . . When desegregation was finally forced by a combination of court rulings and administrative actions, some attempt to subvert the policy should have been expected."[69] Indeed, centuries of denial of educational opportunity to Black Americans did not end with *Brown v. Board of Education* or with the decade and a half of litigation that forced desegregation to finally happen. While Meier and colleagues' ideas and conclusions help shape my perspective, their actual research is limited in its impact. One reason why is that their work dates back to the 1980s, preceding an explosion of school suspensions that occurred in the 1990s and reshaped the field of school punishment, making it unclear whether their work still applies. A second reason is that their analyses are narrow; they considered how Black representation (Black teachers, school board members, etc.) shapes academic and punishment outcomes using very limited quantitative analyses, rather than considering how a legacy of resistance to desegregation shapes punishment while accounting for confounding factors or exploring how this process works on the ground in specific sites. In the chapters that follow, I develop this idea with more extensive and recent analyses to describe and support when, how, and why resistance to desegregation fueled school punishment.

Collateral Damage

Though Black students are far more likely than white students to be punished in school, many white students are indeed suspended and some expelled each year. It might seem odd that I am explaining the common form of school punishment—suspension—as a product of racism, if white students are subjected to it as well. Yet I argue that this makes sense given what we know about how racial oppression tends to operate today.

As I discussed earlier, contemporary racism is often color-blind; it operates in ways that appear to be race neutral but that result in reproduction of racial inequality. School suspensions are an excellent example, because they appear to be a response to student behaviors and thus racially neutral. And yet a large body of research shows us how school staff are quicker to view students of color as disorderly, threatening, or blameworthy, and are far more likely to punish students of color than white students who commit the same offensive behaviors. Thus, punishments are disproportionately applied to one group, despite the fact that punishment policies are written and claimed to be carried out in racially neutral ways. We should thus expect almost exactly what we see: punishment of some white students too but less commonly than Black students. If *no* white students were punished, the mirage of color-blindness would disappear quickly, and punishment policies would not be accepted as racially neutral. In *The New Jim Crow*, Alexander makes the same point with regard to white people being caught up in the racialized war on drugs. She states, "If 100 percent of the people arrested and convicted for drug offenses were African American, the situation would provoke outrage among the majority of Americans who consider themselves nonracist and who know very well that Latinos, Asian Americans, and whites also commit drug crimes. We, as a nation, seem comfortable with 90 percent of the people arrested and convicted of drug offenses in some states being African American, but if the figure were 100 percent, the veil of color blindness would be lost."[70]

It is also important to remember that school staff do not typically intend to punish Black students more severely; instead, it occurs because the racialized social system shapes our perceptions and actions in unintended ways. Without intending to be racially biased, they of course punish white students as well, even if school policies are written in a way that directs their concerns more frequently at Black students and their perceptions of Black students lead them to more frequently view them as causing trouble.

Another reason why it is unsurprising to see white students suspended is that this is how policies work. In a recent article, the penologist Ashley Rubin describes the spread of punishment policies. She describes how punitive "legal templates" become institutionalized, meaning that their continued use over time becomes commonly accepted, taken-for-granted practice.[71] Once punishments attain this status at some locations, they become powerful forces, since schools tend to mimic each other's practices. Applied to suspension, Rubin's analysis suggests that what began in the 1960s as a direct and often intentional response to the unwanted presence of Black students became normative, or taken for granted, in some districts and for some students, and then spread to other districts and applied to other students (just not as commonly).

This process is described by the branch of sociological theory known as "neo-institutionalism." Based largely on the seminal work of the sociologists John Meyer and Brian Rowan, this literature describes how the norms and rules that guide institutions like schools are often based on myths, not evidence of efficiency. In other words, institutions latch onto ideas about what practices are best for their organizations, and they pursue these practices regardless of whether they help them meet any formally stated organizational goal.[72] As Meyer and Rowan state,

> That is, organizations are driven to incorporate the practices and procedures defined by prevailing rationalized concepts of organizational work and institutionalized in society. Organizations that do so increase their

legitimacy and their survival prospects, independent of the immediate efficacy of the acquired practices and procedures.

. . . The formal structures of many organizations in postindustrial society . . . dramatically reflect the myths of their institutional environments instead of the demands of their work activities.[73]

Schools are frequently analyzed in this light, including by Meyer and Rowan. Neo-institutionalism describes how school policies that adhere to myths about what *seems* right gain currency and are adopted by other schools. "New math" does not need to actually help students learn math better; it just needs to be perceived as helping. I argue that the same is true of suspending students: it became commonplace and eventually the modal form of school punishment not because it was effective (it is not!) but because it was seen as an appropriate response to Black students entering previously all-white schools.

This set of ideas also helps explain how the use of suspension spread across the US and endured well beyond the years immediately after desegregation. Like other organizations, schools mimic and borrow each other's strategies regardless of whether these strategies are effective at meeting rational goals, because if they do not, they will be seen as deficient or lagging behind their peers.[74]

The sociologist Charles Tilly's concept of "durable inequality" helps explain the consistent use of suspension since its rise over fifty years ago. Tilly focused on how long-term systemic inequalities arise between groups, including racial/ethnic groups, as well as across divisions based on gender, class, age, citizenship, and others. He argued that those who control access to valuable resources reinforce distinctions between groups and then take advantage of these distinctions once they are presumed to be meaningful. One way they take advantage is through opportunity hoarding, or allowing the dominant group priority access to valued resources, especially those that produce additional value.[75] Education is a primary example of such a resource, because access to education can have multigenerational benefits. Once this pattern of unequal access to opportunity is established, it becomes part of how organizations operate and is emulated by others. Tilly writes, "Durable inequality among categories arises because people who control access to value-producing resources solve pressing organizational problems by means of categorical distinctions. Inadvertently or otherwise, those people set up systems of social closure, exclusion, and control. Multiple parties—not all of them powerful, some of them even victims of exploitation—then acquire stakes in those solutions."[76]

These ideas help us understand how a response to racial desegregation of schools in the wake of *Brown v. Board of Education* is felt today and how it impacts schools and students—even white students—across the US. The spread of punishment to white students means that *all students suffer*, not just Black students, despite the fact that resistance to Black students' presence in schools is at least partly responsible for the initial and continued use of suspensions. This resonates with the argument made by the legal scholar Heather McGhee in her recent book *The Sum of Us*: that racism and the legacy of slavery negatively impact whites too, particularly those who would benefit from a stronger social safety net.[77] While I feel strongly that the pursuit of racial equity alone is sufficient to condemn schools' frequent use of suspension, I realize that others may be more interested only in helping their own children—my analyses show that they too should desire school punishment reform, even out of self-interest alone.

Prior Work on Punishment and Racial Exclusion

As I show in the following chapters, empirical evidence supports my argument that school punishment is shaped by the legacy of racial oppression. My argument also fits within existing theoretical approaches to studying both punishment and racial inequality.

My analyses fit perfectly within a structural race perspective, as I described earlier. One type of structural race perspective, critical race theory (CRT), has been used before to make sense of the limited gains achieved by school desegregation efforts. CRT began after the civil rights era and was inspired by scholars who were skeptical of the lasting gains that would come from the civil rights movement and whether a series of new laws and legal decisions could upend centuries of racial oppression. This skepticism extended to the *Brown v. Board of Education* decision, casting doubt on how effective *Brown* would be in equalizing educational opportunities. In fact, one of the founders of CRT, Derrick Bell Jr., predicted the very problem that I am trying to explain in this book: "Whether based on racial balance precedents or compensatory education theories, remedies that fail to attack all policies of racial subordination almost guarantee that the basic evil of segregated schools will survive and flourish, even in those systems where racially balanced schools can be achieved. Low academic performance *and large numbers of disciplinary and expulsion cases* are only two of the predictable outcomes in integrated schools where the racial subordination of blacks is reasserted in, if anything, a more damaging form."[78]

Bell's prescient words help explain why suspension from school came to be a normal daily occurrence in schools across the US years after he wrote them. In his article on "interest convergence," Bell explains that when social progress occurs (as in *Brown v. Board of Education*), including what appears to be progress toward racial equity, it does so only when it is to the advantage of whites.[79] This is precisely what Meier and colleagues describe as well in their analysis of second-generation discrimination. As predicted, school desegregation was slow and faced opposition among whites who did not want to give Black children equal educational opportunities. Once desegregation finally occurred, schools responded by creating special classrooms for "gifted" students that disproportionately included white students, and they started excluding Black students in greater numbers via suspensions. In other words, desegregation was certainly a mark of progress, though in practice it occurred in a way that hoarded opportunities for white students while removing Black students from schools via school punishment.

My argument is consistent with broader ideas about the historical treatment of Black Americans that do not deal specifically with the civil rights movement or education, as well. Consider, for example, Khalil Gibran Muhammad's widely read book *Condemnation of Blackness*.[80] In it, he describes how anti-Black tropes, based on the combination of racism and flawed social science research, created the stereotype of Black criminality. A flawed understanding of crime and criminal justice statistics supported Jim Crow oppression by convincing whites that Black Americans deserved and required punitive treatment. Similarly, the myth of Black students' disorder and disobedience fuels and justifies suspension rates today. Suspension is most commonly given out for low-level misbehavior such as defiance or class disruption; these are also the misbehaviors that produce the greatest racial disparities in who gets punished. And they follow from tropes of Black youths' defiance and misbehavior.

The field of sociology of punishment demonstrates how the methods and frequency of punishment are social products, not objective or straightforward responses to crime or misbehavior. While the field has historically done a poor job of thinking about racial inequity, it does do a great job of looking at how punishment is informed by structural inequality (such as labor-market shifts) and cultural norms. Sociology of punishment scholarship has taught us, for example, that criminal punishments have varied historically based on ebbs and flows in the availability of laborers and based on cultural norms or sensibilities about what punishments are appropriate and for whom.[81] My argument, that school punishment mirrors and reinforces historical patterns of inequality and norms of who is seen to be *deserving* of punishment, is fully consistent with these ideas.

Recent studies on mass incarceration continue this legacy within the sociology of punishment but offer a more micro approach, showing how local contexts and contests shape punishment. Research shows us that in order to understand how a given state punishes criminal offenders in relation to incarceration rates, who is punished, for what offenses, how severely, and so on, we need to understand local issues such as political battles and racial dynamics.[82] These insights clearly apply to the legacy of racial oppression on school punishments; as I show through case studies of New Castle County, Delaware, and Boston, Massachusetts, school districts in which resistance to desegregation was settled by court intervention and student busing subsequently saw higher school suspension rates, particularly for Black students.

While structural racism is not the only influence on suspension rates, it is both an important and a poorly understood one. Excessive school suspension rates cause great harm to students, schools, families, and communities and, in the process, exacerbate racial inequity. And yet no prior research has been able to explain why we commonly punish students in this nonsensical way—how suspensions came to be seen as a good idea to begin with—and why Black students are so disproportionately punished. We need to understand the foundations of harmful punishment more thoroughly if we wish to create lasting school disciplinary reform.

The link between historical structural racism and contemporary school punishment is also important for equity battles outside of schools. This link demonstrates the continuing relevance of historical racial oppression, undercutting color-blind claims that racism is a relic of a past era. It illustrates how schools today replicate a centuries-old pattern of white supremacy.

A recurrent theme in talks and writing by the literary giant and civil rights icon James Baldwin is that both white and Black Americans are harmed by racism and that both Black and white America have much to gain from recognizing and eliminating racial oppression: "Real freedom for 'white' people could come only when the oppressed were free."[83] His words shape how I think about the importance of systemic racism and school punishments today—that this topic is relevant to all Americans, since the harm that comes to students, schools, and communities affects us all. My hope is that by demonstrating how contemporary school practices are based on historical patterns of oppression and how they continue its legacy, my analyses clarify the relevance of systemic racism to all members of society.[84]

Chapter Outline

I use the remaining chapters to flesh out and support the argument I summarize in this introduction. In chapter 1, I consider the historical context of school desegregation and school punishment, as well as prior research on the link between the two. This body of research includes several studies in southern states, where school segregation took on a different form than in the North. These prior studies clearly illustrate a link between desegregation and punishment, showing that punishment, particularly of Black students, rises immediately after desegregation. They therefore establish a precedent for my argument, though they leave many questions unanswered, primarily because many of these analyses are dated and examine only local contexts. Chapter 2 continues by extending these prior studies with a nationwide and contemporary analysis. In this chapter, Felicia Henry and I report on our analyses of nationally representative data showing that schools in districts that were involved in desegregation-related civil rights lawsuits have higher rates of suspensions, particularly of Black students, today. We discuss the substantive results of these analyses and how they establish an empirical link between historical resistance to desegregation and contemporary school punishment.

Having established an empirical connection between resistance to desegregation and contemporary school punishment, I then explain how this comes about in the next four chapters. These chapters report on archival analyses in New Castle County, Delaware, and in Boston, Massachusetts. I chose these sites for a variety of reasons but mostly because they provide illustration of desegregation's impact on punishment in a mid-Atlantic state and in the North, rather than just focusing on the southern US, as much of the research on desegregation and punishment has done. These chapters offer historical evidence to support and flesh out my argument, demonstrating the emergence of school suspensions following highly contested (and much-resisted) school desegregation efforts.

Chapters 3 and 4 report the results of archival research in New Castle County, Delaware. Delaware is an excellent case study: it is a mid-Atlantic state (neither northern nor southern), the most northern state to have de jure racial segregation before 1954, and the site of one of the cases aggregated into the *Brown v. Board of Education* case (in fact, it was the only one of five sites that constituted the *Brown* Supreme Court case in which the plaintiffs won their lower court cases). In chapter 3, I describe what segregated schools in New Castle County looked like before a massive 1978 desegregation effort and the apparent rarity of school suspensions during this time. Chapter 4 then describes the implementation and response to a 1978 judicial ruling that desegregated the county's schools, merging eleven school districts into a single county-wide school district. I draw from evidence I found in state archives, official records, and discussions with civil rights leaders involved in the desegregation effort to tell the story of what happened after desegregation. As the evidence shows us, immediately after desegregation, schools began to suspend students, particularly Black students, at unprecedented rates because of the strain desegregation put on schools and teachers' inability or unwillingness to educate these students.

In chapters 5 and 6, I describe the results of similar research conducted on Boston schools. Having already reviewed prior research from the South and focused on Delaware in the mid-Atlantic, my case study of Boston illustrates the link between resistance to desegregation and school punishment in the North. While Boston schools were not segregated *by law* in the 1950s and 1960s, they were indeed racially segregated and the subject of a bitter legal battle in the 1970s. In chapter 5, I describe what Boston schools looked like prior to the conclusion of this legal battle, when Black and white students attended different schools. Chapter 6 continues the story of Boston schools by demonstrating what happened during desegregation in Boston and how increases in suspensions were one product of massive white resistance to desegregation. This chapter is informed by archival work in Boston, official archived data, and discussions with legal advocates involved in desegregation. As I demonstrate in this chapter, the dramatic resistance to racial desegregation in Boston meant that Black students were unwanted in many schools and were at much greater risk of suspension as a result.

I begin the concluding chapter by summarizing my argument and how the evidence I unveil in chapters 1 through 5 builds a case to support it. I consider what occurred in the years between desegregation and today, how my argument applies to other minoritized groups of students, and how we might be able to do better for our children. In this chapter, I build an argument for why this toxic legacy should be of concern to all parents, all schools, and all policy makers. I conclude by returning to a broader discussion of racial inequality in contemporary society, using the link between historical resistance to school desegregation and contemporary harms to students as an illustration of the importance of this topic today and of the relevance of past injustices to today's problems.

1

"They Just Want the Blacks Out of School"

Punishment after Desegregation

On June 11, 1963, Governor George Wallace of Alabama stood in front of Foster Auditorium at the University of Alabama. The moment is known as his "stand at the schoolhouse door"—Wallace was there to block the enrollment of the university's first two Black students, Vivian Malone and James Hood. Wallace, whose inauguration address included the famous claim of "Segregation now, segregation tomorrow, segregation forever!" stood defiantly while Deputy US Attorney General Nicholas Katzenbach presented a court order demanding the school allow the two students to enroll. Wallace moved only when confronted by the National Guard, who had been ordered by President John F. Kennedy to ensure that the students were allowed to enroll. During the standoff, Wallace used his platform to denounce racial integration as an assault on the "individual freedoms" of Alabama citizens, stated that he was attempting to maintain the "peace and dignity" of the state, and referred to the nation's movement toward a "military dictatorship." Figure 1.1 shows a photo of the standoff.[1] As I think about Wallace's angry rant while standing in the schoolhouse door, I wonder, in what world is someone trying to preserve forced segregation defending "individual freedoms"?

Wallace was trying to defend segregation at the University of Alabama, not in K–12 schools, which are my focus in this book. But his hypocritical rant captures the anger of a white society forced to change by allowing Black students access to white schools. This anger led many people to resist the change demanded by the *Brown v. Board of Education* decision and still shapes school practices today.

FIGURE 1.1. Governor George Wallace of Alabama stands in the doorway to Foster Auditorium at the University of Alabama, attempting to block the admission of two Black students, Vivian Malone and James Hood. (U.S. News & World Report Magazine Photograph Collection, Prints & Photographs Division, Library of Congress)

It was common for Black students to be denied educational opportunities prior to desegregation, particularly in the South, where schools were segregated by law. Given the brutality of oppression through the institutions of slavery and then of Jim Crow laws, this should not be surprising at all. Segregated, unequal schools were not just a reflection of the southern practice of segregation. The roots of this system were much deeper and more pervasive than just having separate schools, as it was based on deeply entrenched systemic racism and white supremacy.[2] Black children were seen as inferior to white children, intellectually and in other ways: less able to learn and less important to educate, particularly given the few career options available to them.[3] It is important to keep this in mind because it reminds us that deeply held beliefs and perceptions have always created and justified educational inequities and continue to do so today. Historical educational inequities were not just about separate school buildings or less per-pupil funding; they ran deeper than that and were felt in the North as well, even where schools were not segregated by law.

Because *Brown v. Board of Education* attacked this unequal system of education, it was enormously important. With this case, the NAACP Legal Defense and Education Fund struck an important blow to Jim Crow, overturning the 1896 *Plessy v. Ferguson* Supreme Court case that allowed segregation on the basis of the presumption of "separate but equal" facilities for African Americans and whites. In *Brown*, the Court ruled that "in the field of public education, the doctrine of 'separate but equal' has no place. Separate educational facilities are inherently unequal."[4] Though this decision was both unanimous and unambiguous, it offered no advice on *when* or *how* schools ought to desegregate. The following year, in what is known as *Brown II*, the Court instructed schools to desegregate "with all deliberate speed."[5] This vague instruction left it open to states and school districts how and when they ought to reshape previously segregated school systems, allowing opportunities for states and local districts to resist the mandate to desegregate.

Resisting *Brown*

A couple of well-documented examples vividly illustrate the public's violent resistance to Black students entering previously all-white schools in the South: Little Rock, Arkansas, and New Orleans, Louisiana. In 1957, the "Little Rock Nine" was a group of nine Black students who had volunteered to attend previously segregated Central High School. Upon arrival, they were turned away by the Arkansas National Guard, which was ordered by Governor Orval Faubus to prevent the Black students' access to their new school. These nine students were unable to attend school until late September, when President Dwight D. Eisenhower intervened by federalizing the Arkansas National Guard. Guardsmen escorted the nine into school and remained at the school throughout the

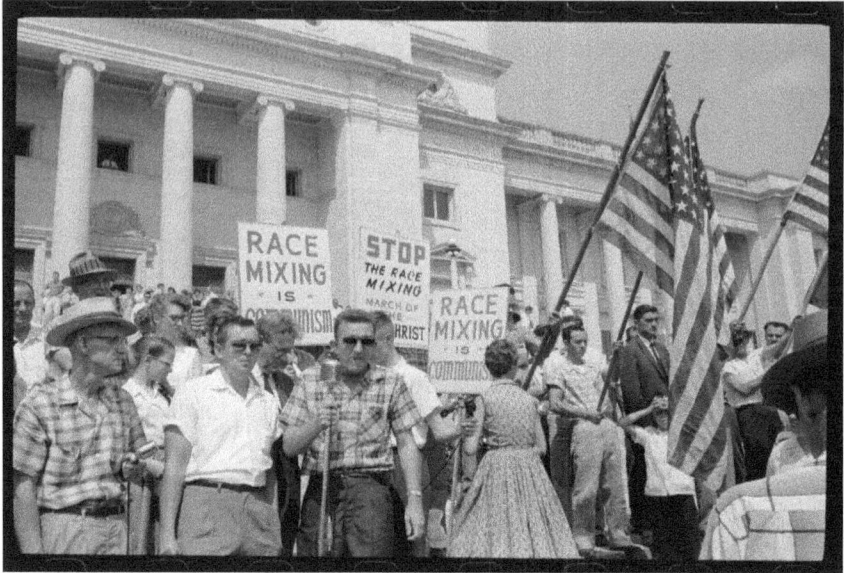

FIGURE 1.2. Little Rock, 1959, rally at state capitol. (LC-U9-2908-15, U.S. News & World Report Magazine Photograph Collection, Prints & Photographs Division, Library of Congress)

school year.[6] They had to walk through angry crowds of white students yelling at them, spitting on them, and threatening to lynch them.

The case of Ruby Bridges is also well known, memorialized in a famous Norman Rockwell painting. In 1960, Ruby and two peers were the first Black students to attend the previously all-white William Frantz Elementary School in New Orleans. Six-year-old Ruby was escorted to school by federal marshals *every day* that school year. On her way in, she had to pass by angry mobs of white people screaming obscenities and racial epithets.[7]

Angry resistance to desegregation was certainly not limited to these famous illustrations, as Black students who led the first wave of desegregation elsewhere, too, were forced to endure picketing, verbal abuse, and even physical violence.[8] But the resistance did not come only from angry white segregationists among the general public. Congressional members from the South expressed their anger through the "Southern Manifesto" that I referred to in the introduction. Its authors—nearly the entire congressional delegation from Alabama, Arkansas, Florida, Georgia, Louisiana, Mississippi, North Carolina, South Carolina, Texas, and Virginia (eighty-two representatives and nineteen senators)—described the *Brown* decision as "unwarranted" and a "clear abuse of judicial power." They framed their complaint in constitutional terms, arguing that neither the Constitution nor the Fourteenth Amendment mentions education. The manifesto stated, "This unwarranted exercise of power by the court, contrary to the Constitution, is creating chaos and confusion in the states principally affected. It is destroying the amicable relations between the white and Negro races that have been created through ninety years of patient effort by the good people of both races. It has planted hatred and suspicion where there has been heretofore friendship and understanding."[9]

The sheer absurdity of this statement, of completely ignoring a history of white terrorism via lynchings and other forms of violence and segregation, while describing race relations in the South during Jim Crow as "amicable" and showing "friendship and understanding," is mind-blowing. While it is true that efforts to comply with the *Brown* decision resulted in protests and even violence, the manifesto ignored the violence of Jim Crow and blamed the disorder on the Court's decision rather than the white supremacist desire to deny Black students access to white schools.

The case of Prince Edward County, Virginia, helps illustrate the lengths to which policy makers and the white public at large were willing to go in order to resist desegregation in the wake of the *Brown* decision. Prince Edward County was one of the five jurisdictions aggregated into *Brown v. Board of Education.* As the sociologist Christopher Bonastia describes in *Southern Stalemate: Five Years without Public Education in Prince Edward County, Virginia,* county officials began to divert funds away from public education immediately after the *Brown II* ruling that schools must desegregate with all deliberate speed. County officials used public funds to create a private educational academy for white students, while eliminating funding for public schools from the county's budget; this administrative sleight of hand required that school funding be approved on a month-to-month basis (since it was no longer written into the annual budget). In 1956, the state assembly passed a law that banned public funding for integrated schools. Then, in 1959, Prince Edward County decided to close its public schools entirely. For five years, all public schools in the county remained closed. The vast majority of white students went to private academies, with tuition for many of them paid for with public funds, while the vast majority of Black students went without any formal education for those five years. This ended only when the federal government intervened by creating a federally funded school system for underprivileged children, run by the US Department of Justice, followed by a 1964 US Supreme Court order that the county must reopen the public schools. The entire county chose to close its public schools for five years rather than desegregate.[10]

Bonastia shows how despite the robust resistance to racial desegregation, it was not explicitly framed as an issue of race. Instead, segregation was defended in color-blind terms. Resisters of desegregation justified their actions by claiming to protect local control of schools, taxpayers' rights, and individual choice. In this way, it bears a striking resemblance to the Southern Manifesto, in which segregation was defended based on constitutional grounds as well as an appeal to the desire for local control of schools. As Bonastia argues, this color-blind defense of Jim Crow provided a template for contemporary resistance to racial equity.[11] It also resembles contemporary efforts by school districts to dismiss racially disparate use of school punishment by claiming that it is both necessary for school safety and a racially neutral response to student misbehavior.[12] In other words, the argument (often used today) that school punishment is administered fairly, given to the students who misbehave the most[13]—despite evidence showing that student misbehavior does not account for disparate rates of school punishment—parallels the arguments given to resist desegregation.[14]

Segregationist academies were another tactic used to resist desegregation across the South. These were private schools open only to white students, which were created during and soon after areas were forced to desegregate. Many were funded with public money, such as in Mississippi, where the state provided a stipend of $240 per student to attend private schools. Religious institutions and banks also facilitated their growth by donating money or space or providing loans to these new academies. Some segregationist academies were clones of formerly all-white public schools, having transported even the prior school's colors, mascot, team name, and student newspaper from the public school that was forced to desegregate to the new segregated school.[15]

Desegregation was resisted throughout the South, not just where schools were closed or where white mobs resulted in armed escorts for Black students.[16] In 1965, eleven years after the *Brown* decision, only 2 percent of Black students in the Deep South attended schools along with white students.[17] A 1967 US Commission on Civil Rights report found that the vast majority of Black students finishing high school in 1967 had never attended a single class with a white student.[18] The 1964 Civil Rights Act empowered the federal government to enforce the desegregation requirement and to withhold funds from school districts that refused to desegregate.[19] Schools gradually rewrote policies to end legal (known as "de jure") segregation. But as schools opened pathways for Black students to enter previously white schools, they tended to do so in limited ways, keeping these pathways narrow and restricting the levels of actual racial integration.[20] One example of this is "school choice" policies that allow families to apply to whichever schools they wish their children to attend. Such policies appear to be fair on their face. But in practice, they are not. Continued racial bias meant that white families' applications were more likely to be approved; preference for sending children to local neighborhood schools meant that residential segregation translated into school segregation; and unequal access to transportation, including school buses, meant that white families had far more flexibility to choose where to send their children. White families were able to use this choice to send their children to schools that were predominantly white.

The problem was not only in the South. In more recent work, Bonastia considers the case of New York City public schools.[21] He finds a consistent and familiar pattern of school board responses to the problem of racial segregation from the 1950s to today: token reforms that appear on their face to be fair but that do little to reduce segregation. As he describes in detail, the New York City Board of Education supported the idea of school integration but was concerned that if it fully integrated its schools, white families would leave the school system. The board responded by creating policies like "open enrollment" and "free choice" that appeared to offer solutions to the problem of segregation but actually did little. Throughout the decades since *Brown*, the board has obstructed actual progress in New York City schools through practices like commissioning studies on the problem of segregation and then ignoring their findings and recommendations, creating school zoning patterns that maintain existing racial boundaries, locating new schools in segregated neighborhoods, and limiting student transfers that would reduce segregation.[22]

It is not just New York. In an analysis of Nashville's experience with desegregation, the historian Ansley T. Erickson illustrates how school segregation is a matter of *policy*, not just a result of individuals' preferences or biases.[23] She describes how educational inequality is not by chance; instead, it is created as a direct result of the actions of politicians and school officials. Decisions on attendance zoning boundaries, how to allocate funds, whose (often, which parents') voices and concerns should be weighed more heavily than others, and where to build new schools, for example, typically favor white families and prioritize their fears about attending desegregated schools.

These patterns continue today. The education scholars Gary Orfield and Erica Frankenberg, for example, clearly illustrate trends in segregation since *Brown*. They describe how southern schools remained 98 percent segregated until the Johnson administration threatened to sue and cut off funds to them following passage of the 1964 Civil Rights Act; after that, the South desegregated rapidly, and it remains the least segregated region of the US. The Northeast, in contrast, has the highest percentage of Black students in schools composed of 90–100 percent students of color. Further, segregation has increased in each region of the US since the early 1990s, in large part because of Supreme Court decisions, like *Milliken v. Bradley* (1974) and subsequent cases, in which the Court overturned desegregation plans and reversed nationwide desegregation policies. In these cases, the Court retreated from its previous stance, arguing that school systems were not responsible for residential segregation across district lines that resulted in school segregation and undermining efforts to actively dismantle the system of racial segregation that characterized schools. Figure 1.3 is a reproduction of Orfield and Frankenberg's analysis of the percentages of Black students who attend segregated schools (i.e., 90–100 percent students of color) by region, over time.[24] In subsequent analyses, they also show that Latino/a students have experienced substantial growth in levels of segregation over time; as of 2011, 43 percent of Latino/a students in the US attended schools with 90–100 percent students of color.[25] Even more recently, the US Government Accountability Office found that 38 percent of K–12 students in the US, about 18.5 million students, attended a "predominantly same-race/ethnicity school," and 14 percent attended "almost exclusively same-race/ethnicity schools" in 2020–2021.[26]

Continued educational segregation is harmful to *all* students, not just students of color. Though research shows that white students' academic achievement is not substantially impacted by integration, they certainly benefit in other ways by being exposed to various life perspectives and experiences. Students of color, and particularly Black students, benefit in many ways from integration. In a recent thorough analysis of data on school segregation and student achievement, the economist Rucker C. Johnson demonstrates the gains made by all students, but particularly

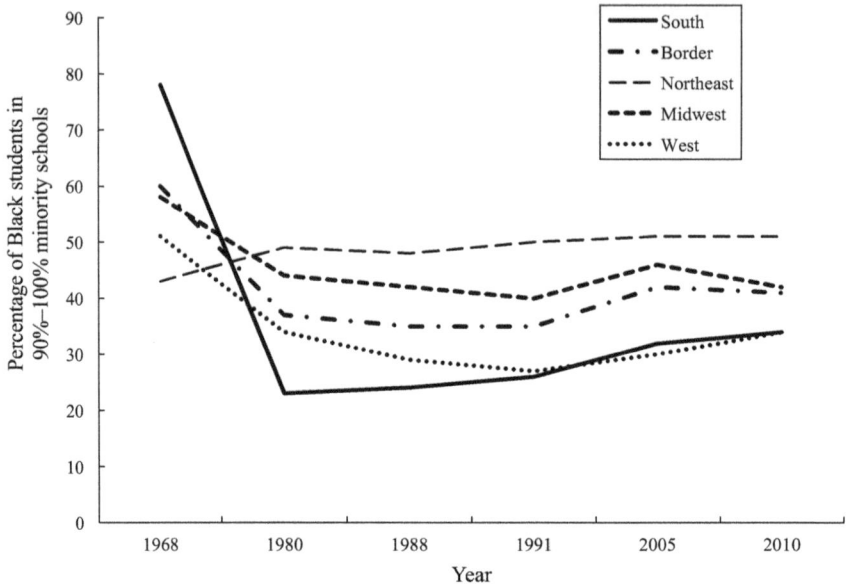

FIGURE 1.3. Percentage of Black students in intensely segregated (90–100 percent minority) schools by region, 1968–2005. (Gary Orfield and Chungmei Lee, *Historic Reversals, Accelerating Resegregation, and the Need for New Integration Strategies* [Los Angeles: UCLA Civil Rights Project, 2007]; Gary Orfield and Erica Frankenberg, "Increasingly Segregated and Unequal Schools as Courts Reverse Policy," *Educational Administration Quarterly* 50, no. 5 (2014): 718–734)

students of color, as a result of desegregation. He shows how desegregation results in increases in per-pupil spending, which itself has many important long-term benefits for students as they continue into adulthood: higher wages, decreases in poverty rates, increases in average family income, increased marital stability, improved health outcomes, and lower incarceration rates. The smaller class sizes and better pay for teachers that come from increased per-pupil spending after desegregation mean more students graduate from high school. Johnson found that these benefits extend to the next generation, since the students who initially benefit from desegregation pass on their advantages to their children.[27] Clearly, desegregation is important for improving the life chances of students while increasing equity of opportunity.

Resistance to Desegregation and School Punishment

Resistance to desegregation was not just demonstrated through protest and continuing racial segregation of schools; it was also seen in rates of school punishment. In 1973, the Southern Regional Council and Robert F. Kennedy Memorial published a study that focused on this problem in the South. Titled *The Student Pushout: Victim of Continued Resistance to Desegregation*, the report was the first widely read study to connect resistance to desegregation in the South to school suspension. The report focuses on the "pushout problem," referring to the problem of students being suspended from school, expelled, or treated so poorly that they choose to escape a hostile environment by dropping out. It directly and explicitly connects exclusionary punishment to resistance to school desegregation: "the pushout problem was widespread and in a large number of cases part of a pattern of continuing resistance to desegregation."[28]

This historic report was based on intensive field research in Georgia, South Carolina, Louisiana, and Arkansas as well as additional research conducted via "University Desegregation Centers" in North Carolina, Florida, Alabama, and Mississippi. It included quantitative analysis of school suspensions in areas that desegregated, as well as interviews and other sources of data. It found that many students who "do not conform," such as "blacks who offend the status quo when brought into a white school majority," are excluded from schools.[29] Black students who were interviewed confirmed that their schools targeted Black students as "troublemakers" and punished them more harshly than white students, particularly as a result of racial conflict. The report states, "Several students complained of discipline resulting from clearly racial motivations on the part of administrators. One said he was suspended for 'talking with a white girl.' Another said he was suspended for 'going with a white girl and sitting and talking with her on the lawn.' A third charged that he was expelled for 'eating lunch on the white side of the lunchroom.' Discrimination, excessively severe discipline and unfair application of authority all drew heavy criticism from students."[30]

One Black student in a Mississippi school who is quoted in the report stated, "Whenever there is a racial disturbance, there are always the blacks who are kicked out. I know of only one time when a white was suspended for fighting. When we had this last racial disturbance and I got kicked out, they gave me 10 days and the white boy didn't get any. Whenever two blacks are fighting each other, both of the students got suspended. Something needs to be done, because it seems to me as though they just want the blacks out of school anyway."[31]

The report's analyses of suspension rates demonstrate increases immediately after desegregation. In Little Rock, Arkansas, for example, there were 500 suspensions of white students and 829 suspensions of Black students in 1968–1969, when they were in separate schools; in 1971–1972, once the schools were desegregated, Black student suspensions nearly doubled (1,504), while white suspensions declined to 377.[32] In Charlotte-Mecklenburg County, North Carolina, suspensions rose from 1,554 in 1968–1969, before desegregation, to 6,652 in 1970–1971, after desegregating. The authors report similar results elsewhere as well.

Not only does this report demonstrate massive growth in suspensions for Black students after desegregation occurred in the South, but it also highlights how Black students are targeted for misbehaviors such as "defiance" and "disrespect."[33] This is still true today; research on racially disproportionate school punishment continues to find that Black students are at highest risk of suspension for the most subjectively defined behaviors, such as defiance of authority. Black students are more likely than others to be misperceived as threatening, loud, or disruptive and to be punished for this subjectively perceived behavior.[34] The *Student Pushout* report concludes, "There is enough evidence to conclude that the use of suspension and expulsion policies for the punishment of infractions of school regulations has greatly increased in many areas in the South over the past several years, and that the increase seems to be directly related to resisting major desegregation."[35]

In the following years, several other studies found similar results that pertain to specific sites, mostly in the South. In a 1978 publication, the education scholar Nancy L. Arnez found that a year after desegregating Jefferson County, Kentucky, schools, Black students were suspended far more frequently than white students, citing a ratio as high as 51.6:1 in one school. This means that Black students in that school were suspended at a rate 51.6 times greater than the rate for white students, immediately following desegregation.[36] Overall, the district's suspension rates increased from 7.9 suspensions per 100 white youths and 17.3 per 100 Black youths pre-desegregation to 16.0 per 100 white students and 69.4 per 100 Black students after desegregation.[37] Arnez quotes a report by the US Department of Justice on Jefferson County Schools, which describes factors that contribute to "complications" following desegregation: "These ingredients are: an unwilling or insincere school administration; parents and other citizens hostile or uncooperative to the desegregation process; principals and/or teachers inexperienced or incompetent, at teaching youth who are neither middle class, nor white. Certainly, some of these ingredients were present in Jefferson County during the first year of school desegregation. . . . Enormous suspension disparities suggest that several of the school principals had little or no experience disciplining minority youth."[38]

In a 1988 article, the sociologists Clarence H. Thornton and William T. Trent analyzed data immediately before and after the 1982 desegregation in Baton Rouge, Louisiana, schools. Contrary to Arnez's findings from Jefferson County, Thornton and Trent did not find a substantial increase in suspension rates overall. However, the *gap* in suspension rates between Black and white students widened post-desegregation. In other words, the school was not suspending more students, generally, but it was focusing punishments more on Black students. Further, when Thornton and Trent analyzed variation within the school district, they found that suspensions rose most after desegregation in the schools that experienced increases in Black student enrollment and that this relationship was even more pronounced in higher-socioeconomic-status schools (i.e., those located in wealthier neighborhoods).[39] In other words, in the most privileged schools before desegregation—those with mostly white, high-income students—the response to Black students' admission was most severe. It is easy to picture these more privileged areas reacting to the admission of Black students with some hostility, exclusion, and fear of what might become of their schools.

Headlined by the report from the Southern Regional Council and Robert F. Kennedy Memorial, several studies were able to examine southern schools by comparing school suspensions before and after desegregation occurred.[40] Each found that Black students were disproportionately punished and that this became much worse after desegregation. Schools that were hostile to Black students' enrollment but were forced to accept them responded by removing many of them through school discipline, often for relatively minor or subjectively perceived behaviors.[41]

Other investigations echo these conclusions, even without the ability to compare suspension rates before desegregation to suspensions immediately after desegregation.[42] Consider, for example, the US district court case *Hawkins et al. v. Coleman et al.*, concerning racially disparate suspensions in the Dallas (Texas) Independent School District.[43] Dallas schools desegregated in 1971 in response to a court order. Though no data on suspensions before desegregation were reported as part of the court opinion, the court noted that the school district began to see the problem of racially disparate suspensions since collecting suspension statistics for 1971–1972, the first year of desegregation.[44] In 1972–1973, Black students made up 38.7 percent of enrolled students district-wide but 60.5 percent of students suspended.[45] The district superintendent, Nolan Estes, testified in the case that "white institutional racism" existed in the district and helped explain the high suspension rate of Black students.[46]

A 1979 article by the education scholar Joe Larkin departed from these other studies by focusing on a northern school district: Milwaukee. Larkin did consider suspension rates in general before and after desegregation, finding not much change initially but a substantial increase in year two. But most of his analyses focused just on the years post-desegregation, because these were the only school years for which the data on suspensions indicated students' race. He found that after desegregation, Black students were suspended at three times the rate of white students and that racial disproportionality in suspension rates was far greater in the schools that had the largest increases of Black student enrollments. Schools that were essentially all white before desegregation and had an influx of Black students showed the greatest levels of racially disproportionate punishment.[47]

Each of these studies addresses school punishment immediately after schools desegregated in specific sites. This focus extended by the mid-1970s, as children's rights advocates became concerned about the problem of racially disparate school punishment on a national level. One report in particular advanced this discussion: *School Suspensions: Are They Helping Children?* by the Children's Defense Fund (CDF) in 1975. This report was based on Office of Civil Rights (OCR) data on 2,862 school districts in 1972–1973, an independent survey of students, interviews with students and educators, and other sources. It documented over one million suspensions in that school year, mostly for relatively minor ("nondangerous, nonviolent") behaviors. The CDF reported that Black students were disproportionately suspended—"at twice the rate of any other ethnic group."[48] Importantly, the CDF concluded that this disproportionate suspension rate was *not* due to different behaviors among Black and white youth and went so far as to state that "Black children often bear the brunt of tensions arising from desegregation."[49]

A September 1974 National Public Radio program, "Options on Education," further illustrates advocates' nascent focus on school suspensions in the wake of the *Pushout* report. Several experts were interviewed on this program, including the director of the OCR, representatives from the Dallas Independent School District, a representative from the American Friends Service Committee, a former chief prosecutor for the Civil Rights Division of the US Department of Justice, and others. Each expert spoke about the problem of disproportionate punishment of Black students. An attorney involved in the Dallas lawsuit I referred to earlier, *Hawkins et al. v. Coleman et al.*, stated, "This is essentially a problem which was begun to be detected in the last 4 or 5 years. It was only this spring that an initial study was released in the student pushout book, which was released through the Robert F. Kennedy Memorial. It essentially found that in school systems that are under desegregation orders or have recently attempted desegregation there seems to be a dramatic rise in the suspension of black students."[50] The director of the OCR likewise indicated that racially disproportionate school suspension was an issue that the OCR had just recently become concerned about; only in 1974 did it start nationwide data collection on school suspensions.[51]

A few contemporary studies continue this line of inquiry by asking whether schools that are currently more segregated have lower or higher rates of racially disproportionate punishment. Two different predictions seem reasonable here. On the one hand, we know that schools with larger populations of students of color tend to be more punitive in general and that students of color are more likely than others to receive these punishments.[52] We might then expect a larger racial gap in school punishment within schools attended mostly by students of color. On the other hand, we know that the introduction of Black students to previously all-white schools decades ago resulted in more school punishment and larger racial gaps in punishment. As I illustrate in my case studies of New Castle County, Delaware, and Boston, Black students were unwelcome in these schools and seen as threats in ways that echo research on implicit bias and other racialized perceptions of students. We might then expect that in schools that are less segregated today, in which sizable populations of Black and white students attend schools together, Black students are singled out for punishment at higher rates.

In one study that explores this question, for example, the sociologists Tamela McNulty Eitle and David James Eitle find that school districts that are more segregated have more *equitable* suspension rates.[53] Their measure of segregation is what is known as a "dissimilarity index"; it captures the proportion of students in the district that would have to move schools so that the schools' racial balance of students mirrors the overall district's demographics. Students in districts with more dissimilarity, or more segregation, have smaller racial gaps in punishment (i.e., smaller disparities in punishment between Black and white students). Other research as well finds similar results, showing that school punishment disparities are greater in schools that are more integrated.[54] My point here is not only that desegregation *was* an important catalyst of rising suspension rates, particularly for Black students, but that it still *is* an important factor for understanding contemporary school punishment, since schools today that are more integrated tend to have worse problems of racially disparate punishments.[55]

The "Discovery" of Suspension

By the mid-1970s, child advocates and education experts showed great concern about the number of students being suspended from schools. The timing of this new concern about school suspensions matters a great deal. On the basis of the few (and somewhat vague) existing historical accounts of school suspensions, the practice first became common in the 1960s. While suspension may have been an option for school administrators before then, all indications are that it was not an option that was used very frequently.[56] As the education scholars Kristen L. Allman and John R. Slate write, "School administrators' use of out-of-school suspension began as a method of reducing student misbehavior in the 1960s and has continued to be used since that time."[57]

Before the 1960s, schools tended to rely on corporal punishment, shaming, or other in-school punishments for students who were seen as disruptive. To a large extent, these practices fell out of favor by the 1960s, as schools became more modern and bureaucratic and students' rights were respected. As the legal scholar Avarita Hanson writes, "With a growing concern for individual rights, school officials in most parts of the country were revisiting school disciplinary measures that largely used corporal punishment coupled with public embarrassment to discipline students. In the larger school populations of the 1960s, corporal punishment was less acceptable and less effective, and into the 1970s school systems began to frequently use out-of-school suspensions and expulsions to rid schools of misbehaving students."[58]

In the book *Spare the Rod*, the education scholars Scribner and Warnick discuss the shift toward suspension as a consequence of the mid-twentieth-century professionalization of educators: hitting children was no longer as acceptable to the new professional class of educators that emerged at that time.[59] The sociologist A. Troy Adams likewise argues that suspension better fit the more modern society and school: "While [corporal punishment] may have been successful with the one-room schoolhouse, it lost its effectiveness with large hierarchically structured schools. The advent of the baby boom, flourishing public educational facilities, swelling school enrollments, and the increased student unrest meant that new disciplinary techniques had to replace the corporal punishment of the past. One of the main practices to which school administrations resorted was the suspension and expulsion of students."[60]

These accounts differ slightly, but they all acknowledge a shift by the 1960s–1970s toward school suspension as a common form of school punishment. The fact that child advocates first began to express concern about the problem of school suspensions in the early 1970s certainly supports these historical accounts of when schools began to suspend students in large numbers.

Whether school suspension replaced corporal punishment is less clear. Corporal punishment has not gone away, since it is still legal in nineteen states today and reportedly used in at least 10 percent of public schools in eight states.[61] Research from the 1970s found that Black students were more likely than white students to receive both corporal punishment and suspensions and that their use was correlated: "schools which utilize high rates of corporal punishment also . . . utilize high rates of suspension."[62] Nevertheless, while it is unclear the extent to which suspensions "replaced" corporal punishment, it is very clear that corporal punishment is used much less today than in the early twentieth century and that suspension became commonly used in or around the 1960s–1970s. The timing of this shift coincides with desegregation. Given the delay in implementing the *Brown* decision, most schools in the US that had been segregated did not begin desegregating until close to 1960 at the earliest—right about the time that schools turned to the practice of suspending students.

By the mid-twentieth century, there was a growing focus on children's psychological health and the need to nurture children that is perhaps best illustrated by the popularity of Dr. Benjamin Spock's influential book *The Common Sense Book of Baby and Child Care*.[63] Corporal punishment no longer fit as well as it had in the past with contemporary child-rearing practices. Many schools decided that they no longer wanted to hit children or have them stand in the corner, since these were no longer acceptable methods, and instead they began kicking kids out of school. But why turn to out-of-school suspensions instead? Certainly, other options must have been apparent to these schools. They could have actually worked with students to correct behavior while keeping them in school, for example. This could have been a moment when schools invested in students' well-being by hiring school counselors who could help students address problematic or disruptive behaviors. It could have been a moment when schools began to work more closely with families to care for children. Instead, it became a moment when schools turned to exclusion, to removing students who were seen as difficult from schools—not helping them, not working with them to address behaviors, not teaching them, but kicking them out. So the relevant question is not whether suspension replaced corporal punishment (the answer to this is unclear) but instead why, once corporal punishment became less popular, schools across the US adopted such an ineffective and harmful policy. Again, I argue that it only makes sense if we see the students who were disproportionately excluded at that time as *unwanted*.

Long-Term Harms of Excessive School Punishment

So far in this chapter, I have argued that resistance to desegregation in the years after the *Brown* case was fierce, at times violent, and impactful. That evidence, mostly from the South, shows that this resistance to desegregation correlates with increased use of school suspensions for Black students in particular, that school suspensions first became prominent during the era of desegregation, and that these problems continue today. These observations set the context for my analyses in the next several chapters, which demonstrate an empirical connection between past resistance to desegregation and contemporary school punishment, as well as help explain how this came to be.

Before moving on, it is important to note the importance of this legacy of resistance to desegregation and its impact on school punishment. Schools' reliance on suspension, particularly for students of color, is a major disruption to the healthy development of young people as well as a crucial source of racial inequity that has multigenerational impacts.[64] A large volume of research considers the current harms of excessive school punishment, most commonly suspensions, on students. This research, often described using the term "school-to-prison pipeline," finds that excessive use of school suspensions harms students, schools, families, and communities.[65]

The most obvious harms come to the individual students who are suspended. Because they are removed from school, they miss out on instructional time, are more likely to be retained (held back) a grade, and are less likely to graduate.[66] But their punishment also labels them as "troublemakers," which can predispose teachers, administrators, and other students to treat them differently.[67] This is probably why studies find that students who are suspended are at greater risk of future school discipline as well as arrest and eventual incarceration.[68] When one considers how each of these hazards—failure to graduate from high school, arrest, and incarceration—can impact one's future job prospects and earning potential, it is clear that suspension harms individual students' futures.

Research also shows that excessive use of school suspension harms entire school communities. Students who attend more punitive schools, including students who are not suspended themselves, tend to have weaker connections to their school and to adults within it and also report higher rates of depressive symptoms than others.[69] When compared to students in schools that are similar in many ways other than their suspension rates, students who have not been suspended but go to high-suspension-rate schools tend to score lower on standardized tests.[70] This is worth restating: frequent use of suspension relates to worse learning outcomes for the students who are *not* suspended as well.

These results make sense when one considers how suspensions influence the all-important school social climate. The term "social climate" refers to students' (and others') sense of belonging, trust, and connections to others. Schools with inclusive social climates are ones in which students feel that they are cared for, listened to, and accepted—these are schools that provide both structure and support for their students, helping them learn and grow in a nurturing environment.[71] But when a school excludes students frequently, particularly if it is in response to minor misbehaviors that cause no threat to anyone's safety (as is typical of most incidents that result in school suspension), that school makes its social climate less inclusive and less supportive. Excessive use of suspension weakens a school's ability to facilitate students' growth and learning—lower test scores, weaker connections to others, and even risk to students' mental health are obvious results.

Families bear the brunt of school suspensions as well. In research based on a series of interviews with parents and grandparents of students who had been excluded from their schools, Thomas Mowen and I found that these families suffered as a result.[72] Much of their suffering was economic, since parents of students excluded from schools were forced to miss a great deal of time at work to pick up their children from the school, attend disciplinary meetings, supervise them while at home, and accompany them back to school. Most of the parents we met worked at fairly low-income, hourly wage jobs and needed to leave work suddenly when the school called. As a result, they lost needed income, and several even lost their jobs. But families also suffered emotionally: many reported how their child's exclusion from school provoked family conflict and even levels of stress that manifested physical symptoms. Some families were even forced to send their children away from home to live with family members in other areas so that they could go to school.

Entire communities are harmed by excessive use of school suspensions as well. In another study, Thomas Catlaw and I found that students who are suspended from school are less likely to vote and to volunteer in their communities fifteen to twenty years later, compared to others who are similarly situated other than their history of suspension. The alienation from civic and community action that can result from school exclusion weakens communities.[73]

These harms demonstrate the enduring racial inequities connected to resistance to school desegregation and the broad importance of the topic. Students of color, and particularly Black students, are at much greater risk of suspension than are white students, meaning that they, their schools, their families, and their communities feel each of these harms more frequently and more deeply than do others. Not only is the benefit of a public education degraded for Black students at several levels, but schools actively contribute to the problem of racial inequality, with long-lasting effects. As the sociologist Mark Warren states in his recent book *Willful Defiance*, the school-to-prison pipeline is "one of the most important mechanisms—if not the most important mechanism—for the reproduction of poverty and lack of power for communities of color."[74] These effects are multigenerational. Young people who are shortchanged a full education are less likely to be able to provide for their children financially.[75] They have less "cultural capital" to bestow on their children, which can put their children at a relative disadvantage in school.[76] They are more likely to burden their families with the pains of incarceration. By catalyzing high rates of school suspensions, resistance to desegregation has continued a multitiered system of education that contributes to ongoing multigenerational inequality. Yes, formal, legal segregation has ended, but its impact continues today, in part because resistance to desegregation shaped school punishment in a way that still today disadvantages Black students, their schools, their families, and their communities.

Conclusion

In the video of Governor George Wallace's stand at the schoolhouse door, his anger is palpable. He was far from alone, as policy makers and citizens resisted school desegregation in ways that were ugly and, at times, violent. Grown men and women protested, yelled racial epithets, and even spit on Black children as they attempted to go to school.

At the start of this chapter, I pointed out the irony of Wallace describing his segregationist effort as protection of "individual liberty." But it is only ironic if we see Black students as human beings whose liberty matters. Clearly, Wallace did not see them as such and was more concerned about the "liberty" of white students to attend an all-white institution if they so choose. The two Black students trying to enroll at the University of Alabama were unwanted by Wallace and his supporters, even if federal courts ruled that the university had to accept them.

This pattern of anger and obstruction was replicated in K–12 public schools throughout the US. The Supreme Court ruled that racial segregation was illegal but did not provide a specific timeline for when schools must desegregate. After more than a decade of schools' delays in desegregation, they were finally forced to act in the late 1960s, right at the same time that schools began to commonly suspend students out of school as a response to real or perceived student misbehavior. This is no coincidence. Researchers and child advocates noticed the connection and drew attention to the fact that immediately after school districts desegregated, they tended to suspend many students out of school, particularly Black students.

Suspending students communicates that they are unwanted in previously white spaces. It is the act of taking the anger of segregationists like

Wallace and redirecting it to a practical end that they desired: removing Black students from schools. And it continues today. When schools
suspend students today, they follow the same blueprint, relying on an
ineffective and harmful practice that removes unwanted students from
school rather than help them or the schools. Wallace's anger is relevant
today, not just in Alabama in 1963.

2

The Legacy of Racial Injustice

Historical Resistance to Desegregation and Contemporary Suspension Rates

WITH FELICIA HENRY

Lucinda Carver is eleven years old. If one can say anything about her, it is that she obeys her mother's orders to the letter. One of her mother's orders is to go to the bathroom before she leaves for school so she won't have to go during class time. Usually Lucinda follows her mother's request. But on one November afternoon, she found herself in the middle of a social studies class needing to urinate. Timidly she asked permission to be excused from the class. The teacher denied her request. Several minutes later Lucinda asked again. The teacher warned her that one more interruption and she would be taken to the principal's office. Fearing an accident, Lucinda rose from her seat and left the room. Upon returning to the classroom the teacher ordered her to report to the principal's office. A three-day suspension followed. The official reason, misbehaving in a classroom and making it impossible for others to pay attention to the teacher.

Rachel, a high school student, left her class to use the restroom but did not return. A school police officer later came in the classroom to collect her belongings. After school, the principal shared that Rachel had in fact been engaged in conversation with him on her way to the bathroom. He recounted that she had "used profanity" in her response to his request about how she was doing that day. He told her to go back to class, after which she told him that she needed to use the restroom. He gave her the option that either she could "go back to class" or he could call the officer to take her home. She chose home. The officer retrieved her belongings, picked her up in his squad car, and drove her to her mother's house. She remained at her mother's house, suspended for the next five school days.

The first of these cases of a student being suspended because she needed to use a bathroom is a quote from the historic 1975 Children's Defense Fund report on school suspensions.[1] The second of these comes from Hannah Carson Baggett and Carey E. Andrzejewski's recent book, *The Grammar of School Discipline*.[2] Despite nearly fifty years separating the two descriptions, in some ways, little has changed. In each, a student is suspended out of school for insisting on using a bathroom and in the process violating a directive to stay/return to class; in each, a student is excluded from school because their bodily need interferes with rigid behavioral expectations. The pattern of school suspension that began in the 1960s and 1970s, as schools were resisting racial desegregation, remains today.

Past battles over race, and particularly battles over racial desegregation of schools, are still relevant today across the US. They were not just immediate, short-lived responses or a problem limited to the South. Instead, these battles laid the foundation for the use of exclusionary school punishment that is still used across the US today. It would be a mistake to assume that the hostile and damaging response to desegregation is limited to the past—that the backlash to desegregation is something that hurt students in the 1950s–1970s but is not relevant to today's schools and students. Instead, resistance to desegregation shaped how educators perceive and respond to student misbehavior in a way that still influences school practice today. School suspension first became popular following desegregation because it was a convenient way to remove students who were seen as problems or who were unwanted by many educators, students, and parents of students in previously all-white schools. But it became institutionalized—suspensions became a taken-for-granted practice that is still today used as the primary response to student misbehavior.

In this chapter, Felicia Henry and I explore this legacy of resistance to desegregation with national-level statistical analyses. Our analyses show that schools in districts in which there were more civil-rights-related lawsuits or government actions suspend more students, particularly Black students, today. In other words, the resistance to desegregation that necessitated legal action left a legacy that is still felt today. If we were to make the mistake of assuming that the racist ideas used to justify separate and unequal Jim Crow schools are solely a relic of the past, something that was fixed when Jim Crow laws were prohibited, then we would blind ourselves to the reality of contemporary school punishments and be unprepared to move forward toward a more equitable and supportive system for all children.

Studying Legacies of Racial Injustice

A structural race perspective reminds us that the legacy of past battles over race shape the present, that racial inequities are embedded deep within social institutions, including schools, and that they do not disappear even when society takes apparent steps toward racial equity. Remember, CRT began soon after the civil rights era, among scholars who recognized the existence of racial inequity despite all the progress made to dismantle Jim Crow. This is because racial inequity is entrenched within social institutions, including schools. Racialized perceptions and patterns of behavior shape institutions like schools in subtle ways that remain hidden unless we make an effort to question why we do what we do.

Consider, for example, school funding. There is no law or policy that explicitly instructs jurisdictions to spend less on average per pupil for schools attended by mostly students of color, compared to schools attended by mostly white students. Such a law or policy would probably be struck down based on the Fourteenth Amendment, which granted all citizens "equal protection under the laws." And yet this is what recent research finds to be the case.[3] This is because schools are funded through local property taxes. Rather than direct full *state* funding for schools, states allow *local* school districts to set their own funding levels, typically collecting this money through property taxes. As a result, areas with more valuable properties (i.e., wealthier areas) have more resources to dedicate to their schools and better school funding. Residents of poorer areas tend to pay much higher tax rates on their properties, but the lower overall values and accumulated wealth in these areas result in less overall funding.[4] Further, low-income areas are more likely to have more tax-exempt businesses, including churches, nonprofit human service organizations, hospitals, and others. In other words, we allow an area's wealth to shape its ability to fund schools, both directly and indirectly. Given the fact that people of color in the US tend to have considerably less wealth than white people do, this means that local school funding tends to be lower in districts where more students of color go to school.[5] States may compensate for inequitable local funding, but often the compensation is insufficient to make up for the gap at the local level.[6]

If we look uncritically at school funding, we might see a race-neutral system that prioritizes local control of schools. But a more critical inquiry shows that the logic at the root of the school funding system is based on a clearly inaccurate assumption of local areas being equally able to fund themselves. Again, poorer areas tax themselves at *higher rates* than do wealthier areas, presumably because they value their children's education so much. But these efforts still leave them at a financial disadvantage.

A structural race perspective, and CRT in particular, can help us make sense of school funding. It would suggest that the system was never designed to actually provide equal funding but only to give the appearance of it. Yes, all students are guaranteed equal protection of the law under the Fourteenth Amendment, which courts have interpreted to mean equal educational provision. This was the basis of the *Brown v. Board of Education* decision. But the devil is in the details, and in practice, schools serving mostly Black students receive less funding, on average, than do schools serving mostly white students. A structural race perspective tells us that racism is embedded within the institution of schooling, and the public at large puts less emphasis and importance on the education of Black students, for whom they might have lower expectations of social and financial success, compared to white students.

It does not require explicit or intentional racism to achieve this differential outcome—the racism embedded in school funding systems makes it happen in spite of constitutional protections and an ostensibly fair funding formula.

To help understand this contemporary problem, a structural race perspective points to the legacy of unequal funding for Black and white students. As NAACP attorneys argued in *Brown v. Board of Education* and as I illustrate in later chapters on New Castle County, Delaware, and Boston, Massachusetts, segregated schools were not funded equally. Current funding inequities may be subtler and less obvious than the racial inequities of school funding in the 1950s. Further, the current disparity in school funding might appear to some observers to be more a matter of community wealth than a matter of systemic racism. But the country's legacy of investing less in the education of Black students—due directly to racist beliefs—suggests otherwise. It suggests that although community wealth matters too, the legacy of racially inequitable school funding impacts current funding.

We can trace the impact of the legacy of racially inequitable treatment on other outcomes as well. In a recent article I wrote with colleagues Geoff Ward, Nick Petersen, and James Pratt, we examined how historical racial violence shapes school punishment today.[7] We considered a specific form of school punishment, corporal punishment, which is still legal in nineteen states, mostly in the southern US. We found that within these states, students—particularly Black students—are at greater risk of receiving school corporal punishments in counties where greater numbers of lynchings occurred between 1865 and 1950. Our analyses account for a large array of school- and county-level factors that might relate to school discipline and help explain rates of corporal punishment, but still, we find a robust effect of lynchings on contemporary corporal punishment. In other words, in counties marred by a legacy of racist violence and terrorism, schools *today* physically beat students, particularly Black students, more frequently than do similarly situated schools with fewer or no lynchings in their past. We interpret these results as demonstrating how past forms of racial violence are embedded in areas and impact how residents of those areas define problems and solutions to those problems. Our analyses show that the United States' history of racial violence is still relevant today—the problems themselves may look different, but the sins of the past shape the problems of the present.

A structural race perspective does not just help us understand corporal punishment and school funding. We could use this framework to analyze contemporary racial disparities in residential patterns, household wealth, employment, incarceration, and so on. With each, we can use a structural race perspective to understand how a history of intentional racial oppression and a deliberately enforced racial hierarchy shape current problems, though in less obvious ways; with each, we see that racial inequity continues today, with subtle racial stereotypes, understandings, and processes resulting in racial gaps despite policies that seem neutral and fair on their face. This is certainly true of school suspension as well. Confronting this legacy of racial oppression may be painful and difficult for some people, but it is necessary to achieve greater equity.

Analyzing How Historical Resistance Shapes Suspensions Today

In collaboration with Felicia Henry, I performed quantitative analyses of nationwide data that span multiple decades to better understand how the legacy of resistance to desegregation impacts school suspensions today. Much like my prior work with Ward and colleagues, we test the relationship between historical markers of racial oppression and contemporary school punishment. A more detailed description of both our research methods and the results of our analyses is in the appendix. In this chapter, we offer an abbreviated version of both, with a focus on their relevance to the broader narrative in this book rather than the technical details.

To do this analysis, we used data from three sources. The first is the Federal Department of Education's Office of Civil Rights (OCR) 2017–2018 Data Collection. All public school districts in the US are required to report data to the OCR on school suspensions and other characteristics of individual schools, such as enrollments, per-pupil expenditures, staffing, and crimes on school campuses. Our second data set consists of US Census data on the racial/ethnic composition of communities that match the school districts surveyed by the OCR. Our third source of data is a data set on desegregation-related court cases and HEW (the federal department formerly known as Health, Education, and Welfare) actions from 1952 to 2002. This data set was assembled and provided by the American Communities Project at Brown University. It includes a list of 3,340 cases, each linked to specific school districts.

Together, these data sources provided us a way to study how the presence of desegregation-related court cases and HEW actions from 1952 to 2002 relate to school punishment in 2017–2018. Certainly, our measure of court cases and government actions is inexact; not only might some cases or HEW actions have been missed, but others would appear multiple times if they were renamed while pending (as was the case in Boston, in which the desegregation case I discuss in chapters 5 and 6 was renamed to correspond to a new head of the school board). To reflect this lack of precision, we use aggregate categories and compare districts with zero cases, one case, and two or more cases. A district would have a value of 1 or 2 on this variable if either of two conditions occurred: (1) lawsuits were filed to open up schools for students of color, or (2) the federal Department of Housing, Education, and Welfare intervened to mandate school desegregation. Given that these both occurred in areas that resisted desegregation, we interpret this variable to indicate resistance to desegregation. We then trace how schools in these same school districts punish students in 2017–2018. Our goal was to test whether a legacy of historical resistance to desegregation shapes the present.

We run statistical analyses to calculate how the number of court cases over a fifty-year span relates to suspensions in 2017–2018. To help ensure that competing explanations are not responsible for the results that we find, we statistically control for several other variables, each of which measures characteristics of schools in 2017–2018. These variables include type of school, age range served, student enrollment, per-pupil expenditures, number of student support staff, rate of students retained, proportion of student body that are white students, and violent crimes in school. We also control for two characteristics of school districts: a measure of intradistrict racial segregation and the percentage of residents within each district catchment area who are identified by the US Census as Hispanic.[8] Finally, we include a variable for region of the country: Northeast, South, Midwest, and West. We use these variables to perform several random-intercept regression models. All of this means that we analyzed the data in a way that lets us assess how resistance to desegregation relates to suspensions today, after taking into account a large number of other potentially important factors, thus helping us to rule out competing explanations of our results (at least those that would be accounted for by the variables we include).

What We Found

Most public school districts (71.2 percent) were not involved in desegregation-related court cases. Of the 95,447 public school districts included in our analysis, 14,370 (15.1 percent) were involved in one court case, and 12,904 (13.5 percent) were involved in two or more. School districts in the South are far more likely to have been involved in court cases. Figure 2.1 shows the number of school districts in each region of the US with zero, one, or two or more identified court cases; 46.6 percent of southern districts were involved in at least one case, a rate far higher than in the Northeast, Midwest, or West.[9]

The timing of court cases varies across region of the US as well, as shown in figure 2.2. Here we illustrate the percentage of school districts in each region that faced a court case (or their first case, if they were involved in more than one) in each of several year ranges. In the Northeast, court cases were fairly concentrated in the early 1960s (1960–1964); in the Midwest, cases were more common in the late 1970s and beyond; in the West, cases are almost all from 1965–1979, peaking in

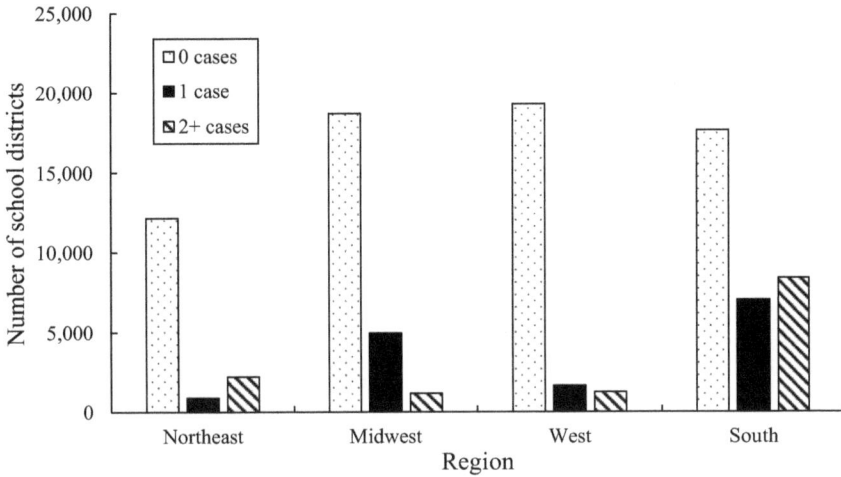

FIGURE 2.1. Desegregation-related court cases, by region.

1975–1979; and in the South, we see that cases began in the 1950s and increased, peaking in the early 1970s. This should not be too surprising—it shows that desegregation was resisted most fiercely and earliest in the South, with resistance peaking in later years farther west and dissipating by the 1980s.

The results of our analyses show that the number of identified desegregation-related court cases from 1952 to 2002 significantly predicts school suspensions in 2017–2018. Schools in districts where there was more litigation have higher rates of suspensions of Black students and more days missed per 100 Black students due to suspension. It is important to note that, as we mentioned earlier, these models statistically control for dozens of school, school district, and community characteristics, factoring out the influence of these other potential causes of suspension rates. Stated differently, our models compare similarly situated schools, comparable in many ways except for their history of resistance to desegregation, in a way that allows us to isolate how court cases relate to school suspensions above and beyond other sources of variation. The results, therefore, are not due to causes such as race/ethnicity of student

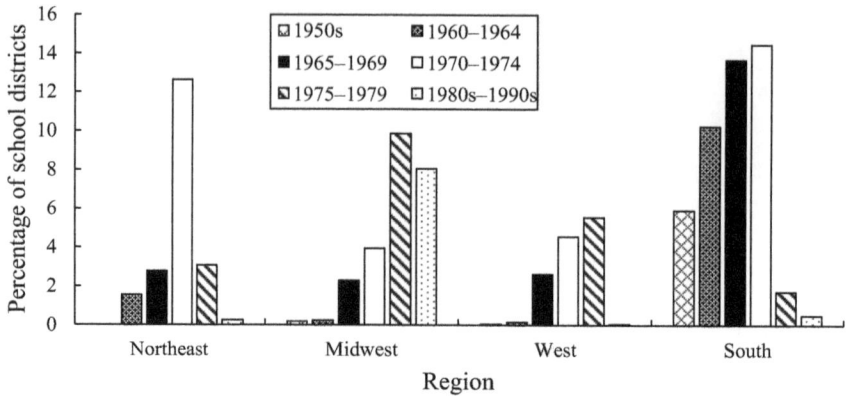

FIGURE 2.2. Timing of first court case in each district, by region.

bodies, school funding, school crime, or any of the many other variables we include, since the models show the estimated effect of desegregation-related court cases after controlling for these other potential causes.

In figure 2.3 we illustrate the relationship between resistance to desegregation and contemporary school punishments by showing the predicted rates of school punishment for Black students in school districts that have different numbers of identified court cases, after controlling for all other variables. As figure 2.3 shows, the predicted suspension rate of Black students goes from a low of 2.6 percent in districts that had no cases to 7.1 percent in districts with two or more cases. The predicted school-wide mean number of days that Black students miss due to suspension (per 100 Black students) is 4.0 in districts with no court cases but goes up to 17.4 in districts with two or more cases.

Other analyses boost our confidence in these results by coming to a similar conclusion. In a recent study, the education researcher Mark J. Chin asks a similar question as we do, seeking to find whether school districts under court-mandated school desegregation orders had higher suspension rates throughout the 1970s and 1980s.[10] Though he uses a subset of cases rather than national-level data and his outcomes end in 1989, his analyses are robust, offering a quasi-experimental approach that provides "the first causal evidence" of the impact that desegregation had on suspension rates. The analyses we have presented here and Chin's analyses complement each other, converging at the same conclusion despite different methodological approaches, years studied, and data used. He finds that suspension rates increased substantially immediately after court-mandated school desegregation, at levels not seen in similar schools that were not under court-ordered desegregation, and that Black students were at particular risk of suspension in these schools. He writes, "In my study, I find that court-mandated school desegregation in the decades following the U.S. Supreme Court decision on *Brown v. Board* led to immediate, sustained significant increases in student suspension rates in integrating districts. These increases were largely concentrated among Black students."[11]

We continue our analyses by exploring whether the impact of court cases varies depending on the timing of cases. In another series of models, we find that having a case (or first case, if there is more than one) in any time period predicts greater rates of suspensions for Black students, compared to districts that had no cases. The strongest relationship is for

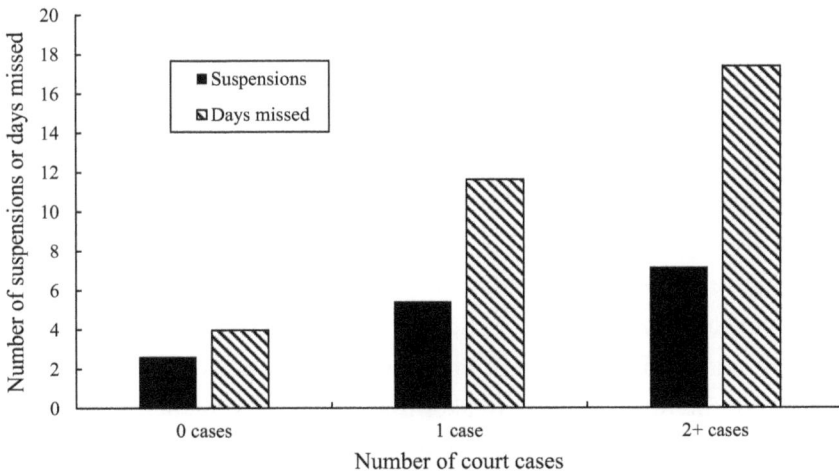

FIGURE 2.3. Predicted percentages of Black students suspended and days missed by Black students per 100 due to suspension.

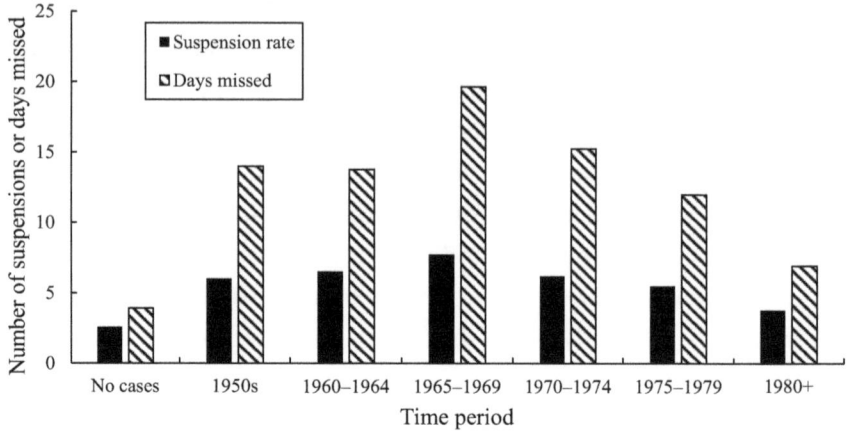

FIGURE 2.4. Predicted percentages of Black students suspended and days missed per 100 Black students due to suspension, by time period.

having a case from 1964 to 1969. Schools in districts with court cases originating after this period have successively lower predicted suspension rates and rates of days missed due to suspensions. In figure 2.4, we graph the predicted suspension rate for schools in districts with a first court case in each year range. While the variation in timing of cases matters, it does not account for the relationship between resistance to desegregation and either Black students' suspension rates or their rates of days missed due to suspensions. In other words, cases initiated in different time periods might have a larger or smaller impact on suspension rates, but across each time period, we form the same conclusion: that historical resistance to desegregation predicts greater use of school suspension today.

In figure 2.5, we offer a contrast by exploring how court cases relate to suspensions of white students. Our models do show statistically significant relationships between litigation and suspensions of white students, but the results are far weaker than the results for Black students. As shown in figure 2.5, the predicted suspension rates are far lower than for Black students, though they are still significantly higher for schools in districts with more desegregation-related litigation. The predicted percentage of white students suspended goes from 2.7 percent in schools whose districts have no court cases to 3.7 percent in schools whose districts have two or more cases. The predicted rate of days missed by white students shows a similar pattern, going from 4.9 days missed due to suspension in schools with no cases to 7.0 days per 100 students in schools with two or more identified cases. When we compare these results to the comparable results for Black students (suspension rates of 2.6 percent if no cases and 7.1 percent if two or more cases), we see that the impact of resistance to desegregation is much greater on punishment rates of Black students. In schools whose districts were involved in no court cases, the predicted suspension rate of white students is slightly higher than that of Black students, but in schools whose districts had two or more cases, the suspension rate of Black students is far higher (7.1 percent versus 3.7 percent).

This last result is compelling but needs to be interpreted cautiously. It does not mean that schools in districts that were never involved in desegregation-related court cases suspend Black students less than they do white students. If one looks at just the bivariate results—that is, before taking any other factors into consideration—we see that in schools across the US whose districts were not involved in any court cases, 7.6

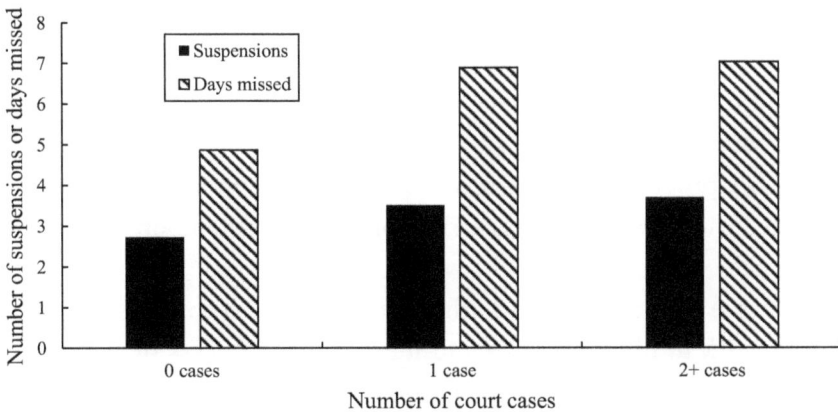

FIGURE 2.5. Predicted percentages of white students suspended and days missed by white students per 100 due to suspension.

percent of Black students were suspended and 3.9 percent of white students were suspended in 2017–2018. In other words, the baseline rate of suspension is much higher for Black students than for white students, mirroring the large number of prior research studies that finds the same result across different locations.[12] The predicted suspension rates shown in the figures we present here are different from these baseline results. Instead of providing the actual suspension rates, they tell us what suspension rates we would expect if all other variables were equal except for the presence of court cases. These predicted rates are therefore a good indicator of how the number of court cases impacts suspension rates, but because all of the variables included in the model are unlikely to be equal across schools, they are less reliable as a measure of overall suspension rates.

Suspensions over Time

Statistical analyses are excellent at seeking out and (where they exist) documenting trends in the data; if done well, they show generalizable patterns for broad areas. But with statistical analyses alone, typically we are unable to flesh out the context underlying these patterns or explain how and why these relationships occur. Here, our statistical analyses demonstrate that across the US, areas of historically greater resistance to desegregation suspend more students today, particularly Black students, and that other characteristics of schools and school districts do not account for this relationship. But they are unable to explain much about the process by which resistance shaped school punishment or how historical resistance has carried forward to contemporary suspension rates.

The case studies I present in the following several chapters do much of the work to fill in this gap and illustrate the process by which resistance to desegregation shaped school punishment in two particular sites. But before moving on, we want to consider what official records can tell us about nationwide suspension rates from the 1970s to the contemporary era. We obtained older data on school suspensions from the Office of Civil Rights. These data allow us to understand how rates of school suspension varied over time and across different schools. Unfortunately, because school districts are not labeled consistently across OCR data sets, we cannot reliably link the data on desegregation-related court cases to the older OCR data on school suspensions. But we can consider how other factors, such as student body race, relate to school suspensions over time. If it is the case that the legacy of resistance to desegregation is felt today in the form of high suspension rates, particularly suspension of Black students, as we argue, then we should expect to see the highest suspension rates in schools with more Black students enrolled. As the criminologists Katherine Irwin, Kay Varela, and Anthony Peguero explain in their discussion of the "racial control model" that they propose for understanding school punishment, "According to our first hypothesis that the racial system will maintain itself, our model assumes that punishment in schools serving mostly students of color is one among many replacements for legal segregation."[13]

In figure 2.6, we look at overall suspension rates from 1974 to 1998 as a function of student body race. More specifically, we divide schools into quartiles based on the percentage of each school's student body that is identified as Black students. This leads to four separate groups: the first-quartile schools have the smallest percentages of Black students, and the fourth-quartile schools have the largest percentages. Figure 2.6 shows that schools with more Black students suspended substantially higher proportions of students. This trend is observed in the earliest data that OCR provides (1974), and it increases leading up to 1998. This is because schools in the fourth quartile—the 25 percent of schools in the US that have the highest concentrations of Black students enrolled—rapidly accelerated their rates of overall suspensions in the 1990s, far outpacing the more modest increase seen in the other three quartiles of schools.

Figure 2.6 illustrates how schools with larger concentrations of Black students tended to suspend more students, compared to schools with

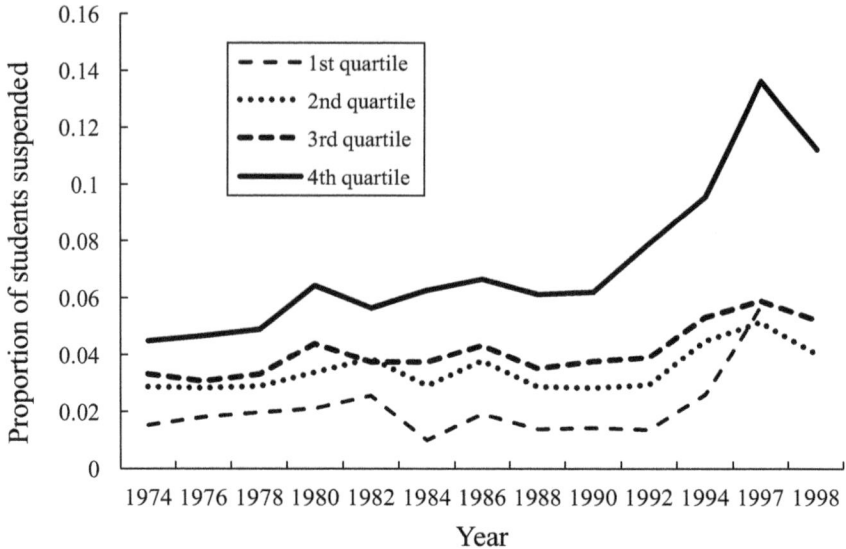

FIGURE 2.6. Mean proportion of all students suspended, by year and student population race (quartiles of proportion Black students). (Author's analysis of data from the Office of Civil Rights, US Department of Education)

fewer Black students in attendance. While some of these "high suspension" schools with large numbers of Black students were probably segregated schools attended by Black students before desegregation, many were also probably schools where Black students arrived after the implementation of *Brown*. Figure 2.6 shows that where Black students attended school after desegregation, suspension rates were high. These results are thus what we would expect if resistance to desegregation fueled a long-term pattern of high rates of school suspension.

The large increase in suspensions during the 1990s is particularly important here. Most prior attempts to understand why schools punish the way they do focus only on this period of time, resulting in explanations about why school punishment increased dramatically, rather than trying to explain why schools adopted the practice of suspension to begin with.[14] During the 1990s, racist fears of juvenile "super predators" dominated policy discourse as schools increasingly "governed through crime" and implemented harsh discipline such as zero-tolerance policies.[15] As figure 2.6 illustrates, the massive increase in school suspensions was concentrated in schools attended by Black students. Schools with the fewest Black students also saw a substantial increase in their rate of suspensions, but they began the 1990s with such a low rate of suspension (less than 2 percent in 1992) that this increase merely caught them up with schools in the second and third quartiles of Black student enrollment, who saw only a modest increase in suspensions during this "get tough" era.

Schools' shift toward harsh school punishment in the 1990s affected all schools; even those with mostly white students adopted new logics and focused much more on security and discipline than ever before.[16] But the rise in suspensions was concentrated in segregated schools attended by Black students. In other words, the practice of school suspension emerged in the 1960s and 1970s as schools desegregated and then became more common in the 1990s, but this growth was particularly felt in schools serving Black students.[17] Stricter codes of conduct and zero-tolerance policies were, on their face, race neutral, in that they did not state that Black students' schools should punish more than others, though this is exactly what happened.

Neo-institutionalism, a theory I discussed in the introduction, helps us understand the continuing use of suspension over the decades. As the theory tells us, institutions like schools often adopt policies because of myths—ideas that support these practices—rather than evidence that these policies are effective or help reach any objective goals.[18] These policies spread across schools, as they become taken-for-granted ways of doing things that are imitated by other schools.[19] Suspending students became a common practice because it was a way to remove unwanted Black students from previously all-white schools. The fact that it was supported by racist myths of Black students' low academic abilities and poor behaviors mattered more than any evidence of effectiveness as a behavior-management tool (there was no such evidence). Over time, it became institutionalized as what schools do and used widely, despite variation in schools' local cultures and climates. The pattern of how suspensions were implemented helped it to become entrenched, as powerful groups such as school boards and administrators used it to hoard educational opportunities and maintain the "durable inequality" between Black and white students.[20]

Conclusion

Lucinda and Rachel, whose stories I tell at the start of this chapter, went to school nearly fifty years apart from each other. And yet their experiences mirrored each other's, as each was suspended out of school for violating the school rules when they needed to use the restroom. Apparently, needing to urinate was as offensive in 1975 as it was in 2021. In this chapter, we use quantitative analyses to help explain how the practice of school suspension has endured over these years.

The data clearly show that a legacy of resistance to desegregation predicts contemporary use of school suspensions. Schools in districts with more desegregation-related court cases or HEW actions in the past have significantly higher rates of suspensions today, particularly for Black students. Importantly, our results control for characteristics such as intradistrict racial segregation, school crime, per-pupil expenditures, and others. This means that the statistical models adjust for these characteristics and report how court cases relate to suspensions after removing the influence of these variables.

We also find that schools with larger concentrations of Black students have consistently maintained higher school suspension rates. This trend is first seen in the first available data, in 1974, and continues today.

These results provide an important piece of the narrative linking historical resistance to desegregation to contemporary school punishment. The fact that we find these results using extensive, nationwide data sets is important. It establishes that the two phenomena—historical resistance to desegregation and contemporary school punishment—are empirically linked. While it is true that school districts everywhere suspend students—and research consistently finds that Black students are at particular risk of suspension—the practice is more common in areas that were sued because of their resistance to racial desegregation. These results are precisely what one would predict based on a structural race perspective since they show how racial inequity is embedded in school systems and has not gone away with apparent progress toward racial equity.

Our analyses add an important component to what scholars have already told us about how desegregation in the South was followed by increased student punishment. Here we extend our understanding by demonstrating that it is not just an immediate effect but a long-term and a national problem as well, since we find that school suspensions are higher in school districts decades after the court battles involving desegregation. Consistent with the title of this chapter, we find that past battles about schools fueled by white supremacy resonate today. These battles are far from a thing of the past, as they have a lasting impact on contemporary school punishment.

Again I need to point out that the effects of this racially inequitable school punishment are multigenerational. The harms caused by kicking kids out of school do not just add up over the years; they multiply. They compound over time, given the reverberations within families and communities and across generations. Children who are denied an education because of resistance to desegregation tend to become parents with lower income and less educational savvy who live in worse school districts. These compounding, multigenerational harms have only grown since the 1970s along with rates of school suspensions.

Our analyses in this chapter offer an important starting point for demonstrating the harmful connection between the legacy of resistance to desegregation and contemporary school punishment. They establish that the connection exists, but they are only one piece of the puzzle because they are unable to explain it. This is a built-in limitation of our analyses, which offer the breadth and power of a historical nationwide view but are unable to explore local dynamics or short-term change. Our statistical models cannot answer the question of *why*; they are unable to explore the local contexts and mechanisms that led to resistance to desegregation influencing school punishment. To answer this question, I turn to case studies of New Castle County, Delaware, and Boston, Massachusetts, in the next several chapters. Considering the specific context and history of the battle over desegregation in each of these locations helps answer the question of *why*.

3

Separate and Unequal

Delaware before Desegregation

> REDDING: You have stated partially—at least you have stated why your
> application was made to the Claymont High School for the admis-
> sion of your daughter. Do you have any other reasons?
>
> BELTON: Yes, I do have some other reasons why I made application.
> To my understanding and my knowledge we are all born Ameri-
> cans, and when the State sets up separate schools for certain people
> of a separate color, then I and others are made to feel ashamed and
> embarrassed, because such separations humiliate us and make us feel
> that we are not as good Americans as other Americans, and I don't
> want my child growing up feeling that she is not as good an Ameri-
> can as any other American, so much so that the school she goes
> to, she has to be separated or set apart to attend a separate, special
> school.

This transcript is from the Delaware Supreme Court case *Belton v. Gebhart* (1952).[1] In it, Ethel Belton describes under oath how school segregation impacts her daughter and other Black students. The plaintiffs in this case were two Black families in Claymont and Hockessin, Delaware, who were challenging the state law that required their children to be bused to segregated Black schools. Belton and her coplaintiff, Sarah Bulah, won their case, which later became part of the *Brown v. Board of Education* Supreme Court case. I begin this chapter with Belton's words because they help convey the sense of lost opportunity that Black families must have felt when prevented by law from going to segregated white schools because they were seen as inferior students and inferior human beings.

The assertion that segregation must make Black children feel worse about themselves is certainly problematic, and it contradicts research demonstrating Black people's resilience, demonstrated by high levels of self-esteem in the face of racial oppression and structural violence.[2] By including this quote, I do not mean to suggest that Black students need white students around them to feel empowered, since that is not the case. Instead, what I think is most important from Belton's comments is the sense that her daughter is being denied educational opportunities because these opportunities are disproportionately given to white students in their segregated white schools. They are the ones whom the state decides to invest in, as their schools receive more resources, more qualified personnel, and other advantages. Belton's daughter is Black, and as a Black child, she was defined by state law as unworthy of attending Claymont High School, which was close to her home but reserved only for white students. Littleton Mitchell, who grew up in segregated Milford, Delaware and became one of the state's most important (if not the most important) Black leaders of the twentieth century, summarized the impact of school segregation in an interview for the documentary *A Separate Place*. He said, "Remember it was the thinking of our legislators that we Blacks were not paying taxes as the whites were paying. And so when that came into focus, we didn't get anything. Didn't have any money. And they didn't appropriate money for it. We were left out in the cold. In fact, we were not considered good enough to be educated."[3]

Why Delaware?

Delaware is a small but fascinating state. As of the 2020 Census, it had only 990,000 residents, but it occupies an important historical role for the US and for the subject of school desegregation. Delaware license plates call it the "First State." When my kids, who have grown up in Delaware, were little, I told them that this meant that the Delaware representative cut in line to sign the Constitution first. That was a lie for my own amusement, though I think they knew I was being facetious. What it really means is that Delaware was the first state to successfully complete the legislative process of ratifying the US Constitution, in 1787. Delaware was also the site of the first successful K–12 school desegregation court case in the US: *Belton v. Gebhart*. This case was the only one of the five cases merged together in *Brown v. Board of Education of Topeka, Kansas* in which the state was appealing a lower court's decision that schools must desegregate, rather than the plaintiffs challenging a prior decision allowing for continued racial segregation. New Castle County, Delaware, which is the focus of my research in the state, was also the site of a metropolitan, interdistrict, court-ordered school desegregation plan.

I use Delaware as my first case study because, even though Delaware's desegregation effort occurred a few years after Boston's (as I discuss in chapters 5 and 6), Delaware is a true "border South state." If the Mason-Dixon line were drawn straight, it would pass through northern Delaware—just barely north of where the University of Delaware lies. Delaware has elements of both the North and the South, particularly when it comes to its history of racial oppression. As the legal scholar Robert L. Hayman Jr. writes, "Delaware represents a useful microcosm of the nation, even, remarkably, when the racial experiences of the northern and southern state diverged."[4] Indeed, one of the best historical accounts of Delaware's experience with desegregation is titled *Between North and South*.[5]

Slavery was legal in Delaware, though the state's history of slavery laws illustrates a complicated and inconsistent pattern marked by tension between abolitionists and defenders of slavery. As early as the 1780s, religious leaders and other abolitionists in the state succeeded in passing state laws that facilitated manumission, or freeing of individual enslaved people, and that banned the sale of enslaved people out of state. And yet slavery remained legal, with legislative efforts to abolish it failing repeatedly. Delaware had a law on the books that prohibited free Black citizens in other states from immigrating to Delaware, but its citizens showed only a lukewarm commitment to this law, since in 1852, they voted down such a rule as a constitutional amendment. Due to a combination of factors, including changing labor needs as well as the inability of slave owners to profit by selling enslaved people out of state, the number of enslaved people declined over the years, so that by the 1860 Census, 92 percent of Black residents were free citizens. The state sided with the Union in the Civil War even though it was a slaveholding state. Yet, during Reconstruction, Delaware's representatives in the US Congress unanimously resisted rights for Black Americans, opposing the 1866 Civil Rights Bill as well as the Fourteenth and Fifteenth Amendments because these efforts provided newly emancipated Black Americans with civil liberties.[6] Violent racial oppression lingered long after slavery ended in Delaware, as it was the last state to formally abolish the whipping post (in 1972); it was not until July 2000 that the final whipping post was removed from public display outside a courthouse in Georgetown, Delaware.[7] It was also the northernmost state in which segregated schools were required by law before 1954. Much of what we already know about the consequences of resistance to school desegregation is based on research in the South; Delaware offers an excellent view of what happened outside (but just outside) the South.

In this chapter, I describe the history of Delaware's segregated school system, up until a federal court ruling that desegregated schools in 1978. Prior studies have provided detailed historical descriptions of Delaware's desegregation process.[8] Instead of repeating these, I focus on the experiences of Black students in being denied educational opportunity and with school punishment, particularly in New Castle County, its largest county and the one that contains a majority of the state's Black residents. Delaware public schools were segregated by law until 1952, when the state's laws changed; after that, they continued to be segregated, though not because of segregation laws, until 1978. While Black students were most certainly denied equal educational opportunities, there is little evidence to suggest that students—Black or white—were frequently suspended or expelled from schools prior to desegregation.

Before *Brown*

In a chapter of Robert L. Hayman Jr. and Leland Ware's edited volume *Choosing Equality: Essays and Narratives on the Desegregation Experience*, Hayman provides a helpful and concise history of educational segregation before the historic *Brown v. Board of Education* decision. As he describes, Delaware public schools were created in 1829 but excluded Black children. Black students were only allowed to attend existing private schools that were willing to admit them (such as Quaker schools) or private schools established for Black students by free Black citizens. By the time of Emancipation, there were only seven schools that Black students could attend, statewide.[9]

Until 1875, there were no public schools in Delaware that would accept Black students. And yet, because public schools were state funded and Black residents paid state taxes, the state's Black residents were funding the segregated, all-white public school system. This changed in 1875, as the state legislature created segregated Black public schools. They were funded by an additional property tax paid only by Black residents of the state. Taxes from white residents paid for the white public school system, while taxes paid by Black residents paid for segregated Black schools— even the state's system of school funding was segregated. Given the low tax base used to fund Black schools due to the overall poverty of Black Delawareans in 1875, Black children's schools received little money and were of much lower quality than the schools for white students that were spreading across the state.[10] A study commissioned years later to study the state of Delaware schools found that in 1917–1918, white schools received $20.13 per pupil, compared to $8.29 per pupil to Black schools.[11] School segregation became further entrenched in 1897, one year after the *Plessy v. Ferguson* Supreme Court decision that allowed for racial segregation under the justification that segregated public facilities were "separate but equal." Delaware's response to the Supreme Court's defense of segregation was to amend its state constitution to mandate separate schools for "white and colored children."[12]

The number of schools for Black students grew in the early twentieth century. In 1917, Pierre S. du Pont, chairman of the board of the DuPont Corporation, created the Delaware Service Citizens, a philanthropic organization that sought to build schools for Black students.[13] Du Pont helped commission a study of the state of Delaware schools by the Rockefeller Foundation. The study highlighted the racially segregated and unequal system for funding schools, which resulted in insufficient funds for Black schools. After the state legislature refused to remedy this gap, du Pont set aside his own money to construct new schools for Black students; he promised to donate all of the funding needed to build these new schools without any additional taxpayer money.[14] His funding resulted in construction of eighty-nine schools for Black students, at a cost of over $10 million.[15]

Du Pont's goal was to provide state-of-the-art school buildings for Black students. His philanthropy resulted in far more schools for Black students and modern school buildings that were vast improvements over the poorly heated one-room schoolhouses, often without amenities such as indoor plumbing, that they replaced. A report and related documentary, *A Separate Place*, distributed by the Hagley Museum and Library in Delaware (on the site of the original gunpowder factory of the du Pont family), conveys the thanks of Black students. The report includes dozens of excerpts of letters sent by Black students in du Pont–constructed schools to Pierre du Pont thanking him for their schools, as well as several reproductions of full letters to him. It also includes the music and lyrics to the 1924 "DuPont Song," written by the teacher J. Matthew Coulbourne in honor of Pierre S. du Pont's contributions to schools as well as T. Coleman du Pont's efforts to improve the state's roadways (see figure 3.1).

While du Pont's contributions helped students learn in modern schools closer to their homes, the state's system of segregation remained

FIGURE 3.1. "DuPont Song." (Hagley Museum and Library, "A Separate Place: The Schools P.S. du Pont Built," accessed 7/21/2023, www.hagley.org)

unchallenged. And, though the number of schools open to Black students grew, these school facilities were still smaller, of worse quality and more crowded than those for whites, offered lower teacher salaries, and had insufficient educational materials to offer.[16] As an example, consider the crowning achievement of du Pont's efforts, the new Howard High School in Wilmington, the state's only comprehensive public high school for Black students when it opened (replacing the old Howard High School) in 1928. The building was large, modern, and expensive, costing over $1 million.[17] But it was built next door to industrial parks, including a tannery that filled the school with the odor of dead animals and "derelict housing."[18] Even the movement's biggest success still subjected Black students to conditions their white peers did not have to face.

Littleton Mitchell, a Black Delaware resident who attended segregated schools before eventually serving as president of Delaware's NAACP, described the Black and white schools in his hometown of Milford, Delaware:

We had a school for whites that was located in a beautiful neighborhood with paved walks and adequate lighting. The school was housed in several buildings; it included grades one to twelve. On the other hand, we had a black school with just five rooms. It was located at the edge of the town. It was not in a location that many residents frequented. The school was surrounded on two sides by cornfields. In the back, there was a pasture with cows and horses. The front of the school faced pens used by a slaughterhouse to hold cows. . . . Milford's white school had manicured lawns. At the black school, grass grew almost up to our hips and was very seldom cut. As far as the playgrounds were concerned, one school had several sliding boards, a number of swing sets, a basketball court, and a baseball diamond. At the black school, there was a field of grass and one pole with six chains attached to it. It was called a "Giant Stride." You could grab a chain, run around, and swing out to circle the pole. . . . The white school had about five maintenance workers; our school had one janitor to take care of the five rooms. The only time our

furniture was replaced was when the other school purchased new furniture. Their old furniture was sent to our school. We also had to use
their old textbooks. . . . It is important to understand that, in Delaware,
the eighth grade was the end of a black student's educational career if he
or she could not afford to enroll in the private high school at Delaware
State, the segregated college for blacks in Dover, or travel to Wilmington
to attend Howard High School.[19]

As Mitchell states, until 1950, Howard High in Wilmington was the
only four-year comprehensive high school that Black students could attend in the entire state. Wilmington, the state's largest city, was in the
northernmost part of the state, which meant that Black students living
in the state's more rural southern areas needed to either move to Wilmington or commute hours each way in order to obtain a high school
diploma. Mitchell commuted to Howard High School from his home
in Milford, Delaware—a distance of sixty-seven miles along the current
highway (which did not exist until 2003). He boarded with a family during the week and hitchhiked home for weekends.[20] By 1953, the state
opened two other secondary schools for Black students. Figure 3.2 illustrates the distance between these schools.

In 1951, the Delaware attorney Louis Redding and cocounsel Jack
Greenberg challenged Delaware's de jure system of segregated schools.
Redding was a Delaware native, Harvard Law School graduate, and the
first Black attorney in Delaware.[21] He was still the only Black attorney in
the state at the time of this case and would be until 1956.[22] Jack Greenberg was an attorney for the NAACP Legal Defense Fund who took
an interest in the case as part of its ongoing strategic effort to overturn
segregation laws across the US. Redding and Greenberg initiated two
cases that were subsequently merged together, *Belton v. Gebhart* and
Bulah v. Gebhart, involving a school in Hockessin, Delaware, and one
in Claymont, Delaware. In both cases, Black parents had asked for their
children to be admitted to white schools close to their homes, rather
than be forced to commute long distances to the Black schools they were

Black Comprehensive High Schools, Delaware

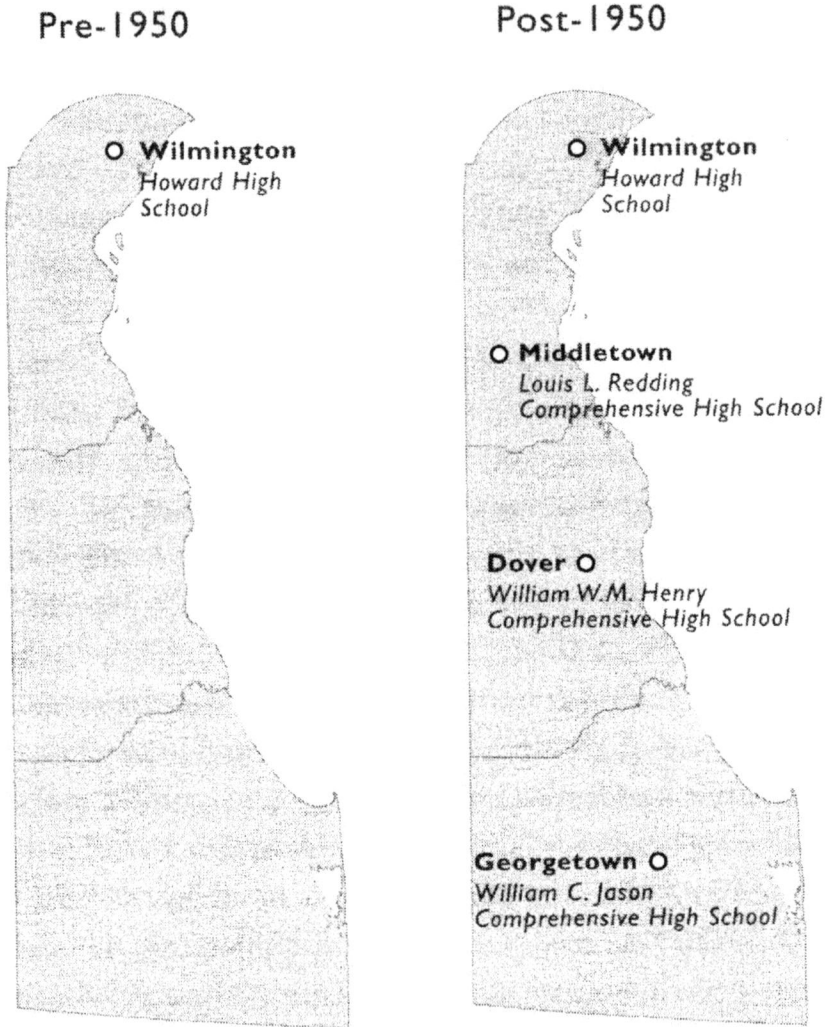

Pre-1950   ### Post-1950

O **Wilmington**
*Howard High
School*

O **Wilmington**
*Howard High
School*

O **Middletown**
*Louis L. Redding
Comprehensive High School*

Dover O
*William W.M. Henry
Comprehensive High School*

Georgetown O
*William C. Jason
Comprehensive High School*

FIGURE 3.2. Black comprehensive high schools in Delaware. (Brett Gadsden, *Between North and South: Delaware, Desegregation, and the Myth of American Sectionalism* [Philadelphia: University of Pennsylvania Press, 2013]; Michael Page, Emory University Libraries)

assigned to; for Bulah, this was an elementary school, and for Belton, it was a high school. The tiny "Hockessin Colored School" that Bulah was assigned to is shown in figure 3.3.[23] Redding and Greenberg won their case in April 1952 in the Delaware Court of Chancery, in front of Judge Collins J. Seitz. In August 1952, the Delaware Supreme Court affirmed the Chancery Court's decision, in *Belton v. Gebhart*.

At the same time, NAACP attorneys arguing similar cases challenging school desegregation in South Carolina, Virginia, Kansas, and Washington, DC, all lost their cases. Their appeals, and the state of Delaware's appeal of the *Belton* case, were all eventually aggregated into the case known as *Brown v. Board of Education of Topeka, Kansas*. Of course, the US Supreme Court officially ended de jure school segregation in May 1954 with its decision on behalf of the plaintiffs in *Brown v. Board of Education*.

FIGURE 3.3. Hockessin Colored School #107, in Hockessin, Delaware. (Hockessin Colored School #107, "Our History," accessed 12/7/2023, https://hockessincolored-school107.org; courtesy of the Delaware Public Archives)

After *Brown*

Unlike southern states that responded to *Brown* with adamant refusal to desegregate, Delaware's response was positive—rhetorically, at least.[24] The two school districts that lost the *Belton v. Gebhart* case had already admitted Black students immediately after the August 1952 denial of appeal, as did at least one other Delaware district.[25] Describing the state's response to *Brown*, June Shagaloff, of the NAACP Legal Defense Fund, wrote, "On June 11 [1954], the State Board of Education stated that as a general policy, it 'fully intends to carry out the mandates of the United States Supreme Court as expeditiously as possible.' At the same time, however, the Board stated that because of differences in tradition and attitudes, some areas would require more time than others."[26] The State Board of Education instructed local school districts to form their own plans for desegregation at that time, less than a month after the *Brown* decision. As a result, districts across the state responded with very different levels of urgency.

Perhaps the most dramatic response occurred in Milford, Delaware, a rural community downstate.[27] The Milford School Board decided to allow eleven Black students into its previously segregated high school immediately after the *Brown* decision. These students began class in September 1954 without incident . . . for about ten days. Community members learned about the students' attendance, were upset about the school's desegregation, and began to protest. Some students suggested that the protest was ignited when white families learned about Black male students' plans to dance with white female students at the upcoming school dance.[28] Bryant Bowles, the self-appointed head of the National Association for the Advancement of White People (yes, the NAAWP), came to Milford and began hosting large rallies with thousands of people attending, protesting desegregation. Parents picketed outside the school and made threats to school officials and the Black students and their families, many students stayed home from school, and the principal temporarily closed the doors of Milford High School.

Governor J. Caleb Boggs intervened to declare that the Black students would leave Milford High until a plan could be worked out that admitted them in a way that avoided public protest. The entire Milford school board resigned in protest after the governor's intervention, and the Black students were forced to leave the high school.[29]

In contrast, the Wilmington Board of Education announced plans for desegregating during the summer of 1954. The plan was reviewed and approved with broad consensus that August. It called for desegregation of primary schools but not secondary schools, since that part of the process would require "further study."[30] The Wilmington Board of Education then passed a resolution in February 1956 that completely banned segregation in Wilmington schools.[31] Other districts in the county (New Castle County) responded in varying ways to the *Brown* decision. Generally speaking, Black students in school districts across New Castle County were allowed to transfer to previously all-white schools in their school zones. Districts dropped de jure segregation and allowed for students to choose their schools but did not take any extra steps to facilitate desegregation.

Thus, after *Brown*, schools in New Castle County ended de jure segregation by allowing Black children to attend schools that had previously been reserved only for white students. In the city of Wilmington, in which the state's Black population was concentrated, this resulted in a growing Black student presence and declining white student enrollment. Figure 3.4 is a reproduction of a graph printed in a Wilmington High School informational booklet from 1965.[32] It illustrates the growth in Black student population and decline of white students in Wilmington High. While a full explanation of this Black concentration in the state's urban area and resulting white flight is beyond the scope of this book, it is important to keep in mind that this occurred at the same time as white flight from urban to suburban areas across the US, spurred by suburban housing restrictions against Black residents, generous loans for white residents (and particularly white military veterans following World War II), and other forms of housing and banking discrimination.[33]

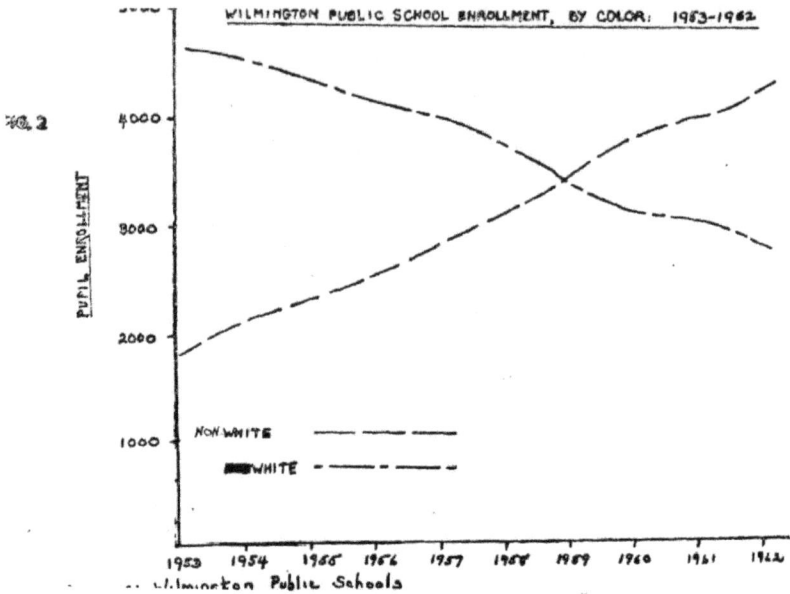

FIGURE 3.4. Graph of Wilmington public school enrollments, by race, 1953–1962. (Published courtesy of the Delaware Public Archives)

Segregated schools attended by Black students received fewer re-sources than segregated white schools. I discussed this problem with Bebe Coker, a Black parent who had three children attend Wilmington public schools in the 1970s before and after they desegregated. Coker is a lifelong activist for social justice and leader; in the 1970s, she worked for the state in social services, a position for which she worked with public schools to help coordinate care for young children.[34] Speaking of schools in Wilmington before they were desegregated by a court order, she said,

> The whole business with desegregation of schools was the fact that, one, you were admitting—the larger community was admitting—that the education, the resources provided in education for the two groups, one was under, the other was over and appropriate. That was the one thing. . . . It was what resources were not being given or what things

were not being shared with us, because either one did not want Blacks to really achieve, or you thought in your propagandized mind that we could not achieve. So I think a lot of times—I say that in all sincerity— because a lot of times we allow the public or the newspapers' participation in what desegregation was all about, to really cover up what the real issues were. The real issues were—were segregated resources, making ours less than, and still finding that people would achieve regardless.

Later in our conversation she returned to this point, adding, "But in Delaware, I—I don't know why I didn't see it initially. I guess it's because I didn't have children when I came here and that kind of thing. And then I began to see . . . differences. But I also was appalled when I saw how inequitable, segregated, so-called segregated schools were in terms of— of particularly the written word at that time, of course, the books and that kind of thing and the things that we didn't have."

The 1965 Wilmington High School informational booklet offers clues about how Black students were perceived in Wilmington at that time. After discussing the growing presence of Black students at Wilmington High, it explains that the median income of Wilmington's white families is far higher than that of the city's Black families but follows that by stating, "A brighter side of this picture is the increase in educational and job opportunities for the Negro in our community. In some areas the opportunities have come faster than there are trained Negroes to take advantage of them. The local banks, retail stores, duPont, Hercules, etc. are 'equal opportunity employers,' and their personnel administrators are constantly asking about prospective Negro employees. The problem is not to place the Negro, but rather to find the qualified Negro to place. This increase in opportunities has stimulated some of our Negro parents and students to a real quest for education."[35]

The stated assumptions that there were insufficient numbers of Black students who were qualified to work at local banks, retail stores, and local companies and that Black families needed "stimulation" in order to desire a quality education are problematic. It is true that deficiencies in the education Black students received at the time left them less prepared than white suburban students for higher education or the job market.[36] But interpreting lower-quality segregated schools to indicate that Black students had limited abilities and lower aspirations reflects racist assumptions about Black students.

Black students who were in the minority in previously segregated schools were treated poorly. In 1971, the Delaware NAACP collected statements from Black students during a "Black Student Seminar on School Problems."[37] While not in New Castle County, the following statements from students in the Indian River School District, which serves the southeastern portion of the state, tell us about the hostility Black students must have felt in previously all-white Delaware schools. Here are a few of the students' statements handwritten on forms by NAACP staff:

A black student is always reminded in classroom by the teacher that they are *black!* in someway. Whenever you're the only black in a class the teacher makes you feel you have to work harder than the others even when your IQ or ability is higher than theirs

Miss Wilder—gym teacher (uses profanity) called her a big girl—can't do much—"a big black"—she dropped out of gym awhile.

Miss Walder (white) called Evelyn Walker a "n****r"—Evelyn was thrown out of class—kicked out of gym permanently

Different punishments—1 kind for black + another for whites—white girl hit her—hit her back. He told to run track—white girl let free

Bussing—Negro boy pushed off of seat when he tried to sit beside white boy "I don't want no n****r sitting beside me." Bus driver did nothing but told a N girl "to keep her nose in her own business"[38]

In the suburbs outside Wilmington, the urban center of New Castle County, there were few Black students enrolled as of 1974. In table 3.1, I show the percentage of white and Black public school students in each of the twelve districts within the county as of September 30, 1974. There were only three districts out of twelve, county-wide, where the student population was greater than 6 percent Black: Wilmington, De La Warr, and Appoquinimink. The De La Warr district bordered Wilmington, was inhabited by mostly lower-income residents, and included a large proportion of industrial land such as the county airport. Appoquinimink was a small district in a sparsely populated rural area at the southern border of the county, several miles from Wilmington.

What table 3.1 tells us is that, other than in Appoquinimink, de jure segregation might have ended, but segregation was still alive and well. Black students were clustered in the Wilmington and De La Warr districts, whereas the suburban schools were nearly entirely white. I do not

TABLE 3.1 New Castle County School Districts' Enrollments by Race, September 30, 1974

District	Black students (%)	White students (%)	Other students (%)	Total enrollment
Alexis I. du Pont	3.4	94.6	2.0	3,310
Alfred I. du Pont	0.7	98.1	1.2	10,982
Appoquinimink	26.1	73.2	0.7	2,452
Claymont	3.5	95.8	0.7	3,504
Conrad	2.6	96.6	0.8	5,674
De La Warr	53.3	45.4	1.3	3,302
Marshallton-McKean	5.0	94.6	0.4	3,931
Mount Pleasant	2.2	96.9	0.9	5,278
New Castle–Gunning Bedford	5.6	93.2	1.2	9,197
Newark	3.9	95.1	1.0	16,640
Stanton	0.7	97.7	1.6	5,597
Wilmington	83.6	12.0	4.4	14,419

Source: Delaware Committee on the School Decision, *Facts and Figures about Education in New Castle County*, May 1975, Desegregation in Delaware Collection, Special Collections, University of Delaware Library.

refer to this as de facto segregation because that term suggests that the outcome is unintended or the result of chance, and there is nothing accidental about it. As James Baldwin wrote, "De facto segregation means Negroes are segregated, but nobody did it."[39] School segregation after the end of de jure segregation is based in part on residential segregation, which is a direct consequence of state and federal policies, not an unintended consequence of individuals' choices of where to live. As the education policy scholar Richard Rothstein details in *The Color of Law*, a combination of federal housing policies, public housing planning, racially restrictive zoning laws, highway construction, and other state and federal government actions actively created the residential segregation we see today.[40]

School segregation was due not only to residential segregation but also to school policy that sought to keep schools segregated. Delaware's 1968 Educational Achievement Act reorganized and consolidated school districts throughout Delaware but excluded Wilmington, segregating Wilmington schools from the newly consolidated districts surrounding it and facilitating white students' avoidance of Wilmington schools.[41] The high level of segregation seen in table 3.1 was the subject of *Evans v. Buchanan*, a lawsuit that eventually forced remedy of the continuing segregation of New Castle County schools. As I describe in chapter 4, *Evans v. Buchanan* resulted in a massive desegregation effort that saw the merger of all school districts in the county other than Appoquinimink into a single, county-wide district, in 1978.

Suspension during Segregation

I pursued a variety of strategies in order to learn about school punishment in segregated New Castle County schools before 1978. I spent time in the Delaware State Archives as well as in the archives of the University of Delaware Library, particularly looking through a special collection of documents titled "Desegregation in Delaware." I obtained all newspaper articles mentioning school suspension from the *News Journal*, the state's paper of record, covering several decades. I obtained data from the US Department of Education's Office of Civil Rights, and I consulted the state Department of Education in order to gather data on school punishment. I found that the data are very difficult to come by. The state's Department of Education claims to have no records of school suspension from before 1978, and in the state archives, I found few discussions of anything having to do with school punishment prior to the 1970s.

While frustrating, this lack of data is very meaningful. Schools are bureaucratic, publicly funded organizations that collect and report data for the general public, so that parents and other taxpayers can see how schools are performing. While schools from the 1960s and 1970s may not have been the data-generating, outcome-measuring machines that schools are today, they were still bureaucratic public institutions that were accountable to their communities: they still collected data, held public meetings, and needed to report on how they were doing. The fact that it is difficult to find records of suspensions or discussions of school punishment from the 1960s or early 1970s strongly suggests that, unlike schools today, exclusionary school punishments were uncommon or at least not central to daily school life. Simply put, the absence of records on suspension amid volumes of materials on school budgets, enrollments, curricula, guidance and counseling, and even drivers' education programs (among many other subjects), tells us that suspension was not seen as an important topic for discussion in public forums or for reporting in official documents.

To illustrate, consider the monthly reports from Delaware Department of Public Instruction's department heads discussing problems and potential improvements to public education, statewide, for fiscal year 1974–1975. The monthly reports I found in the state archives include reports on the following topics or from the following departments: ESEA Title III, Division of Mental Health, ESEA I Administration, Programs for Exceptional Children, Adult Education, Physical Education, Art and Music Education, English, Program Development and Migrant Education, Safety and Driver Education, Social Studies, Library/Media

Services, Supervisor of Elementary Curriculum, Science and Environment Education, Right to Read, Health Education, ESEA Title III Programs, Performance Objectives in Reading, and Language Programs. Despite the long list of individuals and departments reporting, there is nothing about school punishment whatsoever. Even "safety and driver education" refers to safe functioning of a drivers' education program, not a broader school safety program that involves maintenance of security or punishment of students. If a school today were to publish a report on "safety," it would surely discuss policing/security strategies or punishments in response to student misbehavior, but that was simply not the case as late as 1975 in Delaware. These reports also show that the issue is not simply a matter of schools' resistance to reporting performance measures during this time, though schools were in fact resistant to reporting data.[42] These reports include performance measures on many other topics but not on school punishment.

Searching through state Department of Public Instruction archives for this time period, I did find a report pertaining to how schools should manage student behavior. It was from an unnamed department and was titled "Program Goals and Objectives for 1972–73." It appears to be written by Ervin Marsh, who was the state supervisor of student activities for the State Department of Public Instruction. The document describes a series of program goals and objectives, though it is not clear if it was intended to instruct schools statewide or if it was for a particular department or school program. Regardless, it is a fascinating list of recommended school practices and goals that collectively seek to create an environment protective of students' legal rights, empower student leadership organizations, provide drug-abuse education, provide effective student activities, and communicate with the public about student activities. Whatever the specific program was, it was directed entirely at building school climate and student supports without any reference whatsoever to punishment for student misbehavior.

Prior research on the history of school discipline is instructive here. According to historians who study school discipline, early American schools used disciplinary techniques including corporal punishment and physical training. Their goals were to "Americanize" immigrant youth—train them to adopt white, middle-class American behaviors and norms—and to teach other youth skills and dispositions that would suit their likely career trajectories. For working-class youth, this meant physical discipline that would train them to be punctual, obedient factory workers; for wealthier youth, it meant academic training that would put them on a path to white-collar jobs or leadership positions.[43]

Minutes of a December 14, 1967, meeting including the acting assistant superintendent of Wilmington schools illustrates that this historical style of discipline was still being used, to some extent at least.[44] The minutes describe discussions for the New Castle County Vocational-Technical Board to assume responsibility for vocational-technical education of Wilmington public school students. The minutes describe agreement about the responsibilities for each agency. Among them, the Wilmington Board is responsible for "Americanism and Naturalization Programs." The minutes make no other mention of any punishment or student discipline functions. While it is not entirely clear what the "Americanism and Naturalization Programs" consist of, this does suggest that as of 1967, Wilmington schools still considered school discipline to be the practice of instilling particular identities and behaviors in students, not the use of exclusionary punishment to remove students or respond to student misbehavior. If, as prior scholars have described, Americanization and naturalization efforts sought to reproduce a class structure while forcing assimilation into white, middle-class American culture, then they were racist and classist programs, but they were still *inclusive*, in that they sought to include students in the "Americanization" project rather than being *exclusionary* (i.e., removing students from school).[45]

While I did find references in the archives to student discipline, they suggest that exclusionary punishments like suspension were frowned upon and uncommon. For example, in the state archives, I found minutes from an October 9, 1969, meeting of secondary school principals.

There is no specific district mentioned in the document, so it is unclear if the meeting was within a district, county-wide, or even statewide. The first item listed in the minutes is "1. Discipline. Considerable discussion was generated on this topic, particularly as it pertains to publicity." The summary that follows discussion of this item shows a focus on inclusive discipline that seeks to help students and avoid stigmatizing them, not exclusionary punishment like suspension. One item states, "We need to provide another program and facility for unmotivated and aggressive youngsters. (A quote was read from Allen Rusten's letter of September 23 regarding isolation of disruptive students). Although a positive approach must be taken, the principals felt that a stigma would be attached to a program of separatism."[46] This document shows that as of 1969, principals in Delaware had yet to adopt exclusionary punishment as a favored response to student misbehavior. Instead, they were concerned about the stigma students would face if they were removed from school. It also suggests that suspension was so rare that the very term "suspension" was not commonly enough used for the minutes to use this term rather than "a program of separatism."

As another illustration, consider an October 8, 1968, proposal to Governor Charles L. Terry Jr., Wilmington Mayor John E. Babiarz, and the Wilmington Board of Education. The proposal, found in the state archives, is for school aides (monitors) for secondary schools of Wilmington.[47] This document was written just six months after Dr. Martin Luther King Jr.'s assassination. In April 1968, immediately after King was killed, people protested on the streets of Wilmington as in other cities across the US. But unlike in some other cities, Governor Charles L. Terry ordered twenty-eight hundred National Guard troops to patrol Wilmington streets. They continued as what has been called an "occupying force" for nine months until the new governor took office, making it the longest that any US city has been occupied by military forces since the Civil War.[48] It makes sense that students in Wilmington public schools would face hardship that school year, and the proposal begins by stating that there were many "aggressive and anti-social acts" in

Wilmington's secondary schools that year, resulting in some suspensions and arrests. But the suggested response in this proposal to the governor, mayor, and Board of Education was to hire school aides to help support students' needs. The aides were to help supervise students and "develop rapport and lines of communication between student and student, student and teacher, and student and administrator."[49] The proposal states, "The monitor or school aide system provides one avenue of assistance to students, faculty and administration in promoting and maintaining a positive educational and social climate for students in the school."[50] In other words, the proposed response to students' disruptive behavior during a military occupation was to support their needs and improve the school's social climate, not to suspend them.

I spoke about New Castle County schools' use of discipline with Gloria Grantham, a Black teacher and mother of a child in Wilmington public schools and later a researcher studying school punishment (whose research I discuss in chapter 4) and school superintendent. Grantham was a teacher first at Wilmington Friends, a private school in Wilmington, in the early 1970s, before she accepted a job at Burnett Elementary School, a Wilmington public school, in 1975, still three years before desegregation. Grantham confirmed that suspension and expulsion were very rarely used before desegregation. Instead, some schools did use corporal punishment, but more frequently, they tried to resolve conflicts and address student misbehavior by supporting students—until school desegregation and the growth of suspensions.

> GRANTHAM: The assistant principal at the time. And he said, 'We don't like to send kids home, because we would only be sending them to the street.' And I love that because we never suspended kids at Wilmington Friends either. It was never an option that was given. The objective was, if your kids got into trouble, we would work with them and counsel them and help them change their behavior. But there was no such thing as suspension.
>
> KUPCHIK: Is this at Burnett?

GRANTHAM: Yes. Sometimes they would send the kids home at that time at Burnett. They would send them home for an afternoon sometimes or a day. But they didn't like to do that. They didn't like to put them out of school.

   . . . Yes, the kids were punished in a way that they would get yelled at or sat in a chair or separated. . . . I think schools got more into suspension much later, once I got into the deseg[regation] and I left the teaching position.

During the late 1960s and 1970s, the state (and nation) also showed concern about student drug use. I found detailed records of the state's approach to preventing student drug use and the state's expenditures on drug education programs from 1971 to 1973. These programs focused on educating students about the harms of drug use, training teachers how to recognize and respond to student drug use, and supporting students' health. With one exception, I found no references to punitive or exclusionary responses to students who use drugs; rather, the focus was entirely on prevention and treatment. That one exception was a transcript of a speech by Paula D. Gordon for the Delaware drug educators' retreat that Delaware's junior senator at the time, Joseph R. Biden, had printed in the *Congressional Record*. The speech is consistent with the other materials from Delaware's Department of Public Instruction in that it stressed the harms of drug use and the need to educate and support students. The reference to punitive responses was that they ought to be *avoided*:

Non-punitive approaches need to be adopted in schools to supplant purely legalistic actions such as expulsion and suspension. Alternatives to such action need to be provided which focus most importantly on helping the individual to break out of the cycle of drug taking behavior or to cease experimenting with drugs and other harmful substances. In lieu of prosecution, in lieu of being remanded to the juvenile authority, in lieu of suspension or expulsion, the young person can be remanded to counselling, to other forms of care or guidance that may be appropriate, and to special programs and activities designed to help redirect his or her energies and attentions along more constructive lines.[51]

Eschewing punitive approaches to student drug abuse and focusing entirely on treatment and education is a far cry from the zero-tolerance school policies that spread in the 1990s, which focused entirely on exclusionary punishments like suspension and law enforcement.[52]

It is also difficult to find descriptions of school suspensions in the local newspaper, the *News Journal*. My search of the paper, going back to 1940, found very few mentions of "school suspension" or "suspended from school" prior to the late 1960s. The newspaper articles that did mention suspensions prior to the late 1960s often described incidents in other locations. Until 1968, the few articles mentioning suspension of Delaware students tended to describe incidents in which students were suspended for hair length, dress (e.g., wearing a "Beatles suit" to school), or truancy.

This trend shifted with the start of the 1968–1969 school year, with several *News Journal* stories about students suspended for violent interactions in school. Many described interracial violence that resulted in suspension mostly of Black students. Importantly, many Black students were living under a military occupation for much of that school year, given the National Guard occupation of Wilmington at that time. It hardly seems surprising that students who must literally walk past tanks and armed soldiers patrolling their community, watching over them as if they were potential enemy combatants, might engage in conflict in their schools.

Overall, the earliest media mentions of Delaware suspensions were about generational cultural conflict, with students wearing long hair or styles of dress that schools found inappropriate. After Dr. King's assassination, civil unrest protesting a violently racist society, and a racially motivated military occupation of Wilmington, media accounts began to report on school suspensions assigned in response to violent conflict in schools. From news media records, it seems that (a) school suspensions were very rare until the late 1960s, and (b) when they became more prominent, it was largely a response to racial conflict and oppression of African Americans in Wilmington.

To summarize so far, there is very little indication that suspensions or other forms of exclusionary punishment were used frequently or were a focus of schools before New Castle County schools desegregated in 1978. Records from the 1960s and 1970s, including department reports and documents outlining strategies for combating student drug use, barely mention exclusionary punishment. In the local news media, as well, suspensions are rarely mentioned, and when the topic does finally receive more focus, it is in the context of racial conflict that spills over from the streets to the schools in the wake of Dr. King's assassination, military occupation of Wilmington, and the response to centuries of racialized violence.

It is also difficult to find reports of actual numbers of suspensions. The US Department of Education's Office for Civil Rights collects data on schools in an attempt to assess and evaluate education equity through nationwide surveys. These surveys began in the 1960s, but they did not begin to collect information on suspensions until 1972–1973.[53] This is the earliest date for which I could find suspension data for New Castle County. While the lack of data do not mean that no students were suspended, the lack of attention to reporting suspension data suggests that it was not a focus of schools or very common.

The OCR does report on suspensions for three years prior to the county's desegregation: 1973, 1974, and 1976. I show the proportion of students suspended, overall, for these three years in figure 3.5. Here I have separated the data into three trend lines: one for the Wilmington School District (which by then was almost entirely Black students), one for the De La Warr School District (which was divided between Black and white students), and one for all other districts in the county that housed nearly all white students and that later merged into a single county-wide district. A few conclusions can be drawn from this figure:

1. Overall suspension rates are relatively low during this era of continuing school segregation, at least by today's standards (and, as we shall see in chapter 4, by the standards of Delaware in 1978, immediately after desegregating).

2. Suspension rates increased between 1973 and 1976, as school desegregation was an issue being debated in court, among school boards, and in communities.

3. The De La Warr district—the only one among these that was desegregated at this time—had the highest suspension rates by far. In contrast, the primarily white school districts had the lowest overall suspension rates.

In figure 3.6, I present the suspension rates for Black students, specifically. The lines for both Wilmington and De La Warr are similar across the two figures, telling us that the overall suspension rates and Black student suspension rates are similar. The Black-white relative rate indexes for these districts confirm this. A relative rate index is a way of comparing the rate of punishment (taking the size of that student group

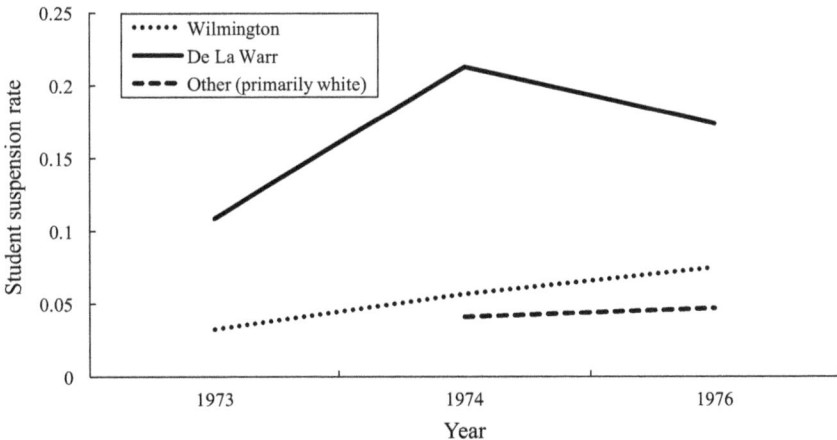

FIGURE 3.5. Office of Civil Rights data reports: proportion of all students suspended, 1973–1976. (Author's analysis of data from the Office of Civil Rights, US Department of Education)

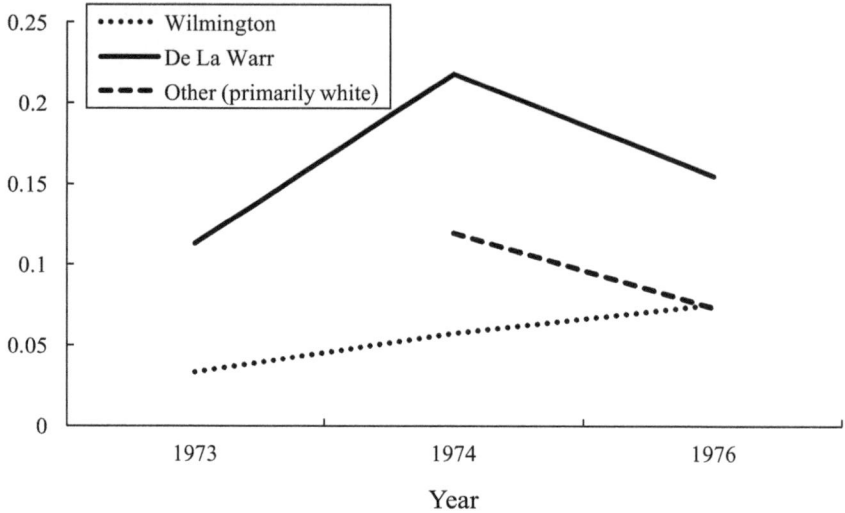

FIGURE 3.6. Office of Civil Rights data reports: proportion of Black students suspended, 1973–1976. (Author's analysis of data from the Office of Civil Rights, US Department of Education)

population into account) for one group of students relative to another. Here I calculated the suspension rates of Black students relative to that of white students. In 1974, the relative rate index was 1.14 in Wilmington and 1.03 in De La Warr. Since an index of 1.0 indicates that the rate of Black students' suspension is equal to that of white students, we see that Black and white students have similar suspension rates in these two districts. But the other districts in the county show a different pattern. Here we see very different lines across figures 3.5 and 3.6, with the Black suspension rates far higher. Indeed, the 1974 Black-white relative rate index is 3.08 in these primarily white districts, meaning that Black students received suspensions at a rate more than three times higher than that of white students. In other words, the districts within the county in which Black students had already been attending schools in large numbers showed relative parity, but in the districts that were almost entirely white, the few Black students enrolled were at much greater risk of suspension.

Conclusion

Despite the end of formal, legal school segregation in Delaware after the *Brown* decision, Black students in New Castle County, Delaware, still tended to go to segregated schools—before everything changed in 1978. There is little evidence that suspension was used frequently at all in the years before 1978. School suspension was not an issue that Delaware schools reported on or collected data about, and it was not commonly reported on in the news media. School strategies, even responses to drug use and efforts to address school climate, prioritized student treatment and empowerment, not school exclusion. What little data on school suspensions prior to 1978 that we do have show low suspension rates. All signs indicate that before desegregation, suspension was simply not a common school practice. This does not mean that it was never used, only that it was not common, unlike today.

A lot can be said about how poorly Black students were treated in Delaware before 1978. They were denied access to better-resourced but segregated white schools and forced to travel great distances to get to school, particularly students who wanted to attend the only Black public high school before 1950. After *Brown*, they were still denied educational opportunities through continuing segregation and treated with hostility once their schools desegregated. And yet, despite this horrible treatment, schools were still using inclusive discipline then, not exclusionary discipline like out-of-school suspension. I do not mean to glorify this era or downplay the vitriol and obstacles that Black youth must have faced getting an education in a border South state during Jim Crow. And yet despite the many problems Black students faced before desegregation, unlike students today, they did not attend schools where they were kicked out if they acted out.

Of course, this is precisely what a structural race perspective would have predicted. Actually, to be more accurate, it is exactly what the founding critical race theorist Derrick Bell literally did predict: that desegregation would be followed by school discipline and expulsion. CRT leads us to predict that apparent civil rights victories, like racial desegregation of schools, will be implemented and reacted to in ways that find new avenues for racial oppression.

Before desegregation, school discipline was an educational tool used to help shape identities, not a means for removing unwanted students, which came later. These identities might have been racialized or classist constructs, such as when schools attempted to use discipline to train Black, immigrant, and poor students for future roles as manual laborers.[54] But they were inclusive; they saw students as bodies to be molded, not problems to be excluded.

As we will see in chapter 4, this changed in Delaware with desegregation. The writing was on the wall for this change. The high suspension rates I show in figure 3.5 for the De La Warr School District are an indicator of it. De La Warr was the only actually integrated district in New Castle County: in 1974, 53 percent of its students were Black, and 45 percent were white. And its rate of suspension was far higher than that of Wilmington, with mostly Black students, or the white suburban districts. Sadly, by kicking kids out of school in large numbers before the massive county-wide desegregation in 1978, De La Warr was ahead of its time.

4

An Issue on Day One

Delaware after Desegregation

> It wasn't an issue until the [desegregation] order was imple-
> mented. And then it was an issue the first day. I mean kids
> were actually suspended from school or suspended off the
> bus the first day of school. And that continues to happen in
> all four districts every year.
> —Councilman Jea Street, personal correspondence, 2021

On the first day after the court-ordered desegregation, New Castle
County schools began suspending students, according to Jea Street, a
New Castle County councilman. Street was one of the most vocal and
effective advocates for Black students during the late 1970s in Delaware,
when he was director of the Parent Education Resource Center. As Street
describes, *immediately* after New Castle County schools desegregated in
1978 due to a federal court order, the school administrators responded
by removing Black students from previously all- or mostly white schools.

After *Brown v. Board of Education*, segregation laws were no longer on
the books in Delaware, but the schools were still racially segregated. Due
to racist housing policy, bank loan practices, and real estate practices
(among other factors), and facilitated by school policy, Black and white
children attended different schools.[1] By the mid-1970s, the Wilmington
School District was composed almost entirely of Black students, while
most of the other districts in the county hosted almost entirely white
students. The exceptions to this were the De La Warr district, which
neighbored Wilmington and hosted near equal numbers of Black and
white students, and the small Appoquinimink district, which was at the

southern end of the county. In this climate, suspensions and other exclusionary school punishments were rarely reported or discussed in school reports. The available evidence suggests that suspension rates were very low—at least outside of the sole desegregated district in northern New Castle County: De La Warr.

All of this changed in September 1978. The *Evans v. Buchanan* case resulted in a mandatory desegregation plan. The US district court's ruling required a merger of all school districts in New Castle County other than Appoquinimink into a single district in which students were bused between areas. This federally ordered desegregation plan did not eliminate racialized school systems; it just restructured them. Suspension rates skyrocketed—resistance to desegregation was the catalyst for sudden and substantial growth in suspension rates, particularly for Black students.

I continue in this chapter by describing *Evans v. Buchanan*—what it was about, how it was resolved, and how schools and communities reacted—since this case set the stage for the rise in suspensions that Street called out. I then return to Street's observations about how suspensions followed desegregation and how every piece of evidence supports exactly what he told me. The aftermath of school desegregation only makes sense if we understand that Black students were kicked out of newly desegregated schools because they were unwanted in these previously white spaces.

Evans v. Buchanan

In 1956, parents of Black children who were denied admission to Claymont (Delaware) district schools sued the state Board of Education (Madeline Buchanan was the board chair). The US district court agreed that the board had not made sufficient effort to desegregate following the *Brown* 1954 decision and ordered it to do so. After years of proposals and negotiations, eventually, in 1961, the district court approved of the state's desegregation plans. But the state took a step backward in 1968, when the Delaware legislature passed the Educational Advancement Act. This act isolated the state's Black students by restructuring school districts across the state—except for the city of Wilmington, which was specifically excluded from the act and separated from all other districts. *Evans v. Buchanan* was then reopened in 1971 at the request of the parents of Black students from Wilmington, because of the continuing level of segregation that they argued resulted from the Educational Advancement Act.[2]

In 1974, a three-judge panel sided with the plaintiffs and ordered the Delaware Board of Education to devise a new educational plan that included the city of Wilmington; the state was ordered to redraw school district boundaries and attendance zones in a way that would create a desegregated school system. The case was upheld on appeals, concluding only after the US Supreme Court refused to hear it in 1976 and again in 1977.[3] During this time, several alternate plans for achieving this reorganization were presented, discussed, and reviewed by the court.[4] The final desegregation plan that was approved by the court merged together all school districts in the county except for the southernmost district, Appoquinimink, into a single New Castle County School District. Figure 4.1 shows a map from 1975 that shows the location of each of the previous twelve school districts in the county.

Students in the new New Castle County School District would attend schools in both the suburban areas and in the city of Wilmington. The court approved a "9-3 plan" that required that each student would attend an assigned school in the suburbs outside Wilmington for nine years and attend school inside Wilmington for three years. Wilmington students were bused to schools in the suburban areas in either first through third grades or seventh through twelfth grades, depending on which part of Wilmington they lived in. Most students from suburban areas were bused into Wilmington for grades four through six, though students from one area came to Wilmington for grades one through three.[5] The primary benefit of the plan was to reorganize in such a way that the mostly Black Wilmington students would attend school along with the

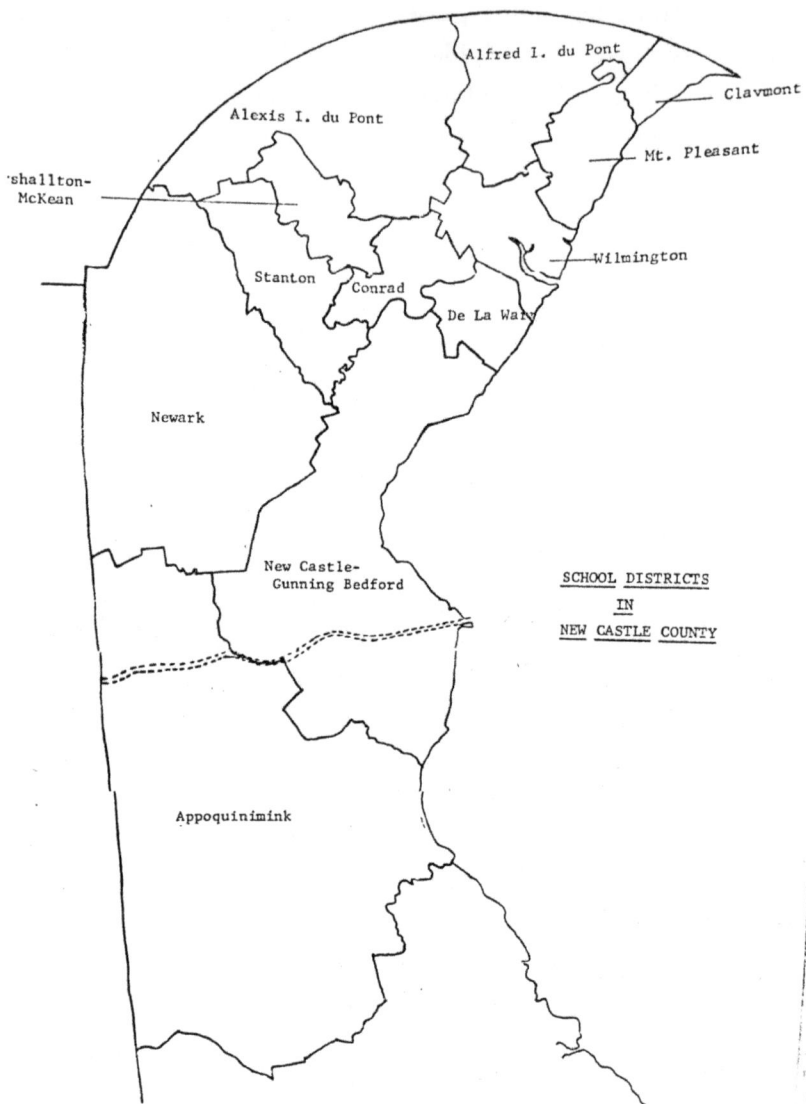

FIGURE 4.1. Map of New Castle County school districts before 1978 court order. (Delaware Committee on the School Decision [1975] *Facts and Figures about Education in New Castle County*, Desegregation in Delaware Collection, Special Collections, University of Delaware Library)

mostly white students from the surrounding suburbs, rather than being educated separately in racially identifiable, that is, segregated and distinct, school districts.

Despite widespread concerns, near-unanimous disapproval from suburban parents, and uneven support from Wilmington parents, the school merger went into effect.[6] The reorganized county-wide school district began its school year peacefully and without public protest in September 1978. Though schools across the county formed a single district, they were subdivided into four regions within that district. In 1981, the Delaware legislature again redrew school district boundaries by separating the county-wide district into four new districts, matching the four regions established three years earlier as part of the county-wide district. They were the Brandywine, Christina, Colonial, and Red Clay School Districts.

The court ruling requiring school desegregation and mandatory busing elicited anger and concern. The state legislature opposed the desegregation plans and passed resolutions expressing its opposition but offered no alternative solutions.[7] Parent advocacy groups, such as the most vocal antibusing group, the Positive Action Committee (PAC), as well as a large number of other community groups, formed to either support desegregation or oppose it (figure 4.2). In 1974, Delaware's US Senator Joseph R. Biden voiced his opposition to busing as a method of desegregation in an address to the US Senate, stating, "Busing, it seems to me, is a dubious triumph of technique over substance. By and large our children's education suffers and our energies are diverted from finding formulas and ways of achieving the goal of fair and open and equal opportunities for all in our schools."[8] Research over the years since then shows that our children's education does not suffer but is enhanced when schools are desegregated.[9]

The desegregation planning stage, in which different parties debated various desegregation strategies, had lasted for years and was highly visible. The Delaware Committee on the School Decision was formed in order to study and communicate with the public about the issue of

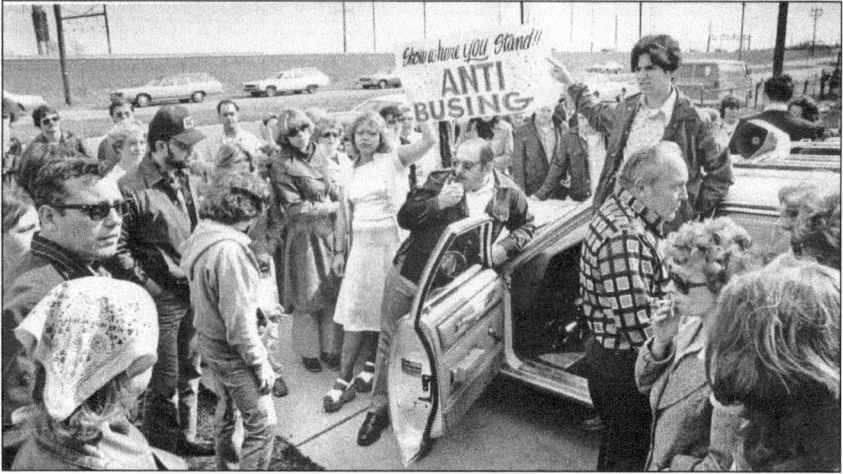

FIGURE 4.2. Protests against busing as a desegregation plan in Delaware. (Delaware News Journal–USA Today Network)

desegregation; committee members consisted of students, parents, clergy, community leaders, civil rights advocates, and many others. Notes and memos from the Committee on the School Decision show that by 1975, New Castle County had begun preparing for desegregation. For the most part, vocal resistance to the court desegregation order was about busing more than desegregation itself. More than twenty years since the Supreme Court's *Brown* decision, most white suburban parents seemed to accept the fact that schools would be desegregated—or at least they did not voice anger at this in and of itself. But the busing of Black students from Wilmington into suburban schools, and particularly the busing of white suburban students into Wilmington, generated fear and resentment.[10]

Other public concerns surfaced as well, particularly in the public forums dedicated to discussing various desegregation plans, and came from both Black and white parents. This long list of concerns included violence in and around Wilmington schools (that suburban children would now be exposed to), fear and suspicion among Black and white students and teachers, and the potential for Black students to be treated with hostility in suburban schools.[11] The potential for both interracial conflict and harsh treatment of Black students in newly desegregated schools was acknowledged in several planning documents, along with concerns about ensuring fair treatment and protecting students' dignity.

The court had requested that the schools include a human relations program as part of the desegregation process, because of its concerns about interracial conflict, unfair treatment of Black students, and the potential for Black students to be targeted for school discipline in newly desegregated schools. About one hundred human relations specialists were hired for schools in the newly formed New Castle County School District in the months before the 1978–1979 school year began.[12] The state Department of Public Instruction wrote, "A Human relations program should be instituted at the district level to coordinate district-wide human relations activities. The district level staff must provide direction to individual school buildings in providing the necessary services (e.g., multi-cultural/non-sexist curriculum, group dynamics, conflict management skills, values clarification techniques, interpersonal communication skills, leadership training . . .) that permit learning in an environment that is non-threatening, where students may see themselves respected for their own worth, and which encourage students to respect the rights of others."[13] Clearly, those who were planning the county's desegregation effort were concerned about the potential for disproportionate school punishment once the plans went into effect. Though school punishment is rarely mentioned in documents prior to 1978, once the court and schools began planning imminent desegregation, it immediately became a frequently voiced topic of concern.

Desegregation in New Castle County did not happen piecemeal or quietly, making it an ideal case study: it allows us to examine what happens when a formerly segregated school system undergoes enormous change in a visible and sudden way. While there were undoubtedly many consequences of Delaware's school desegregation, in the following sections, I focus specifically on evidence of suspension rates after desegregation, based on official data and observations of the people involved, and how we can explain these increases in suspensions.

Reports of School Suspension Data

Councilman Jea Street's description of how schools began suspending students after desegregation is supported by all available data on the subject. Schools' reports of their use of suspension clearly show that the numbers of school suspensions increased dramatically immediately after desegregation. A portion of state funds allocated for the desegregation effort was used to fund a study, called the Special Student Concerns Project, by the Rockefeller Foundation that included a district-wide analysis of school suspensions after desegregation. The report describes an increase of 223.2 percent in suspensions for Black students between 1975–1976 and 1978–1979, the first year of the New Castle County School District. It also describes how Black students tended to be suspended for similar reasons as white students but more frequently and for more days on average. It states, "These data along with information gained from interviews with school personnel raise some questions concerning possible reluctance on the part of administrators to deal with minority group students and a tendency to avoid the problem by keeping them out of school for longer periods of time."[14]

The report shows that county-wide, the percentage of students suspended who were Black increased from 25.9 percent before desegregation to 48.5 percent immediately after. Further, since this report provides data on both racial-group-specific enrollments and suspensions as reported directly by the New Castle County School District, I am able to calculate suspension rates (based on racial-group-specific population sizes) for white and Black students using its data. Figure 4.3 shows these rates for 1975–1976 and 1978–1979. Here we see that the rate of Black students' suspensions increases dramatically during the period of desegregation, while the rate of white students' suspensions increases only

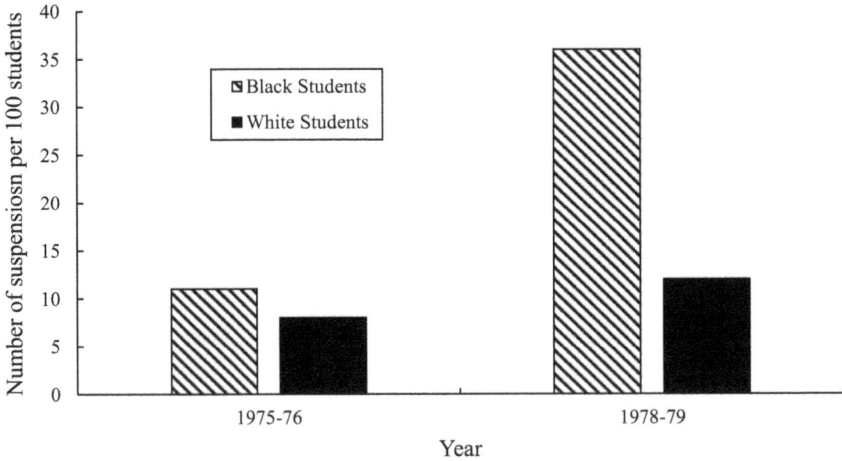

FIGURE 4.3. Rockefeller Foundation report data: suspension rates by race, 1975–1976 and 1978–1979. (Author's analysis of data from Gloria Grantham, Albert Miller, and Claire Fitzpatrick (1979) *An Interim Report of the Special Student Concerns Project: New Castle County Delaware*. Dover: Delaware Department of Community Affairs and Economic Development. Desegregation in Delaware Collection, Special Collections, University of Delaware Library)

slightly; the Black rate is 210 percent greater after desegregation compared to before, while the white rate increases by 39 percent.

The newly formed New Castle County School District also reported suspension data to the US Department of Education's Office for Civil Rights (OCR), which I analyzed and compared to suspension rates as reported by the OCR in earlier years. The suspension rates reported by the OCR for the new New Castle County School District are far lower than the rates published in the Special Student Concerns Project report. It is impossible to know for certain which data are more valid, though I have much more confidence in the Special Student Concerns Project report data. These data were reported directly to the researchers doing the analysis at that time, rather than reported to a national clearinghouse, entered into a system, and archived for decades. Further, a 1979 report to the county by the same lead author (Gloria Grantham) and using the same data set offers analyses that demonstrate far greater detail to these data than to the OCR data.[15] The data set on which the Special Student Concerns Project report is based includes the month of infraction, type of infraction, specific punishment, location within the school, and school identity, none of which are available in the decades-old OCR records. While I cannot be certain, this greater detail does lead me to assume that these data are more credible than the different numbers reported by the OCR. Nevertheless, I show the OCR data results in figures 4.4 and 4.5; these figures begin with the same data shown in chapter 3 (figures 3.5 and 3.6) but add new lines for the newly formed New Castle County School District (years 1978 and 1980) and then for the four new school districts that were created out of the county district in 1981 (years 1982 through 1994, reported every even year).

Figure 4.4 shows the suspension rates for all students, while figure 4.5 shows the rates just for Black students. These figures offer a more complex view of changes in suspension rates, leading to a few observations:

1. Suspension rates in the county-wide district and the four new districts were higher than the suspension rates pre-desegregation in both Wilmington and the primarily white districts.
2. When looking at just suspension rates of Black students (figure 4.5), this increase post-desegregation, and particularly after the county schools were separated into four districts in 1981, is striking.
3. According to the OCR data, the total suspension rate does not reach the De La Warr district's high pre-desegregation suspension rate until 1994. The suspension rate of Black students reaches the pre-desegregation De La Warr district level in 1992 and surpasses it in 1994.

Thus, even though the OCR data show considerably lower suspension rates than were reported by the Special Student Concerns Project,

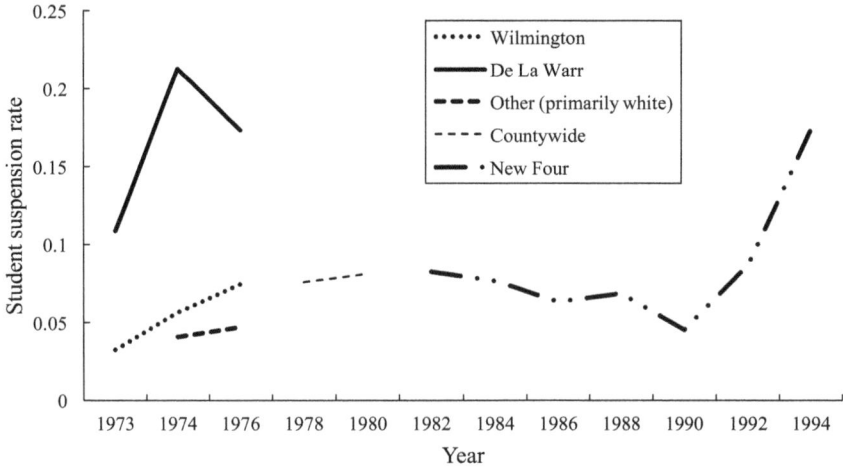

FIGURE 4.4. Office of Civil Rights data reports: proportion of all students suspended, 1973–1994. (Author's analysis of data from the Office of Civil Rights, US Department of Education)

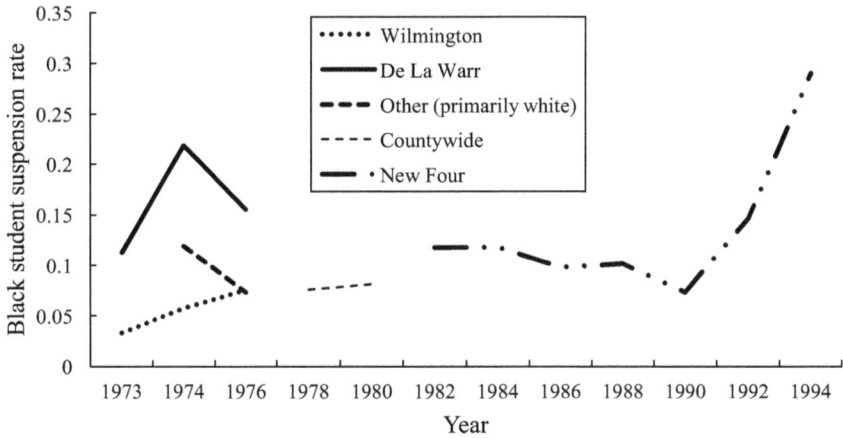

FIGURE 4.5. Office of Civil Rights data reports: proportion of Black students suspended, 1973–1994. (Author's analysis of data from the Office of Civil Rights, US Department of Education)

we still see an increase post-desegregation for all but the district (De La Warr) that was already desegregated.

Other Evidence of Increased Punishment

My research through Delaware archives offers several reasons to have confidence in the conclusion from the Special Student Concerns Project report: that school suspensions increased dramatically immediately after desegregation. In contrast to my inability to find records of school board reports or other discussions of school punishment in the 1960s or early 1970s, the issue becomes a prominently discussed concern during and after desegregation. Observers and child advocates at the time of desegregation also sounded the alarm about the rise in suspensions, particularly for Black students, immediately after desegregation.

On-the-Ground Observations

Jea Street, the current New Castle County councilman whom I quote in the epigraph to this chapter, was one of the most vocal and effective advocates for Black students during this era of desegregation. At that time, he was director of the Parent Education Resource Center. He later led the Coalition to Save our Children, and he has been involved as an advocate for Black children since December 1, 1974. When he and I discussed evidence of school suspensions immediately after desegregation, he said,

> Well, I mean, the fact of the matter is you go right to the beginning, in that, following the existence of the Wilmington School District, where there were no out-of-school suspensions that were at least reported in the last year of operation of the Wilmington School District. In the first year of school desegregation, the '78–'79 school year, and as documented in the Special Student Concerns Advocacy Project by Dr. Gloria

Grantham, there was a 200 percent increase in the out-of-school suspension of Black children and a 75 percent increase in the placement of
Black children in special education. And except for the year that the state
and the Coalition were in court over unitary status in 1994, it never went
back. The lowest it ever was, was that year that we were in court, and that
was seven thousand. In the initial year, it was ten thousand. And it never
went back. Neither did the placement rate in special education. And not
only suspensions but suspensions, expulsions, and arrests. And I'd never
heard of school-related arrests for disciplinary matters until we entered
the school desegregation order. . . . As we went forward, the OCR report in the Christina School District in December 2012—well, the prior
school years that they investigated, Christina had seventeen thousand
kids and twenty thousand suspensions. And the OCR determined that
they discriminated in discipline district-wide at all levels. So what else is
there to say? It's crystal clear—it's never changed. And I don't know what
else to tell you.

When I asked the councilman specifically about suspension rates
in Wilmington prior to 1978, he said, "My recollection is, well, during the four years that I was an advocate [1974–1978] primarily in the
Wilmington School District, we didn't have any suspensions."

Even board members of the newly formed New Castle County School
District expressed concerns about suspensions just after desegregation.
The Special Student Concerns Project's 1979 report summarized staff
interviews with the five board members; when describing board members' perceptions of the success of desegregation, school discipline was
the first concern that was mentioned: "Assessing how well desegregation
went this year, all the members felt it was a major factor that students
were transported peacefully and without any major incidents. There are
some problems to be worked out concerning discipline, curriculum, and
the lack of integration among students and staff and all members agreed
there is a big job ahead for next year as far as strengthening the entire
process."[16]

Project Confidence Group

The 1980 final report from the Project Confidence Group provides a clear illustration of the new concern about suspension that arose after desegregation. This group was formed soon after desegregation by Delaware House Resolution No. 172, which requested that the state Department of Public Instruction establish a review committee to "bolster the level of public confidence" and study performance of schools in New Castle County.[17] The Project Confidence Group researched only a few key issues: numbers of teachers, instructional supplies, *suspension rates*, test scores, school organization, and performance incentives for school administrators. In this report, the Project Confidence Group reports on the results of interviews and surveys with district administrators. The report states, "There is concern, however, among teachers, administrators, students, and parents relative to the suspension rates and the discipline in the schools. Out-of-school suspension rates have fluctuated since 1977–78 from 7 percent to 17 percent in 1978–79."[18]

Though school suspension was barely acknowledged in archived materials before the mid-1970s, it was a large-enough concern to be one of the few issues included in a state-legislature-mandated study about areas that needed to be resolved in order to boost public confidence in the schools.

Reporting to the Court

When the state Department of Public Instruction presented its plan in 1981 to reorganize from the newly formed New Castle County School District to the four new districts that were within it, plaintiffs raised concerns. One of them, according to a Department of Public Instruction report, was that the reorganization "fails to address two major problems: 1) 'resegregation in classrooms apparently caused by ability grouping and tracking' and assignment of students to special education programs without valid testing; and 2) a disproportionate discipline of Black students."[19]

These concerns were part of the court record within the years immediately following desegregation. Because of them, the 1981 court order allowing the creation of the four new school districts required that the Department of Public Instruction regularly report data on school suspensions to the court. Though several pieces of information were requested by the court, suspensions were the first item listed in these regular reports, even before student enrollments; to be clear, these regular reports to the court prioritized reporting of suspensions over reporting of how many Black and white students attended each recently desegregated school.

The court also urged the state to perform a study of school discipline, student ability grouping and tracking, and assignment to special education curriculum, so as to better understand these issues and instill credibility in the local school boards. The Department of Public Instruction commissioned such a study, which analyzed data on incident reports as well as from interviews and surveys. The report analyzes discipline incident data from the 1979–1980 and 1980–1981 school years, so we cannot use it to compare schools before and after the 1978 desegregation action. But the results are still important, for they show that suspension rates were high overall and particularly high for Black students. Black students in 1980–1981 constituted 26 percent of the student population in the New Castle County School District but received 47 percent of all suspensions. Black students were also more likely to be suspended multiple times, making up 60 percent of all students given multiple suspensions. When including all students, there were 8,558 out-of-school suspensions, resulting in 22,478 student days lost to suspension in that school year. A total of 14 percent of Black students and 7 percent of white students were suspended at least once, a rate that the report notes is much higher than the national average or in any of seven midwestern states used as comparators in the report. Finally, the report found that most disciplinary incidents resulted in suspension rather than other behavior-management strategies: "Seldom are other optional disciplinary techniques used."[20]

The report conducted by the Delaware Department of Public Instruction therefore finds that in the years just after desegregation, New Castle County suspension rates were more than twice the national average, with Black students having a much-higher rate of suspension than white students. It is also worth noting that the suspension rates reported here were at a level consistent with what was reported by the Special Student Concerns Project (in its report; see figure 4.3) and much higher than those I derived in my analysis of Office for Civil Rights data (figures 4.4 and 4.5).

Media Reports

My analyses of news media reports of school suspensions also suggest that the practice became common only after desegregation. In chapter 3, I discussed the rarity of articles on school suspension found in the Wilmington area's paper of record, the *News Journal*, prior to the era of civil rights protests and subsequent military occupation of Wilmington. The number of articles about school suspension increased dramatically with the 1978–1979 school year—the first year of county-wide desegregation. Some of these articles describe specific incidents that resulted in suspension or efforts to revise school rules generally. But several of them explicitly describe concerns over racially disproportionate use of discipline. For example, in a June 1978 article published in the months just before the desegregation plan went into effect, James D. Thomas, Delaware's director of the state Human Relations Office is quoted as stating, "Past experience throughout the United States indicates clearly that disciplinary action against minority students increases substantially once desegregation occurs."[21]

In March 1980, the *News Journal* published a front-page article in the Sunday paper about inconsistent discipline. The article referred to the fact that the New Castle County School District had no administrator to coordinate discipline across schools, no budget category to fund school discipline efforts, and a lack of uniformity. It also refers to the district's "alarmingly high suspension rate, a rate that is particularly high among minority students," and the fact that "one of every 12 secondary students—and one in every five black secondary students—was suspended at least once during the first four months of the school year."[22]

Continuing Legal Action

The Delaware schools returned to court in the 1990s when the state Board of Education sought unitary status, or freedom from federal court oversight. The plaintiffs, a parent-based "Coalition to Save Our Children," argued against unitary status (i.e., for continued court oversight) because they claimed that Delaware schools had not eliminated all vestiges of segregation. A central part of their argument was that students of color were disproportionately punished in the recently desegregated New Castle County schools. Judge Sue L. Robinson apparently was unconvinced, since she granted unitary status, thus ending the court's supervisory role in Delaware schools.[23]

The Coalition's argument demonstrates the widespread concern about high rates of suspension, particularly for students of color, in the years following desegregation of Delaware schools. Others agreed. In a foreword to a 2014 report on resegregation of Delaware schools, the education researcher and well-known expert on desegregation Gary Orfield writes of Judge Robinson's decision, "I have long thought that the lower court's decision was one of the most superficial and unbalanced among the cases I have read."[24]

The available evidence strongly and consistently demonstrates that school suspensions increased dramatically after the county's 1978 desegregation and that Black students were at particular risk of school suspension. A rigorous report documents stark increases in suspension and racially disproportionate suspensions; the court overseeing desegregation requested regular reports on school suspension due to its concern; the topic became a frequent item of discussion in the news media; student advocates who opposed unitary status a decade later saw high suspension rates as evidence of limits to the county's desegregation efforts; and observers on the ground reported the problem in desegregated schools. The pattern is clear, but the question that remains is, Why did suspensions increase so much after desegregation?

Explaining the Rise in Suspension

A structural race perspective reminds us that racial inequities are embedded within social institutions, including schools; that they are often unintended but follow a historical pattern of racial hierarchies; and that when institutions like schools change, they tend to do so in ways that benefit or maintain advantages for the white majority.[25] These insights, and particularly the way that they lead to a nuanced understanding of racialized social systems, help explain why suspension rates jumped so dramatically in New Castle County, Delaware, as schools desegregated. Explaining the rise in suspension after desegregation is more complex than suggesting that school punishment is an intentional outcome of school staff oppressing Black students.

It is important to keep in mind that desegregation was one part of a series of social changes and disruptions that caused anxiety and tension. As the stress on schools, communities, and families increased, schools responded by excluding students, particularly Black students. The response allowed schools to show that they were taking action to maintain order during a time of disorder. At the same time, intentionally or not, they were preserving opportunity for white students who no longer had access to segregated schools and limiting Black students' opportunities to learn in these schools.

As Amanda E. Lewis and John B. Diamond demonstrate in their analysis of contemporary schools, historical structural racism has and continues to shape institutional practices, or how schools go about educating and managing students. These practices then inform how individual students are treated.[26] This causal chain helps us understand how a systemic racial hierarchy influences individual teachers' and school administrators' actions. Teachers and administrators might be simply responding to the problems in front of them in ways that seem to them to be fair and reasonable. Indeed, according to student advocates and others involved with New Castle County's desegregation experience, most of the exclusion of Black students was not an intentional act of circumventing an unpopular court decision by removing students who were unwanted. Instead, in many classrooms and schools, it was a result of a subtler process, such as misrecognizing Black students' behaviors or responding to broader anxieties, each of which is shaped by historical structural racism.

Misrecognition

Often, Black students were seen as different or deviant. Their entrance into previously all-white (or mostly white) schools was a dramatic and sudden change. It is not surprising that many school staff saw the very presence of Black students as disruptive. Many educators also viewed these students as foreign and misinterpreted or misrecognized Black students' behaviors to be threatening or deviant. These perceptions of Black students as disruptive and alien are a direct result of structural racism; because schools had previously been understood to be white environments and educators' expectations were based on white students' behavioral norms, any deviation from these learned expectations was perceived as foreign, hostile, or problematic in other ways.[27]

Gloria Grantham describes this problem well. Grantham was a former Delaware teacher who then directed the Special Student Concerns Project for the county and was responsible for the most extensive study of the immediate effects of desegregation in Delaware. Her research began before desegregation occurred and continued until 1980, and it included analyses of school records, surveys of students, and interviews with teachers, administrators, and others. In my discussion with her about why suspension rates skyrocketed immediately after desegregation, she told me,

So here's where the disparity comes in, that kind of behavior in schools and deseg[regation]. So I'm in [a suburban school district in New Castle County]. [The district catchment area] is a closed community. These people and children grew up in [that area] all their lives. These teachers know them, their friends or their parents and neighbors. They're in their neighborhoods. But the danger of that was, you now have kids that you don't know, and they're Black, and they're coming into your school. They were seen as interlopers. "Why are they here? We don't want them. They don't belong. They need to go back to the city." They weren't prepared. And this was the main thing.

I spoke with the political scientist Jeffrey Raffel, who was instrumental in studying and advising the desegregation process as it was unfolding, about exclusionary punishment after desegregation. His comments mirror what Grantham noted about staff being unprepared and less tolerant of Black students' behavior: "Yes, there was resentment from suburban parents. . . . But it never occurred to me—I saw no evidence that the people in this system would be punishing people because of that. They might have been less tolerant. But I think, . . . what I saw was that they were less able to cope. Definitely many were less able to cope. Then some of them may have been less tolerant without even realizing."

The *News Journal* offered a similar description in the 1980 Sunday article on inconsistent discipline that I described earlier:

> Though there are no statistics to show whether student behavior is better or worse in the new district, administrators privately blame the dislocations caused by desegregation for many of the disciplinary problems.
>
> Schools such as William Penn, where administrators and teachers are accustomed to blue collar youths, seem to have had few problems. Suburban schools in wealthy areas, however, are now dealing with different types of students. Teachers and administrators may need to learn as much as students about different types of students and about discipline, officials say.[28]

These observations mirror contemporary research studies showing that still today, teachers misrecognize behaviors, speech, and dress of Black students. Teachers often view Black students' speech and behaviors as threatening or disruptive and their style of dress and other cultural dispositions as disrespectful.[29] Though Black students value education as much as other groups do overall, their behaviors are often misrecognized or wrongly perceived to indicate attitudes and intentions that are hostile to the school or to teachers. As Grantham indicated of New Castle County teachers in 1978, today's Black students are at risk of being seen by teachers as foreign or not belonging, and as a result, they are disproportionately punished for not conforming to expectations.

Current research finds that Black students are at greatest risk of being punished for minor, subjective offenses such as "defiance" or "insubordination." This is because the subjective nature of deciding whether a student has committed such an offense allows more room for racialized perceptions to influence teachers' judgment of wrongdoing, as compared to a relatively more objective offense, like possession of a weapon or fighting. This research result is accepted widely enough that it has been the basis for laws in some states, such as in California, in which Senate Bill 419, passed in 2019, prohibits schools from suspending anyone up to the eighth grade for willful defiance or disrupting school activities.[30] In 1979, the New Castle County Special Student Concerns Project's *Interim Report* stated a similar observation based on the experience with desegregation there and particularly its finding of reasons for Black students' suspensions: "These data along with interview results tend to suggest a sensitivity of school personnel and possibly students to particular categories of behavior to which a suspension consequence will result. The behavioral dynamics involved in defiance, for example, which is exceedingly high for Blacks, may well reflect an interpersonal strategy whenever defiance in Black students becomes a much less tolerable and expected form of behavior than the same behavior in Whites."[31]

This misrecognition was not limited only to perceptions of behaviors. As Delaware schools desegregated, many teachers viewed

Black students as academically deficient as well. Bebe Coker, the activist, parent, and social service coordinator working in Wilmington schools during desegregation, described this problem to me during our discussion:

> KUPCHIK: Were there other problems in terms of how Black students
> were treated after desegregation?
> COKER: Well, . . . I would say that there were those who thought that
> Black children learn differently. You could tell. . . . I always had the
> feeling that the white teachers thought they had to teach us one
> way and their children another way. I don't know why, but I always
> had that feeling. And to tell you the truth, to this day, I have that
> feeling. They don't think we learn in the same way. I recognize that
> there are those youngsters who bring a different level of resourced
> background to a given situation. Anybody does. But that doesn't
> mean that you can't learn or you should not be placed on the scale
> that you're supposed to be, to be on chapter 1, chapter 2, chapter 8,
> et cetera. But there are still those persons that just don't believe that
> Black children are capable of a certain level of learning or an accept-
> able level of learning or an expected level of learning.

As she describes, many teachers saw Black students as less able to learn and shortchanged their education, a problem that continues today.

Grantham echoed this description, as she found that white teachers in newly desegregated schools resisted Black students' presence because they assumed that Black students were academically deficient:

> GRANTHAM: [White teachers] did not think [the Black students]
> were prepared for them in the suburbs. That was the word that I
> would hear a lot. "These kids are from the city. They're not pre-
> pared well for our classrooms." And that's what I would get a lot at
> the time. I wasn't teaching at the time. At the time, I was working
> through the deseg[regation] with the whole New Castle County

administration. And I would hear this from various teachers
as I visited and worked with schools.

KUPCHIK: And you think that's not true? The kids were prepared?

GRANTHAM: Oh, definitely, like I said, many of them were. But the
problem with it was this: the students, like the ones I mentioned
that went on to college to good schools, these kids were going to be
successful. They were super bright. They had a very difficult time,
but they managed to get through it. It was the average kid who
carried the brunt of many racial disparities that occurred during
desegregation.

She continued to describe the impacts of this racist assumption. Before
getting to know students and gauging their academic abilities, teachers assumed that Black students were "not good enough" to be in their
schools. This was hurtful to the Black students, who felt the teachers' hostility. It also resulted in the schools' inequitable use of school
punishment:

GRANTHAM: Mostly it was the emotional and mental anguish and
anxiety that they pressed into the kids. That's what schools became
for them.

KUPCHIK: And that was because of hostility from white teachers,
primarily?

GRANTHAM: From the whole culture, this whole acculturated thing,
of "You're just not good enough. You don't belong here. Don't do
anything wrong. These rules are for you, not for our kids." And the
injustices that come with that, that kids would do things to them, but
they would be the ones that were the victims. I mean that they would
be the ones that were the perpetrators, even if they were the victims.
It was just a mess. It was a mess.

As Black Delaware students entered previously all-white spaces after
1978, they were perceived as foreign and deficient. Teachers, even many

who might have supported desegregation, often saw them as different, not part of a community previously characterized by similarity and trust and not as capable or well behaved as white students. As a result, school staff turned to exclusionary punishment (i.e., suspension) far more often than would have been seen as appropriate if working with a community that was characterized by similarity. As Raffel points out, this might not have been intentional. But racial bias need not be intentional for it to result in punishment that oppresses people of color.[32]

Broader Anxieties

The suspension of Black students immediately after desegregation is about more than just misrecognition, however. It is also important to understand the social context at that time and how it may have influenced school staff members' judgments about maintaining order in their schools. Desegregation must certainly have caused anxiety among explicitly racist white families who did not want their children's schools to accept Black students. But the dislocation and anxiety that it caused was far broader than that.

As Raffel found, most white families in New Castle County supported the idea of desegregating the county's schools. But they resented being *forced* to do so by court intervention, and even more, they strongly opposed mandatory *busing*: in 1978, only 9 percent of suburban parents polled favored or strongly favored busing, while 89 percent opposed or strongly opposed it.[33] It is important to keep in mind that the desegregation plan was not just about educating Black and white children together. It also meant massive changes of school attendance and a complete redrawing of school district boundaries. These are enormous changes, especially considering that many people might have bought their homes specifically to live within a particular school district (which no longer existed as of fall 1978), and they might have been invested in their locally elected school boards (which were all dissolved as well). Given how extensively many families plan for their children's education, it is easy to see how upsetting it might have been for these plans to be entirely changed from one school year to the next.

Black families in Wilmington were not necessarily supportive of the county's desegregation plan either. In Raffel's research on attitudes toward busing and desegregation, he found that in 1978, only 48 percent of Wilmington parents who responded to a poll (most of whom were Black) favored or strongly favored busing, while 43 percent opposed or strongly opposed busing.[34] Instead of attending schools in their communities, their children were now going to be bused into suburban school districts, some several miles away, for nine out of twelve grades. This meant earlier wake-up times and long bus rides for many, greater reliance on buses (making after-school activities more difficult), and increased difficulty for parents to attend school functions or meet with teachers. Further, merging the former Wilmington School Board—which by 1978 was dominated by Black community leaders—with the surrounding white school districts meant that Black Wilmingtonians lost what was at that time the primary source of the Black community's political power in the entire state. There were good reasons for Black parents and community members in Wilmington to be wary of the desegregation plan; while desegregation offered the hope of better educational opportunities, in practice it was disruptive to schooling, parenting, and the Black community's political power.

Teachers, too, faced great disruption with the desegregation plan. The plan not only changed student attendance patterns but also included compulsory staffing changes in an effort to desegregate teachers. Because most Black teachers had been in Wilmington schools prior to desegregation, many teachers were forced to move schools, and some Black teachers lost their jobs as a result.[35] Other Black teachers were transferred to suburban schools, and many white teachers took their place by being transferred from the suburbs to Wilmington schools. Not only did this result in resentment among many teachers who did not appreciate being forced to relocate their jobs to entirely new schools that are much farther away, but it also raised problems with equity of salary that resulted in a teachers' strike. Before desegregation, teachers in Wilmington received higher pay, on average, for the same level of experience, compared to teachers in suburban schools. The desegregation plan meant that these teachers now worked alongside others who were paid on a lower pay scale. The teachers' union demanded that the salaries be leveled for the sake of equity, but the state claimed not to have sufficient funds to do so.[36] This resulted in a six-week-long strike, from mid-October through November 1978, until a compromise ended the impasse.[37]

There was real disruption to the schools that were forced to accept Black students. That is not in question. But what is important is that this disruption resulted in punishment for the Black students who were the face of the change. This is precisely what a structural race perspective would predict, of course. As Victor Ray writes in his theory of racialized organizations, "Once racialized hierarchies become a taken-for-granted aspect of organizations, they are enforced by Whites' 'sense of group position.' Threats to the organizational hierarchy—for example, the hiring or promotion of non-Whites, affirmative action policies, or diversity programs—are often seen as illegitimate intrusions into the normal, meritocratic, neutral functioning of organizations."[38] Here, the inclusion of Black students into formerly all-white schools is the threat to the organizational hierarchy. These students were seen as an "illegitimate intrusion" and were removed via school suspension in large numbers.

Certainly, students faced difficult adjustments as a result of desegregation through busing as well. The merger of eleven districts into one, busing of students, and transfer of teachers must have been an unsettling process in the best of circumstances. The fact that some teachers and students resented their forced transfer and others undoubtedly wanted to preserve a segregated school system meant a lot of tension and resentment for students to navigate in the fall of 1978. Observers at the time noted the impact of these tensions. For example, the Special Student Concerns Project's *Interim Report* noted the following about human relations specialists in the newly desegregated schools: "Most Specialists agree that the majority of [misbehavior] incidents occur because of frustration on the part of students or as a result of students' lack of knowledge concerning the norms of the school."[39] While not common, at least a few *News Journal* articles at the time of desegregation described interracial student conflict.

It is important to place the massive shift in schools in 1978 within a broader political and economic context as well. The 1970s were a time of important political and economic challenges that, according to the legal scholar Jonathan Simon, reoriented the American public's relationship to government. In his influential book *Governing through Crime*, Simon argues that the upheaval of the late 1960s and 1970s—including the Watergate scandal, exit from Vietnam, and civil rights protests, among others—led to an erosion of public trust in government and a crisis of the New Deal political order. In the resulting void, policy makers realized that public support could be built, but on fear, and they began "governing through crime" in ways that mobilized fear in support of their political agendas.[40] The anxiety and distrust that Simon describes also characterizes what residents of New Castle County must have felt in 1978. In the years immediately preceding school desegregation, the country experienced Watergate, a rocky exit from Vietnam, an oil crisis, and rising crime rates. The 1970s also saw the start of postindustrialism, when the economic and labor model shifted away from an industrial base, leaving many low-wage earners unemployed.[41] My point is that there were already several major shifts and crises going on before desegregation that undoubtedly raised levels of anxiety and distrust of state institutions such as schools. An immense change to the county's educational system could only have added to this anxiety.

Anxiety does not necessarily or directly result in exclusionary school punishment. But it does help us understand why school suspensions rose. Throughout the 1970s, county residents experienced anxiety and trauma based on important national events, while at home, their children's schools were being completely restructured in order to allow Black students the opportunity for inclusion in previously white schools. If Black students' inclusion is viewed, consciously or not, as another source of disruption that adds to the sense of anxiety amid social change and upheaval, then it is easy to see how many school staff might have seen these students' exclusion (via suspension from school) as a reasonable response. Moreover, it is a response that is supported by the forces of structural racism. Remember that a structural race perspective tells us that when times change and institutions progress, they tend to do so in ways that maintain advantages for white people. Responding to anxiety and upheaval by suspending Black students certainly fits this pattern.

Different Behaviors?

An alternate possible explanation for the high suspension rates observed after desegregation is that students in general, and Black students in particular, behaved worse than they did while in segregated schools.[42] It seems likely, particularly given the few *News Journal* reports I referred to earlier about interracial conflict among students, that desegregation did result in more student fights or in Black students responding defiantly to hostility aimed at them. In my discussion with Raffel, he referred to such defiant behavior as a function of the displacement of Black students to schools in which they felt they did not belong. He stated,

> Who owns the school? Whose school is it? . . . Can we still call our—is our nickname for the school still going to be Warriors or . . . whatever, you know, some name, or are we going to change that to blend . . . ? So what's our cheerleading squad going to look like? Are they going to do the more traditional, white schools' cheering or the Black schools', et cetera. The vast majority of African American kids were bused out to the suburbs. And so they were going to schools that weren't theirs. They weren't in their neighborhoods. They were further away. It wouldn't be a shock to think that that might cause behavior that that would lead to more suspensions, right?

Raffel also pointed out to me the fact that many of the Black students entering previously segregated white schools were not prepared for the academic rigor of their new schools. He described some of the schools in Wilmington before desegregation as dysfunctional, with lax academic standards and ineffective leadership. An outside evaluation of Wilmington's schools in 1973, conducted by Mark Shedd, ex-superintendent of Philadelphia schools, and a field research team from the Harvard Graduate School of Education, agreed. In the report, Shedd criticized the Wilmington schools for being ineffective and inefficient, with 80 percent of children more than one grade level behind in reading by grade six. Shedd also raised concerns about a lack of parental involvement in Wilmington schools, bloated district-level administrative staff, poor delivery of district-wide services to the school level, and lack of coordination between schools.[43] Black students who moved from these underperforming schools to higher-performing schools in the suburbs must have faced a difficult transition. Not only would expectations have changed, but so might their workload. These stressors, and the difficulty and stress caused by not understanding the academic material in their classes (which might have been at a much more advanced level than they were prepared for, because of the prior school they attended), might result in higher rates of misbehavior among Black students.[44] Further, Raffel had found that behavioral expectations differed across previously segregated schools as well. Black students who had been in Wilmington schools prior to desegregation and then traveled to suburban schools encountered stricter standards of behavior in their new schools, which resulted in more frequent school punishment.[45]

Raffel raises excellent points, particularly because he was observing responses to desegregation in real time, and I accept his observations as fair and accurate. But I would argue that despite each of these factors, staff members' negative responses to the Black students who entered their schools were still important. Disruptive behavior from Black students who feel unwelcome and ill at ease in their new schools is, to a large extent, a consequence of the resistance to desegregation and the hostile climate that the incoming Black students faced, not the direct result of internal student behavioral dispositions (i.e., not a matter of their character or typical behavior). While it might be the case that student misbehavior was worse after desegregation, the sudden jump right at the point of desegregation suggests that desegregation itself is related, not just other influences such as community crime rates or baseline behavioral differences between groups of students that are unrelated to desegregation.

Certainly, a sudden shift in behavioral and academic expectations might have led to more negative and defiant behaviors from Black students. But the fact that schools chose to respond with exclusion rather than inclusion, by punishing these children who bore the brunt of desegregation and a history of oppression rather than embracing them and addressing the problems they faced, speaks volumes. Desegregation was stressful, to say the least. Suburban school staff could have responded to the many real difficulties that resulted in different ways. Teachers and school administrators have agency—there was a range of responses they could have chosen, including less punitive and more inclusive options than suspension. They could have responded by welcoming the students who entered their schools, making them feel wanted, easing them into new curricula, and working with them to address any behavioral issues that might arise. They could have seen these students as children placed by adults on the front line of a centuries-old battle against racial oppression, not problems to be excluded. Such a response would mean not just kind actions by individual teachers but a host of school supports such as teacher aides, mentoring, and tutoring. Indeed, many teachers did their best to warmly embrace the incoming Black students, and the state provided this type of support in the form of the human relations specialists who worked in the schools to ease the transition and help students.[46] And yet schools still resorted to suspension at a level not previously seen, showing that a common response to desegregation and the stressors that came with it was to exclude Black students.

Furthermore, though the change in academic and behavioral expectations that came with desegregation might help explain some of the problem of racially disproportionate punishment in 1978, it offers little explanation for the continued problem of racially disproportionate punishment in following years. In other words, if the problem of racially disproportionate suspension rates was because of an adjustment to suddenly changed academic demands or standards of behavior, then we would have seen the problem dissipate in subsequent years as students became accustomed to schools' standards and expectations. Instead, as we have seen, racially disproportionate suspension rates only continued in the decades that followed.

There is no way to determine with certainty whether Black students' behaviors were problematic after desegregation to such a degree and in a way that justified massive jumps in suspensions. The only data we have (flawed as it is) come from schools' reports of disciplinary incidents, not actual student behaviors, so they measure schools' responses rather than students' actions. In my discussion with Grantham, I asked her about the possibility that suspension rates were so high after desegregation because of misbehavior primarily among Black students. In response, she stated simply, "That's not true." She elaborated by comparing her experiences teaching at an exclusive predominantly white private school in Wilmington and at a public school with almost all Black students just before desegregation and said of both groups of children,

All adolescent kids—I don't care where you are, what color they are—their behavior is very similar. They don't use good judgment because they're adolescents. They don't—they haven't lived long enough to benefit from the experiences during adolescence, bad or good. And so they just do stuff. Now, if they can live through adolescence, then they start to calm down, because all of those experiences mean something. They may get into a lot of trouble. . . . Because, . . . as Piaget puts it, they're transitioning into formal operations. But the fact that I now have a little bit of foresight and the fact that I'm observing adults very closely and especially my parents. I'm an excellent observer, but I'm a very poor interpreter of what I see. So I think if I'm fourteen and my parents get on my nerves, I'll just go out and get a job and live somewhere else. I'll just buy myself a car, and I'll do this and I'll do that. It's like, you know—it's just—it's just who they are. They want to wear what they want, where they want autonomy, they want this, they want that, but they don't use good judgment. And that's all kids.

In other words, she recognized that all adolescents behave immaturely and that Black and white students showed similar types of misbehavior.

In a later conversation, Grantham returned to this point and argued against race-neutral explanations of the spike in suspensions immediately after desegregation. Here is her explanation for why teachers perceived Black students as defiant and academically deficient:

It's race primarily. Here's my statement on it: *It is race.* So we start there. Because white people wanted to say, the white population of teachers wanted to say, "It's a class issue, not a race issue." Wrong. It's a race issue. Class only enters after race, because when you put class with class, of which there were so many middle-class, upper-middle-class African American families, educated, and their children, they all suffered, because if they were a part of the deseg[regation], they were still seen first as Black. And once you're seeing—once this color thing that upsets the white population so much, once they see this [points to her skin], it's somehow you're—you're not good enough. "You cannot be where our kids are." That's where you saw the flip and "We'll protect our children from you." And that's the other thing that it's always set up, as "We need to protect our white children from the Black children who are here." And that's first and foremost on our minds that "these are the people who will hurt our children, fight our children, rob our children, mistreat our children. And they're here and they're interlopers, and they're actually in our school. And we are being forced to teach them." And they just—the white teachers were afraid of them. You can't teach kids when you're afraid of them. There was a myth that these Black boys will somehow hurt our white teachers or offend them or upset them, especially at the high school level. And it's like, give me a break, these are kids! You know, for those white teachers who were the adults and who saw kids for who kids were, they loved them. There was no problem. That's always how it's been with white and Black teachers. Teachers are wonderful people, and when they are taught to do their jobs well and they understand people and different races of people, everybody does well. It works for all of us. And that was the case. There were so many white teachers who loved the kids, period, and did such a great job with them. And once the culture took over, as you know, "We have to nip this in the bud immediately. We have to suspend them, get them out." It just became another way of segregating, the suspensions, as they rose higher and higher. Just, "Anything they do, just send them home. Anything they do, just send them home" or "expel them or put them out."

As she describes, the racial bias held by many teachers resulted in schools sending Black children home. Teachers viewed Black students with suspicion and fear but were forced to teach them; suspension became a way for them to try to protect their schools and white students from the newly admitted Black students.

More than a decade later, the state argued in court that higher rates of misbehavior, not racial bias, explained disproportionately high rates of school punishment for Black students. When the state Board of Education requested unitary status in the 1990s, the plaintiffs argued that the high rate of school punishment for Black students was one of several indicators of continuing discriminatory treatment. The expert witness testifying on behalf of the state, Charles Achilles, argued that while Black students were more likely to be suspended than white students in the county schools, this was due to the equitable application of the schools' codes of conduct, not discriminatory treatment. To support this argument, he presented evidence that the level of racially disproportionate suspensions was lower in New Castle County than in the

US overall, based on national data from the Office for Civil Rights; the rate of disproportionate discipline was consistent across the four school districts in the county; and that application of school codes of conduct was consistent regardless of administrators' race. The court accepted this argument and found that "the codes [of conduct] are not applied in a discriminatory fashion."[47]

Perhaps the racial disparity in punishment was acceptable to the court because the court assumed that this was an inevitable consequence of Black students' more disruptive behavior. Research since then across multiple sites shows that such an assumption is simply false, since if there are behavioral differences between Black and white students (which itself seems doubtful overall), these do not explain racial disparity in school punishment.[48]

It might be true, as Achilles testified, that the problem of racially disparate punishment is less severe in New Castle County than in other places across the US or even than the national average. But that does not mean that it is not problematic—it just means that the problem is widespread! The same is true for the fact that punishments are consistent across administrators and school districts: it is absurd to argue that discriminatory treatment is acceptable just because the discrimination is consistent. Those of us who grew up in the 1980s were told to "Just Say No" to drugs, that just because one's friends use drugs is not a good reason for you to do so.[49] It is not clear to me why this same logic does not apply to school discipline; just because New Castle County schools' peers disproportionately suspended Black students, that does not mean that it is acceptable for schools in New Castle County to do so.

Conclusion

Councilman Jea Street's comments at the start of the chapter echo all the evidence I could find. Immediately after New Castle County schools were desegregated in 1978, suspension rates skyrocketed, particularly for Black students. Black students entering previously all-white schools were seen as "interlopers," strangers in an environment that was unaccustomed to them and uncomfortable with their presence. While it may not have been an intentional strategy by most teachers to exclude Black students from newly desegregated schools, the evidence shows that this happened frequently and cannot be explained away only by referring to student behavior or other factors.

Granted, all of this occurred during a moment of great change and anxiety. Resistance to Black students entering previously all-white schools was not the only influence on school punishment. But the evidence shows that it was an important one. Desegregation was about *inclusion*: civil rights advocates wanted Black students to be included in the schools that provided opportunities to white students. Given what a structural race perspective tells us about the reproduction of systemic inequality over time, it should hardly be surprising that this court-mandated project of inclusion was met with a wave of *exclusion*: exclusion from school via suspension.

Suspending students does not improve their behavior, nor does it help schools maintain orderly environments in the long run. But it does communicate to students that they are not wanted in school. And it preserves opportunities for white students at the expense of Black students, in ways that reverberate across generations. Many of the Black students who bore the brunt of resistance to court-ordered desegregation and were suspended from schools in New Castle County became parents who were underemployed because of their own educational gaps and who were less connected to their children's education. The immediate growth in suspension after desegregation was clearly impactful, both then and today. In my discussion with Grantham, she spoke clearly about the multigenerational harms that suspensions caused for Black families in Wilmington:

> Oh, it was awful. I mean, responses to desegregation destroyed three generations of African American students. And the results of that is what we are seeing today. They literally—I mean, I have kids now that—oh,

I don't know if I told you—I went back to teaching last year. . . . And this population of students show residual effects of desegregation. And we're still seeing the residual effects of all of those bright, bright children who were just devastated by deseg[regation]. I mean, they were put out. They were seen as interlopers. They were misunderstood, and they were—they were just the victims of people who didn't believe that they could do it.

Nearly fifty years after New Castle County schools desegregated, the Black community still reels from the impact of low expectations, harsh punishment, and denial of real educational opportunities that took shape in the wake of desegregation.

New Castle County, Delaware's experience with desegregation follows the pattern of events that a structural race perspective predicts: policy change is enacted in ways that maintain racial inequality because a racial hierarchy is baked into institutions like schools. Desegregation was supposed to level the playing field by providing Black students access to the best schools, which had been reserved for white students. But once Black students were in those schools, staff misrecognized their behaviors and saw them as problems to be managed. They turned to suspension as a solution to the increased stress and disorder brought by desegregation. In this way, desegregation did not end racial inequality in Delaware; it just restructured it. Again I turn to Bryan Stevenson's words: "Slavery didn't end. It evolved."[50] As one system of racial oppression ended in New Castle County, it was replaced by another; after 1978, New Castle County schools were desegregated but marked by a racially inequitable system of punishment that removed Black students from school.

5

The Cradle of Liberty?

Boston before Desegregation

On May 22, 1856, US Senator Charles Sumner from Massachusetts was beaten unconscious on the Senate floor by Representative Preston Brooks. Sumner was an outspoken abolitionist. Three days earlier, he had delivered a lengthy and fiery abolitionist address on the Senate floor using language that compared the South's institution of slavery to prostitution. Then on the twenty-second, Representative Brooks of South Carolina walked onto the Senate floor, where Senator Sumner was stamping copies of the speech he had delivered, and began to beat him with a metal-topped cane. Brooks hit Sumner repeatedly as Representative Laurence M. Keitt (also from South Carolina) stood by with a drawn gun. Brooks was expelled from the House and then reelected to it. After a long recovery, Sumner spent another eighteen years in the Senate.[1]

I bring up this incident to illustrate the history of Massachusetts, and Boston in particular, as a site where independence and equality have historically been celebrated. Boston is known as the "cradle of liberty" because the Revolutionary War began there, not only with its first battles but also with the first strategic planning of revolutionary efforts. Nearly a century later, Sumner was celebrated in Massachusetts (including multiple reelections) after being nearly murdered for delivering a scathing abolitionist address.

Massachusetts was also the first state to legally desegregate schools, in 1855. This law followed a lawsuit, *Sarah C. Roberts v. The City of Boston* (1849), in which Sarah Roberts's parents sued the city in an attempt to integrate city schools. Sarah, who was Black, had to pass by five primary schools on her way to the only school in Boston that admitted

Black children. The Robertses lost their legal case, but the case mobilized school integration advocates and sparked a sustained boycott of segregated Black schools. The pressure worked, and the state legislature passed the nation's first school desegregation law. In fact, this law was even referenced as an example of a successful school integration effort in Chief Justice Earl Warren's written decision for *Brown v. Board of Education*.[2]

Boston is home to many prestigious academic institutions and is known for being a politically liberal city. Its residents (and senator) were abolitionists when the nation was divided over whether it was acceptable to own human beings, and the state of Massachusetts led the nation in legislating desegregation. Massachusetts was the *only* state won by the liberal George McGovern against Richard Nixon in the 1972 presidential race. It has strong credentials as a progressive state that supports equality. If desegregation were to proceed peacefully and without harm to students anywhere, one would expect it to happen in a place with such a pedigree, making it an excellent site for studying how desegregation unfolded in ways that led to the problem of excessive school punishment. The northern, liberal character of Boston also offers an important contrast to chapters 3 and 4, which focus on the border South state of Delaware.

Despite the city's laws prohibiting de jure segregation, its pedigree, and its reputation as the "cradle of liberty," Boston was also a site of egregious school segregation and racial injustice. In the years before a federal court mandated a controversial desegregation plan for Boston schools in 1974, Boston residents, politicians, and advocates debated about where and how Black students should be educated. The state legislature worked to help schools desegregate, only to face local efforts to undermine or reverse the legislation and maintain segregation (while denying its existence). And yet the subject of school punishment barely surfaced as a topic on the agenda—until the 1974 desegregation plan took effect, that is. Despite the many differences between the northern, abolitionist, liberal state of Massachusetts and the border South, slave-owning state of Delaware, I found that their histories with deseg-regation and punishment mirror each other's.

Racial Segregation in Boston Schools in the 1960s

Despite Boston's moniker of the "cradle of liberty," it has a dark history of racial oppression. Earlier I noted that the state's 1855 law prohibit-ing de jure school segregation was cited in the *Brown* decision as an illustration of desegregation success; ironically, the 1849 *Roberts* case challenging school segregation in Boston—the one in which the court refused to rule for the plaintiffs seeking integrated schools but that spurred the passage of the 1855 desegregation law—was itself cited as the existing legal precedent on which *Plessy v. Ferguson* rested. The 1896 *Plessy* Supreme Court case, of course, established "separate but equal" as legal, solidifying legal segregation and justifying Jim Crow laws. On the basis of this precedent and the historical treatment of Black residents in Boston, the historian Zebulon Vance Miletsky calls Boston the "original site of Jim Crow segregation."[3]

Boston's history is complicated, marked by both successful efforts to foster racial equity and racial oppression. Even after equity-oriented legislation, such as the very progressive 1855 law that legally integrated the state's public schools, Black students still received inadequate educa-tion that paled in comparison to what white students typically received, and usually in schools that were segregated. This is precisely what a structural race perspective would predict—or more precisely, it is the historically repeated pattern that structural race theories try to explain. Whether we are considering federal civil rights laws or Massachusetts's law prohibiting segregation, legal advances toward equality repeatedly fail to stop racial oppression; they only cause it to change form.

In the historian Ronald Formisano's rich description of Boston before and after desegregation in the 1970s, he details the discrimination in housing, employment, and education that shaped Boston in the 1950s and 1960s. He describes the flight of white Bostonians to suburban enclaves, facilitated by federal loan programs and highway construction and enforced by discriminatory lending practices. While this pattern happened throughout the US, Boston's experience was marked by extensive technology-sector growth just outside of Boston, in areas that were far more accessible to white residents.[4] Not only were Black residents increasingly clustered in Boston rather than in the thriving suburban areas, but this pattern was replicated within Boston as well, with white and Black residents tending to live in racially identifiable neighborhoods due to racist bank and realtor practices.[5] As Formisano writes, "In the wake of Martin Luther King's assassination, Mayor Kevin White had persuaded a consortium of Boston banks (BBURG, Boston Banks' Urban Renewal Group) to provide $27 million in mortgages to low-income black families. Unfortunately, realtors and bankers quickly exploited the program to make money and to turn a thriving Jewish neighborhood into a black ghetto. BBURG selected Mattapan, which ran through two Irish neighborhoods and was a thriving self-contained Jewish community, and 'redlined' it—granting mortgages to blacks only within that corridor."[6] Again and again, in Boston and elsewhere, we see that apparent progress is subverted by racially disparate treatment in ways that preserve the racial hierarchy.

The structures of racial discrimination that shaped the pattern of wealth distribution and residential segregation that we still see today also led to segregated schools. Boston public schools mirrored this pattern, even if the law had—for over one hundred years by this point—prohibited legal segregation of schools. As the historian Matthew Delmont states, "Americans' understanding of school desegregation in the North is skewed . . . , emphasizing innocent or unintended 'de facto segregation' over the housing covenants, federal mortgage redlining, public-housing segregation, white homeowners' associations, and discriminatory real-estate practices that produced and maintained segregated neighborhoods, as well as the policies regarding school siting, districting, and student transfers that produced and maintained segregated schools."[7] Delmont points out how segregated

Boston schools were not the by-product of racially neutral residential patterns, of people deciding freely where to live. Instead, they were the result of school policies in addition to racist practices in financial and housing markets.

In 1965, the Kiernan Commission—an advisory Commission on Racial Imbalance appointed by the Massachusetts commissioner of education, Owen Kiernan—found that most of the segregation in education that existed throughout the state was in Boston. The Kiernan Commission's report found that there were fifty-five "racially imbalanced" schools statewide, with forty-five of them in Boston.[8] In the 1960s, Boston schools were, for the most part, racially segregated, with Black children educated in inferior and overcrowded schools.

Robert A. Dentler and Marvin B. Scott, the court-appointed experts that advised Judge W. Arthur Garrity on the Boston desegregation case I describe in chapter 6, help illustrate how segregated Boston schools were. In their book *Schools on Trial*, they write,

> From the onset of the federal civil action suit, no one associated with the Boston public schools disputed the fact that they were extremely segregated. . . . The system included 201 schools in 1973. A total of 160 of them were segregated in the sense that their student racial compositions were identifiably, indeed extremely, divergent from the racial composition of the student population as a whole. Of eighteen high schools, only one, Boston High School, a special occupational training site, reflected the composition of the high school student population as a whole. Eight of the eighteen were between 85 and 96 percent white, and three were between 75 and 98 percent black, within a system where about two-thirds of the enrolled high school students were white. Of the 150 elementary schools in 1973, 62 were 96 to 100 percent white and 32 were 85 to 98 percent black.[9]

My own reproduction of the Boston Public Schools Official Racial Census for high schools from October 1972, table 5.1, shows a similar distribution, with few city high schools that either showed parity or were representative of the student demographics within the city's school system overall.

Segregated Black schools were underresourced in a variety of ways. Students were educated in overcrowded buildings that were older and in greater need of repair than the schools attended by white students.[10] Through the 1950s, average per-student spending was $340 for white students compared to $240 for Black students.[11] A 1963 statement written by Paul Parks, a member of the Education Committee of the Boston NAACP, lists a variety of concerns about the state of Boston's segregated schools attended by Black children. The statement identifies problems

TABLE 5.1 Boston Public Schools Official Racial Census—High Schools, October 1, 1972

School name	White students (% of enrollment)	Black students (% of enrollment)
South Boston	99	1
East Boston	95	5
Charlestown	94	6
Roslindale	94	6
Boston Latin	93	7
Girls' Latin	89	11
Boston Technical	83	17
Hyde Park	81	19
Brighton	71	29
Boston High	67	33
Jamaica Plain	51	49
Copley Square	46	54
Dorchester	42	58
Boston Trade	26	74
Trade High for Girls	24	76
English	12	88
Jeremiah E Burke	1	99
Girls' High	1	99

Source: Author's reproduction of raw data from Boston Public Schools' *Administrative Circular*, No. 26 (1972–1973), found in the Department of Education files, Boston City Archives.

such as overcrowding, cracked walls, leaking roofs, flooded hallways, faulty ventilation, unsanitary toilets, "basement classrooms that are unfit for pupil use," and inadequate per-pupil funding.[12] In the PBS documentary *Busing Battleground*, the Boston civil rights leader Ruth Batson describes the comparison between the schools that Black children, like hers, attended and those attended by white children: "I became chairperson of the NAACP public school committee. I gathered a group of people around me, and when we would go to white schools, we'd see these lovely classrooms, small number of children in each class. The teachers were permanent. We would see wonderful materials. When we'd go to our schools, we'd see overcrowded classrooms, children sitting out in the corridors, and so forth."[13] Segregated schools also meant a largely segregated teaching force. Dentler and Scott also provide data on the racial segregation of teachers in Boston public schools. Only 5.4 percent of Boston public school teachers in 1973 were Black, and most of them were assigned to segregated Black schools.[14]

The well-known writer and activist Jonathan Kozol wrote his first book about segregated Boston schools. *Death at an Early Age* is Kozol's account of his year as a long-term substitute teacher in a Boston school.[15] The book, which won the National Book Award in 1968, is a heart-wrenching account of an underfunded, overcrowded school in which students are treated as unworthy of a quality education. While teaching a fourth-grade class in a segregated classroom in Roxbury (a predominantly Black neighborhood in Boston), Kozol was repeatedly frustrated by the injustices students faced. His "classroom" consisted of a corner of the school's crumbling auditorium, separated from other "classrooms" within the same auditorium space by blackboards that operated as temporary walls. The school lacked basic supplies, and its infrastructure was a mess. Its teachers spoke of Black students as "animals" and public schools in Black neighborhoods as "zoos." Kozol was required to use textbooks that either disparaged Black people or ignored their historical oppression. Kozol's efforts to push back against this system, to affirm Black students' worth and the importance of Black history, and to teach critical thinking were all rebuffed by school administrators, who refused to believe in the ability of their students to learn. With eight days left in the school year, he was fired for teaching Langston Hughes's 1940 poem "Ballad of the Landlord." The story of his firing sounds like something that could happen today, as it foreshadows the contemporary anger that teaching about racism might upset white students and the subsequent trouble that teachers can get into for doing so.[16] One of the few white children in Kozol's class told his father about the Langston Hughes poem, which is about a Black tenant's dispute with his white landlord that ends in court with the judge's verdict: "JUDGE GIVES NEGRO 90 DAYS IN COUNTY JAIL." The father complained to the school's principal, and the principal fired Kozol for teaching the poem.[17] Ironically, the poem itself gives voice to the excessive punishment that Black people face when they try to protest their plight.

The local Boston NAACP and other advocates for Black students' right to a quality education began to address the problem of segregated, inferior schools for Black students in the early 1960s.[18] As Formisano details, in 1961 they asked the Massachusetts Commission Against Discrimination to investigate Boston schools, but the commission concluded that race was not a factor in school assignments or quality. The NAACP's next step was to directly engage in talks with the Boston school superintendent, Frederick J. Gillis. But Gillis refused to engage in serious discussions about segregation, stating that since the school department did not classify students by race, it could not assess the NAACP's claims. By 1963, the NAACP petitioned the Boston School Committee, asking for recognition of the existence of segregation, improved teacher training, improvements to Black schools, and an end to discrimination in hiring teachers and administrators. Despite concrete evidence showing segregated schools, the School Committee refused to admit that Boston schools were de facto segregated or to discuss reforms.[19] The disagreement escalated, leading to a June 18, 1963, boycott of schools sponsored by the NAACP and another schools boycott in February 1964—the Kiernan Commission formed in response to this latter boycott.[20] As Russell

Dever, an education researcher who was asked by the court to study school discipline during the 1970s legal action, reports, Black leaders initially just wanted the Boston School Committee to acknowledge the existence—without blame—of de facto segregation and to work to improve the schools Black students attended. But the School Committee steadfastly refused.[21]

The School Committee and State Respond

In 1965, the Massachusetts state legislature passed the Racial Imbalance Act. It came about just a few months after the Kiernan Commission released its report documenting segregation in Boston schools. The act required that in order for schools to receive full state funding, they must show "racial balance," which was defined as having between 50–100 percent white students. If school districts contained schools with a majority of students of color, the district was required to submit plans for desegregation.[22]

And yet the Boston School Committee still refused to take action to desegregate Boston public schools. As Formisano writes, "For nine years after the passage of the Racial Imbalance Act, the Boston School Committee . . . refused to take steps to bring about any significant school integration. Through delay, counterattacks, and the most transparent obfuscation and tokenism the committee held the line against a growing black population. Meanwhile, the number of racially imbalanced schools climbed upward."[23] As Formisano continues to describe, the Boston School Committee responded with denial and delay. It refused to implement relatively minor reforms, such as integrating schools located between Black and white neighborhoods. Even though the NAACP and others had sought only this modest level of reform, nothing on the scale of the mandatory desegregation through busing that would eventually follow in 1974, the School Committee responded as if it were under full attack and stonewalled. The committee challenged the Racial Imbalance Act in court, continuing until the Supreme Court declined to hear the case in 1968. Given that the committee was forced to submit plans for how it would desegregate schools, it submitted convoluted plans that changed little, resulting in continuing negotiations with the state board in charge of enforcing the law. As Matthew Delmont describes, "The Racial Imbalance Act played out in Boston like a local version of the Civil Rights Act, promising on paper but with little impact on the city's schools."[24]

Each year, associates of School Committee members in the state legislature filed bills to amend or repeal the Racial Imbalance Act. Hearings to debate the act were held in several different years as the debate over it continued and political opposition to it grew. Governor Francis Sargent vetoed several legislative attempts to revoke the act, until May 1974, when the governor decided to replace the Racial Imbalance Act with a new plan that relied on voluntary busing of students of color into white neighborhoods.[25]

While the Racial Imbalance Act was in place and the political maneuvering to undermine or repeal it was ongoing, the number of Boston schools defined as racially imbalanced grew. The act became law in August 1965. In 1965–1966, there were forty-six Boston schools classified as imbalanced. The number grew steadily, reaching seventy-five imbalanced schools in 1972–1973. The percentage of students of color who attended these imbalanced schools grew from 68.2 percent in 1965–1966 to 78.9 percent in 1972–1973.[26]

Instead of addressing the problem of school segregation, the Boston School Committee denied that any problem existed. It responded to critics by arguing that the schools already were de jure desegregated. In defense of its position, it cited the fact that Massachusetts law prohibited formal segregation and pointed to the city's school choice program. In 1961, the Boston School Committee had instituted an "open-enrollment" policy that allowed students to enroll in a school of their choice, provided there was space available. Committee members repeatedly used the existence of this policy to insulate themselves against charges of segregation.

Yet multiple observers, as well as the judge (Garrity) who would eventually intervene to desegregate Boston schools, recognized the limitations of the open-enrollment policy. Black parents were typically misinformed about their open-enrollment options and were often unable to obtain information they needed to make better-informed decisions about their children's education.[27] Open enrollment did not come with transportation, meaning that a student who decides to enroll in a better-performing school that is farther from their house must find their own way there. As a result, Black families with few resources were unable to take advantage of any opportunities that school choice might have provided.[28] Furthermore, there was consistent evidence that open-enrollment applications from Black students were routinely denied by school principals or by the School Committee.[29] As Formisano states, "The committee had paid lip service for years to open enrollment but in practice made it difficult for black students to use it, while routinely granting transfers for white students whose parents knew the system."[30] Thus, the open-enrollment policy—the very policy used by the School Committee to deny claims of segregation—actually increased segregation. Black families had little ability to choose schools, while white families were empowered to obtain better schools for their children.

I found a document in the Boston City Archives that captures some of the Black families' concerns about how their children were treated in Boston schools and the School Committee's denial of any problem. The document is a transcript of a 1965 meeting between members of the Boston School Committee, the superintendent, and representatives of the US Department of Health, Education, and Welfare (HEW). The HEW representatives were meeting with school representatives because a complaint had been filed with them alleging racially discriminatory treatment in Boston schools. The HEW representatives did not discuss specific allegations or who made them, since the purpose of the meeting was simply to inform the School Committee that they would be investigating the allegations. But two issues did come up in the conversation. One was that Black families were unable to access the open-enrollment program that was on the books as a way to provide choice to all families; the other was discriminatory treatment within schools. Ruby Martin, the special assistant to the assistant secretary of HEW, began:

> MARTIN: I would like to get to the specifics that we learned about yesterday. One of the first things was the ineffective mess of the open-enrollment policy, that Negro parents are not told where the empty seats are. When they find out where they are they are told that there are no empty seats. It happens frequently and on a large scale.
> SUPERINTENDENT: A Superintendent's Circular which describes the Open-Enrollment Program was sent out May 7, 1965 and it explains how they may take advantage of Open-Enrollment.
> MARTIN: How do you find out where the empty seats are?
> SUPERINTENDENT: Another document sent out in September will be updated and the impact of the changes in this policy will be reflected. It will go to every principal and department head.
> MARTIN: It does not get to the Negroes.[31]

Later in the meeting, Martin described a few of the other complaints that HEW received regarding how Black children were treated in schools:

> I should list the kinds of things that people said were discriminatory acts within the schools that are predominantly Negro, the kinds of things they thought constitute violations of Title 6: Assignment of teachers—teachers in the predominantly Negro schools are usually the newest, least prepared and least experienced; the bulk of temporary teachers; teachers are not of the same caliber as those in the predominantly white schools. They have no idea how teachers are assigned. They have suggestions and ideas. They consider it a very serious problem. There was a long discussion on punishment administered within the Negro schools; instances where Negro children have been sent to the hospital as a result of punishment.[32]

At no point did Martin suggest that Boston schools needed to be rezoned to ensure racial parity. She was instead discussing whether Black students were treated fairly in schools and whether they had equal access to the open-enrollment policy set up to help families. The School Committee representatives responded defiantly, with one representative, Joseph Lee, even suggesting that the committee favored Black students: "Our whole point is discrimination is in favor of youngsters in difficulty. We have all manner of special courses, teachers, Operation Head Start, etc. We spend much more time, 20% more on the Negro child than on the white child. We should not favor the Negro child but should favor the child having difficulty whether Negro or white."[33] His response is an excellent illustration of "color-blind racism": claiming that because the committee provides additional resources to students in need and spends more time on Black students than on white students, therefore it cannot be accused of racial discrimination.[34] Apparently it did not matter to him that the system segregated Black students into inferior schools, where they were mistreated and had less experienced teachers.

As I write about this today, I shake my head in disbelief (yes, I am actually shaking my head at this moment). It just seems so ridiculous for so much energy to be invested in fighting against commonsense measures to make schools more just places. Remember, the NAACP and others had requested relatively modest reforms. Initially, they were not asking for an overhaul of Boston schools or for the School Committee to reassign large numbers of students. They wanted an admission that de facto segregation existed and small changes with regard to student assignments. Mostly they sought better funding and other resources to support the schools attended by Black students. Their primary goal probably would have been to have teachers like Kozol have an actual classroom with walls, rather than having to share an auditorium space with other teachers. And yet the School Committee fought tooth and nail to deny the existence of segregation and to block any type of student reassignment or school reform.

The School Committee was not alone in its fight. Perhaps the most telling indicator of public opposition to desegregation was the popularity of School Committee member Louise Day Hicks. Hicks was from South Boston and the most visible and vocal opponent of school desegregation. When she was up for reelection in 1963 in the general School Committee race, she received the most votes of all candidates. After the election, she concluded, "The people of Boston have given their answer to the de facto segregation question."[35] A majority of the voting residents of Boston seemed to support this fight against desegregation.

Some historians have explained this resistance to change as being due to neighborhood tradition, culture, and control. Formisano, for example, whose excellent historical research informs much of this chapter, essentially argues that the opposition to desegregation was a product of social class, neighborhoods, culture, and religion. He describes how Irish Bostonians had overcome a history of oppression to gain political power in Boston and saw the effort to desegregate schools as a concession of some of this power, which they resisted.[36] It is true that, as I describe in chapter 6, much of the (at times violent) opposition to school desegregation in Boston centered in the Irish Catholic enclave of South Boston, as its schools were merged with those of the predominantly Black adjacent neighborhood, Roxbury. As Formisano describes, the Irish Americans in South Boston interpreted desegregation reforms as interference into their way of life, an attack on their neighborhood and traditions. Since school segregation was largely a function of neighborhood segregation, challenges to student assignment were interpreted as challenges to the local community itself, both in and outside South Boston.[37]

Perhaps this sounds somewhat familiar? It strikes me as a close parallel to the call to "make America great again" and the slogan's appeal to tradition and local control as reasons to oppose reforms that redistribute resources to others, particularly Black Americans. Like the current desire to push back against "wokeness" and social changes that empower traditionally marginalized groups (people of color, LGBTQ individuals, and others), South Boston residents opposed reforms that they interpreted as an attack on their community's boundaries and that they thought might provide opportunity to Black students at the cost of their own children's education.[38]

To be sure, some of the voices against desegregation were not couched in color-blind terms but phrased in explicitly racist ways instead. Kozol quotes statements made by Joseph Lee, member of the Boston School Committee, after the Kiernan Commission's 1965 report:

> Lee defended to the hilt the nature of the present set-up. "It seems to me," he said, "the pupil from the unprosperous Negro family is usually backward in school, otherwise there wouldn't be any concern or any state commission report for the overcoming of his backwardness." He maintained as well that "white children do not want to be transported into schools with a large proportion of backward pupils from unprospering Negro families who will slow down their education. . . . White children do not want large numbers of backward pupils from unprospering Negro families shipped into their present mainly white schools, either."[39]

Though Formisano describes the reaction as being about fear, not explicit racism, he (perhaps unintentionally) illustrates the important role of explicitly racist tropes in shaping the resistance to desegregation in South Boston ("Southie"): "Irish Catholics' perceptions of the unrestrained sexuality of ghetto culture further intensified fears of blacks. Many whites associated ghetto blacks with promiscuity, teenage pregnancy, single-parent families, and prostitution. Irish Catholics, for a variety of reasons, have tended to be puritanical in sexual matters and have cloaked 'sins of the flesh' with an aura of taboo. Desegregation raised the specter of friendships and even sexual intercourse between Southie's white daughters and black males, about whose sexual prowess Boston's white men believed old myths and made nervous jokes."[40]

While I am sympathetic to the argument that white residents of Boston were nervous about the changes that were coming, including loss of local (neighborhood) control of schools and introduction of conflict into their children's schools, the resistance to desegregation was very clearly about race. Unlike Formisano's interpretation, Delmont argues that race was the central driving force behind resistance to desegregation in Boston. The debate eventually became focused on busing, which was the means used to address desegregation, but Delmont states that this was a red herring—a smokescreen that allowed segregationists to avoid talking directly about race. Indeed, Delmont's book *Why Busing Failed* is largely an analysis of how real problems about segregation and structural inequality were hidden by framing the problem as one about busing. After all, as Black parents and Black education advocates pointed out, buses were used frequently to transport students before desegregation, with little controversy. Most white people had no problems with busing when the buses were transporting Black children past their local segregated white schools, miles away to the segregated schools for Black students. Rather, busing was an issue invented as a distraction and one that allowed whites to defend segregation in a color-blind way, by appealing to parents' desires to defend their local neighborhood schools. Delmont quotes Julian Bond, the cofounder of the Student Nonviolent Coordinating Committee and a Georgia state legislator, as saying, "What people who oppose busing object to, is not the little yellow school buses, but rather to the little black bodies that are on the bus."[41] By framing the issue as "busing" in a way that violated parents' rights to have their children go to local schools, the Boston School Committee sought to maintain a dual system of education that protected whom they saw as their constituents, while sacrificing the Black students, whose education was less important to city leaders and residents at large.

Evidence of Suspensions before 1974

There is consistent and clear evidence that in the years leading up to 1974, Black students were largely secluded at segregated schools in inferior, overcrowded, and outdated buildings. As Kozol's exposé vividly describes, Black students received little love from the Boston Public

Schools system. But there is very little evidence that they were commonly removed from schools via suspension.

Neither out-of-school suspension nor in-school suspension seem to have been commonly used throughout the 1960s. The 1958 Boston Public Schools Code of Discipline, for example, detailed how and when corporal punishment could be used but did not mention school suspension by name. It did include a single paragraph that states, "A teacher may temporarily exclude from the classroom to the office of the head master or principal a pupil whose continuous misbehavior is such as to prevent a teaching-learning situation for the class. Such exclusion shall continue, but for not more than one school day, until the head master or principal has consulted with the teacher regarding the pupil's status. A pupil who is excluded from the classroom shall be escorted to the office of the head master or principal or to whatever supervised area may be designated by the head master or principal."[42]

While the Code of Discipline clarifies the possibility of excluding a student from school, the practice was limited to a single day, and the student was still kept in school at the head master's or principal's office, rather than out-of-school suspension. Clearly, the Code of Discipline did not intend for suspension to be used frequently.[43] As in schools elsewhere, corporal punishment was the far more common mode of student punishment.

This record is consistent with Kozol's description of Black students' treatment in the school where he taught. Kozol addresses the use of corporal punishment several times throughout *Death at an Early Age*, criticizing it for being degrading, based on racial hatred, and ineffective at addressing student misbehavior. He mentions suspension only once in the book, in reference to a five-day suspension given to a student.[44] At no other point does he discuss the use of school suspension, despite his extremely critical tone in describing racially biased and abusive treatment of students.

By 1970—well into the ongoing debate about Black students and desegregation of Boston schools—Boston school practice seems to have changed. This assessment is based on changes to the Code of Discipline at least. In 1970, a new Code of Discipline was published, and this one showed a noticeable shift away from corporal punishment and toward suspension.[45] The 1970 code establishes that "an administrative head may suspend a student in accordance with the procedures in Section III whenever the pupil has engaged in criminal conduct, serious or repeated violation of school rules, disruption of classes, injury to others or intentionally placing others in fear of injury, malicious damage to property of others or the use of profane or obscene language."[46] In the following section (Section III), the code establishes limits to suspensions: up to three school days for students under sixteen and up to five days for students over sixteen years of age.

I discussed school punishment prior to desegregation with Barbara Fields, a Boston Public Schools teacher before and during desegregation and then head of the Boston Public Schools Office of Equity. She stated, "I would bet before [the 1974 desegregation court case for Boston, *Morgan v. Hennigan*] no one had paid any attention to discipline. And also, I think because the schools were segregated, then they felt no need to actually do so." She continued to describe how suspension was not a central feature of segregated schools because in Boston, the teachers were segregated as well; white teachers did not frequently suspend white students, just as Black teachers did not frequently suspend Black students.

I searched through annual reports from the superintendent of the Boston Public Schools for discussions of suspensions. These annual reports, which are available online, offer reports from multiple divisions within the School Department.[47] For example, the 1972–1973 document includes reports from each of the following departments: music, arts, and aesthetics; school lunches; special services; science; audio visual instruction; custodial; vocational educational and industrial arts; kindergarten; physical education; and libraries. The document then includes a section titled "Highlights of Other Departments," which includes blurbs about adult educational and recreational activities, board of examiners, curriculum development, and Title I programs. It contains no mention of school punishment or of school suspensions. The 1971–1972 super-intendent's report does include a brief description of "safety and trans-portation," but safety is limited to "fire drill procedures, traffic patrols, driver education, and classroom and assembly visits by police and fire departments."[48] In contrast to today's schools, in which school discipline is a paramount concern—even an organizing principle, if some prior researchers are to be believed—school punishment was not viewed as important enough to mention in annual reports.[49]

Following my exploratory strategy when researching Delaware schools, I also searched the Boston paper of record, the *Boston Globe*, for mention of school suspensions before the 1974 mandatory desegregation reform. It is worth noting that while it is the largest circulating Boston paper, some people might view the *Globe* as partisan (liberal) and not representative of what all Boston communities considered newsworthy. I would suggest that this makes it an even better source for my purposes; since I am looking for evidence of the use of suspensions before deseg-regation, particularly for students of color, would it not be best to look in the source that was at that time most dedicated to shining light on the plight of students of color?

My search for *Boston Globe* articles mirrored my search in the New Castle County, Delaware, news media: it produced very little before the 1970s.[50] I did find a total of forty-six articles in the 1960s that discussed suspension. Many were not about Boston public schools, and those that were about Boston schools most commonly discussed hippie students suspended for violating their school's hair policy or dress code. News articles discussing suspension increased considerably in the 1970s, par-ticularly as desegregation went into effect. But before 1974, it was rarely a topic of news coverage in the *Boston Globe*.

First Calls for Disciplinary Reform

Today, school punishment is a common focus among civil rights and racial justice advocates. The NAACP's website lists a handful of topics on which the organization is focused. One of them, "education innovation," lists four areas under "what we're fighting for." Of these four areas, two relate to school suspension.[51] Other racial justice or civil rights advocacy groups feature the issue of racial justice in school punishment or the "school-to-prison pipeline" as well. It is a well-known, common focus for those who are concerned about the treatment of students of color in contemporary schools.

And yet it is difficult to find any mention of the problem of school suspensions in the archived records describing the very tumultuous 1960s and early 1970s of Boston. From the early 1960s until 1974, the Boston NAACP and other local groups were advocating for Black children's educational rights through public relations campaigns, protests, and even boycotts of schools. They challenged School Committee elections and petitioned to the city and state legislatures. But the issue of school punishment was not on their radar or high on the agenda of the students who were fighting for justice themselves. I found in the Boston City Archives a flier for a student demonstration in November 1970. Event cosponsors include the Black Panther Party Boston chapter, the Black Student Federation, the Massachusetts Law Reform Institute, and the Student Mobilization Committee, among others. The flier describes protest of school rules prohibiting political speech and meetings. The second page of the flier lists twenty-three items in a Student Bill of Rights, drafted by the Greater Boston High School Rights Committee. Figure 5.1 reproduces this list. This Bill of Rights focuses almost entirely on rights of speech and assembly and other political issues. Of the twenty-three items, only one addresses student discipline (number 8), but rather than pointing out the use of suspension or racially biased punishments, it demands due process when the school takes disciplinary action (in whatever form).

Perhaps the most robust and visible early challenge of school suspension is the 1970 report *The Way We Go to School: The Exclusion of Children in Boston*, written by the Task Force on Children Out of School. The Task Force was chaired by Hubert E. Jones, who later went on to lead the Boston Freedom House, an important racial justice advocacy

SCHOOL BILL OF RIGHTS

(drafted by the Greater Boston
High Schools Rights Committee)

High School students shall have:

1. The right to freedom of speech in school.
2. The right to leaflet on school property.
3. The right to hold unauthorized meetings in school.
4. The right to hold legal peaceful demonstrations on school property.
5. The right to hear non-student speakers of the student's choice on school time.
6. The right to form organizations whether or not the purposes and ideas of those organizations are agreeable to the school administration; these organizations shall be protected with the same rights and privileges as all other student clubs and organizations.
7. The right to hold school assemblies on topics of the student's choice on school time.
8. The right to due process; all students shall have counsel if they so wish and a trial with a jury of students pending any disciplinary actions. All students shall have the right to appeal any decisions of a disciplinary nature.
9. There shall be an end to the use of police in schools to settle disputes.
10. The right to open school elections; no student shall have to fulfill arbitrary administrative requirements before running.
11. The right to control the school newspaper without administrative censorship (except those restrictions placed on all newspapers concerning libel and obscenity.
12. The right to publish and distribute non-official student publications in school; these publications shall be protected by the same rights and privileges as official school publication.
13. The right for teachers and students to collectively participate in deciding school policies and regulations.
14. The right for teachers and students to collectively control and determine curriculum.
15. The right for students and teachers to veto any administrative decision concerning the firing of a teacher.
16. The right for students and teachers to veto an administration's rejection of available government funds.
17. The right to strike.
18. The right to abstain from attendance at official school meetings and assemblies.
19. The right to refrain from saluting the flag.
20. The right to freedom of dress; the right to wear buttons, armbands and other symbols of political and moral beliefs.
21. The right to see at any time all files and information concerning the operation of the school; each student has control over his or her own personal file.
22. There shall be an end to discrimination in school on the basis of race or sex.
23. All students shall be protected, as any other citizen, but the U.S. Constitution and the U.S. Bill of Rights.

FIGURE 5.1. Reproduction of Student Bill of Rights. (Flier for student demonstration, Boston City Archives)

organization that still serves the city of Boston. The vice chair was Donald T. Donley, dean of the School of Education at Boston College, and the other nineteen members consisted of clergy, school administrators, mental health professionals, civil rights attorneys, educators, and youth advocates in and outside state agencies. It was formed in 1968 to address the problem of "exclusion from, and within, the school system."[52] The report was the culmination of over a year of research.

The Way We Go to School is an extraordinary document that was ahead of its time. It documents for the first time in Boston (as far as I am aware) the fact that children are being removed from schools, discouraged from coming, or placed in "special classes designed for the 'inferior'" on a daily basis.[53] It tells the stories of several such children in powerful, evocative testimonials. But even in this focus on excluding students from schools, the report says very little about punishment for student misbehavior via suspensions. Instead, it focuses on three broad categories or types of exclusion. The report lists them using the following terms:

1. Children who are out of school or who have never been to school. The children in this category come primarily from cultural minorities; many of them are Spanish-speaking. Most of these children cannot go to school because the School Department has failed to establish educational programs for them;

2. Children who are not allowed to attend school, or who are made to leave school. This group is composed of children with physical handicaps such as those who are crippled; it also includes girls who are pregnant. Generally, these children are not allowed to attend school even though, in the opinion of many experts, they are capable of participating in normal school activities;

3. Children who have unique needs which are inadequately or inappropriately met within the school system. Children in this category include those who are mentally retarded, emotionally disturbed, and perceptually handicapped. The School Department often confuses

them by labelling a retarded child as disturbed, or vice versa. One re-sult is that "special classes" become a catch-all for children with vastly different needs.[54]

The report does acknowledge the problem of excluding students who are disruptive in class, are disrespectful to teachers, fight, or misbehave in other ways.[55] But it does not provide counts of such in-stances or details on them; instead, it argues that exclusion is counter-productive, that principals' use of suspension typically does not follow the procedures listed in the Code of Discipline, and that improving school climate and instructional techniques are more appropriate and effective responses to (and ways to prevent) student misbehavior. Im-portantly, this discussion represents a relatively brief section within the larger report; even the discussion of exclusion in response to stu-dent behavior focuses primarily on treatment of students classified as "mentally retarded."

The Way We Go to School was an insightful, important document. It made a powerful argument against removing students from school and for more inclusive educational practice. And yet it says very little about the use of school suspension as a punishment for student misbe-havior other than for students who are diagnosed as disabled or labeled as needing medical/instructional/therapeutic interventions. Further, while it addresses the problem of "cultural minorities," the concern is more focused on immigrant students and those with limited English proficiency rather than the disproportionate punishment of Black stu-dents. To be clear, The Way We Go to School is impressive in all ways. I do not mean my comments to be any form of slight or criticism. In-stead, I am pointing out that this well-researched document advocat-ing for students' right to stay in school and receive a quality education speaks very little about the problem of school suspensions for misbe-havior among students without disability diagnoses or about the pun-ishment of Black students in particular, issues that would be the focus of attention just a few years later. The fact that this forward-looking document offered little focus on these future areas of great concern suggests that in 1970, school suspensions were still not very common.

Conclusion

As the 1856 near-death experience of Senator Charles Sumner illustrates, Massachusetts policy makers and citizens have always shown support for racial equity. The state prohibited slavery, its policy makers advocated for prohibition across the US, and it boasts the nation's first school desegregation laws. Despite this historical pedigree, concentration of universities in Boston, and liberal populace, schools in Boston were segregated until 1974. Black students received far fewer resources and a lower-quality education in substandard buildings compared to white students, on average. Black students in Boston were denied equal opportunity of education, limiting their ability to compete for jobs and future opportunities, such as the ability to bestow educational and financial advantages on their children.

Rather than fix the problem or even acknowledge it—without blame!—the Boston School Committee denied its existence. It hid behind the fact that the schools were, by law, desegregated and that students had access to open enrollment, all while maintaining racially segregated school assignment plans and blocking Black families from taking advantage of open enrollment. It even subverted state law that required racial balance in school enrollment, ignoring requirements to restructure schools. The citizens of Boston supported these efforts by reelecting outspoken opponents of school desegregation such as Louise Day Hicks.

And yet, despite this contentious history of segregation and racial oppression in Boston Public Schools, there is little evidence that schools used out-of-school suspensions frequently. Suspension as a school punishment is barely discussed by youth advocates like Jonathon Kozol, civil rights organizations protesting the treatment of Black students in Boston schools, or investigative reports such as that by the Task Force on Children Out of School. It appears only rarely within articles published in the *Boston Globe* and is not included in annual superintendent reports. Mirroring my findings in New Castle County, Delaware, my archival work indicates that despite rigid racial segregation of schools, out-of-school suspension was not a commonly used punishment in Boston before the 1970s.

6

Unprepared

Boston after Desegregation

Given what happened during desegregation, I just found that the school district and the system wasn't prepared. I think prior to deseg[regation], I think there was a different relationship that families had with schools, where parents always told kids, "I don't want to hear from that school." And I think suspensions weren't the first tool schools used. But during desegregation, during busing, I think what happened there was people were totally unprepared and—and things were so, not only confusing—people were never placed in that situation of dealing with racially—racial tensions being as they were at South Boston High School and some other schools.

This quote comes from my discussion with Albert Holland, the first Black administrator to work at South Boston High School, the flash-point of resistance to desegregation. He began working there in 1975, as Boston schools were implementing a court-ordered desegregation plan. As he describes, schools were "totally unprepared" for the level of conflict—among students, between staff and students, and between community members and students—that occurred, and as a response, they suspended students en masse.

Following years of advocacy on behalf of Black students, in which the NAACP and others sought recognition of continuing school seg-regation and improvements to schools serving Black students, the NAACP filed suit in 1972. Judge W. Arthur Garrity's 1974 ruling in the case, *Morgan v. Hennigan*, required immediate desegregation by reas-signing students and transporting them on buses to their new schools.

The hateful, violent protests that erupted are well known, having been a feature of national news. Perhaps the most iconic image of these protests is the Pulitzer Prize–winning photograph *The Soiling of Old Glory*; in it, we see a white protester using an American flag as a weapon against a Black man, an attorney named Ted Landsmark. The contrast within it is clear and unsettling. We see an act of racial violence and a clear look of hatred on the face of the attacker, contrasted with symbols of liberty: the American flag and the setting of City Hall Plaza in Boston, with the Old State House, the original colonial seat and Massachusetts state capitol, in the background.[1] But what is less well known is the change in school punishment that immediately followed desegregation. As we saw in Delaware, as Black students began attending formerly white schools in Boston, many were excluded via suspension—a practice that by all available evidence seemed to be much less common in the years before desegregation.

Morgan v. Hennigan

Throughout the 1960s and into the early 1970s, the Boston School Committee was steadfast in its refusal to either admit that Boston schools were racially segregated or take meaningful action that might help Black students.[2] As a result, the Boston NAACP filed *Morgan v. Hennigan* in 1972. After two years of litigation, Judge Garrity released his decision on June 21, 1974.[3] He found that Boston schools were indeed segregated and that the Boston School Committee had actively maintained and extended this segregation. According to Ronald Formisano in his detailed history of the case and its aftermath, the ruling itself was widely supported or at least uncontested. The evidence of continuing school segregation was clear. Segregation was clear enough for the state legislature to pass the Racial Imbalance Act of 1965, nearly a decade before the judge's ruling, and the problem only continued to grow after the act. It is easy to understand why the decision itself was accepted, even by those who disliked it.[4]

In contrast, Judge Garrity's *remedy* to the problem was detested by many people. The judge ruled—in late June—that Boston schools must immediately desegregate by reassigning students to different schools in ways that would integrate them. With less than three months to go before the new school year started, Boston was forced to take action. While this first phase of desegregation was ongoing, starting in September 1974, the judge asked the School Committee to prepare a permanent plan (known as phase 2), to begin in September 1975, that would allow it to have some control over how the schools desegregated. But in December 1974, three of five members of the School Committee voted against adoption of the committee's own plan for school desegregation, forcing the judge to plan and oversee implementation of desegregation himself.[5]

The plan for the first phase of desegregation had been developed by the state Board of Education. It involved only a subset of Boston schoolchildren, as it required reassignment of seventeen to eighteen thousand students, with citywide reorganization to be planned as part of phase 2. This subset included the movement of students between Roxbury High School and South Boston High School. Roxbury was a relatively low-income Black community, whereas the neighboring community of South Boston was home to many working-class white Irish Catholics. The busing of students between these communities became the flashpoint in the conflict over desegregation, with South Boston High School as the site of the most violent protests.[6]

As Robert A. Dentler and Marvin B. Scott, two experts assisting Judge Garrity with planning and implementation, describe, the development of a permanent desegregation plan was difficult, due in part to the decentralized organization of Boston schools: "Indeed, no one even had consolidated authority over the system. The superintendent was in charge of curriculum and program matters, but little else. The business manager was in charge of the budget and expenditures. He reported directly to the school committee, independent of the superintendent, as did the chief structural engineer (in charge of plant repairs), the chief custodial engineer (in charge of plant maintenance), and the secretary for the committee. In addition, the associate superintendent for personnel was detached from control by these officers and often dealt directly with city hall and with school committee members."[7]

Not only was the system administratively complex and dysfunctional, but the School Committee was unable even to produce an accurate list of students attending Boston schools upon the judge's request. The court appointed a panel of masters that sought advice and devised the permanent plan. It created a series of nine (later consolidated into eight) community school districts within the city. Desegregation occurred within each community district, which meant that students reassigned to new schools would still be relatively close to home, rather than having to travel long distances on buses to schools. Within each community district, school assignments were based on clusters of "geocode units," which meant that students were assigned based on their immediate neighborhoods and in ways that allowed them to still attend school alongside their neighbors but move, as a group, in ways that rebalanced the schools' racial and ethnic mix of students.[8]

Unlike in New Castle County, Delaware, in which an unpopular desegregation plan was implemented peacefully and without obstruction or mass protest, Boston residents began protesting against desegregation the week before school opened in 1974.[9] These protests turned violent on the first day of school, with violence continuing even after phase 2 took effect the following school year. The School Committee member Louise Day Hicks and others who were opposed to segregation had formed a group that would lead the protests: ROAR (Restore Our Alienated Rights). While much of the violence was in South Boston, other areas were affected as well.

ROAR called for a boycott of the schools to open the year, though many parents continued to hold their children out of school even after then. Formisano estimates that attendance citywide fluctuated between forty and sixty thousand students daily out of a potential enrollment of eighty thousand.[10] Many boycotted or protested peacefully; others picketed the newly integrated schools with signs bearing racial epithets; others threw rocks, bottles, or other items at buses carrying Black students. On the first day of school, eighteen buses sustained damage from objects hurled at them.[11] To illustrate, this powerful story of the attack on one bus is told in a 2014 *Boston Globe* article, from the perspective of its driver:

This was Richardson's first day as a bus driver. He'd been driving an ice cream truck all summer but was looking for winter work when he spotted the help-wanted ad in the newspaper. He was 25 years old, a Boston native, and he had no idea there was trouble brewing. No one ever warned him. No one had prepared him for what he might encounter, or advised him how he might best handle it. He'd picked up the bus about 7 a.m. in the yard in Neponset, and he'd been handed a paper, telling him which bus stop to go to. He had never been to South Boston High School in his life, but that was where he was going now.

He emerged from the rotary and turned right onto Dorchester Street. As soon as he made the turn, he saw the crowd in the street. At least 100 people blocked the way, yelling and gesturing in anger. Before he could react, he heard a thud, the sound of something heavy striking the side of the bus. A second later, glass shattered behind him. And he heard the children on his bus start screaming.

What the hell is happening? he thought. Richardson had grown up in schools that were mostly white. At the elementary school he'd attended in East Boston, he'd been one of only three black students in the building. He had never had a problem because of his race; for most of his life, most of his friends had been white. He'd spent lazy afternoons on the beach in Southie and could not recall hearing a harsh word there. Now, it seemed he was entering some other, uglier world. The kind of hate he'd seen on TV, in the South but never in his city—it was here now, right in front of him. But there wasn't time to dwell on his shock. He had to get the children out of harm's way, as fast as he could.

He kept rolling up the street, more bricks slamming into the sides of the bus. They're tearing us up, he thought. People on the street were at the back door of the bus now, trying to pull it open. "Hold the door!" Richardson hollered at the kids in the back of the bus. "Hold on, don't let them open it!"

He could hear people outside yelling racial slurs. He could hear the children on the bus, crying harder. He took a left, trying to find a way out. He drove to the end of West Eighth Street and ran into D Street. There, at the corner, he realized his mistake. They were surrounded by another crowd, bigger and more furious than the first. Bricks were flying, with few windows left to stop them. Richardson told the kids to lie down on the floor, but the kids were lying down already.

He turned left on D Street, left again onto Dorchester Avenue. At Andrew Station, the MBTA train stop, he saw other school buses gathered. He wasn't the only driver who had been forced to turn back. The police were there, and ambulances, medics pulling shards of glass out of children's heads. Richardson steered the ravaged bus to the curb and parked it.[12]

Marches against busing continued for months, as did violence between Black and white students within schools as well, as Black students were routinely harassed and attacked by white students. The protests, racist rhetoric, and violence that erupted in Boston became a national news story.

Back in Court about Suspensions

In June 1974, the *Morgan v. Hennigan* plaintiffs won their case. This decision was then affirmed in December 1974 by the Court of Appeals, where it was renamed *Morgan v. Kerrigan* to reflect the new head of the School Committee, John J. Kerrigan.[13] Judge Garrity continued to oversee the desegregation effort for years to come and to decide on related issues that arose in the years after his 1974 ruling.

Judge Garrity did not issue any findings related to school punishment in his June 1974 *Morgan v. Hennigan* decision—that decision was about racial segregation and the inferior educational experiences of Black students and did not focus on suspensions or other school punishments.

FIGURE 6.1. Antibusing rally at Thomas Park, South Boston. (Photo by Spencer Grant, 1975)

In April 1975, only months after busing began, the issue of school punishment was introduced by the *Morgan* plaintiffs in a *Motion for Further Relief Concerning Student Discipline.* Plaintiffs accused the Boston schools of using suspensions "to perpetuate systematic and widespread discrimination against plaintiffs and the members of their class."[14] As relief, they requested that independent hearing officers make suspension decisions, following procedures to ensure due process; records of suspension and expulsion during the 1974–1975 school year be expunged; failing grades that resulted from suspension be expunged and tutoring provided to students; the schools report suspension data to the court on a monthly basis; and the schools refrain from racial discrimination in school discipline.[15]

This motion provides strong support for my argument in two ways. One, its very presence indicates the sudden emergence of school suspensions as a problem—and a racially inequitable one—immediately after desegregation and as a direct result of resistance to desegregation. Two, it provides otherwise-unavailable data. The motion was written during an era in which suspension rates were not regularly or systematically reported and archived by the schools or state, and it provides a trove of supporting arguments, analyses, and data that carefully document the sudden problem of suspension, particularly for Black students who entered previously white schools.

The plaintiffs argued what is essentially my thesis: that after being forced to admit Black students to previously white schools, the schools resisted by suspending Black students at high rates. The *Memorandum in Support of Plaintiffs' Motion for Further Relief Concerning Student Discipline* accuses the Boston schools of having "done everything in their power to keep black children from attending school with white children. Prevented by this court from locking the door, they have, through the suspension device, created a revolving door that sends black children home almost as fast as they arrive at a 'desegregated' school."[16] After supporting this argument by presenting data on suspensions immediately after desegregation, the memorandum concludes, "These statistics reveal that since the school system has been required to assign black and white children to the same school, it has been retaining the white character of its schools by denying black children education through discriminatory use of the suspension process."[17]

Statistical Evidence: Suspension Rates

The evidence supporting these claims came in two main forms: affidavits of students and teachers who observed or experienced unfair, harsh, or racially motivated discipline and the statistical analyses of suspension data provided by the plaintiffs' expert witness, Paul V. Smith. Smith was an educational data analyst for the Children's Defense Fund and an EdD candidate at Harvard at the time.[18] In April 1975, he presented data on suspensions of Black and white students from September 1974 (the start of desegregation) through January 31, 1975. After taking the average student attendance of Black and of white students into account, he found that in the months immediately following desegregation, Black students were suspended at a rate of 46.2 suspensions per 100 students, while white students were suspended at a rate of 21.7 per 100 students. Other reports, as well, such as figures reported in the *Boston Globe*, showed that suspensions rose from two thousand during the 1971–1972 school year to more than eight thousand in 1974–1975.[19]

The following year, Smith provided a report as an affidavit that analyzed data from the entire 1974–1975 school year. In it, he provided more detailed reports of suspension rates across schools that were and were not part of phase 1 of desegregation, as well as comparisons across specific schools and to earlier school years. Smith found that the citywide Boston high school suspension rate was 38.9 suspensions per 100 students in average daily attendance, far higher than the national average of 17.1 per 100 students. Boston's citywide rate in 1974–1975 was also much higher than the citywide rate of 1972–1973 (21.0 suspensions per 100 students). For Black high school students, the 1974–1975 citywide rate was 64.6 suspensions per 100 students, compared to 28.5 per 100 white students.[20] I illustrate these results in figure 6.2.

When considering just high schools that were included in phase 1 of desegregation, suspension rates are even higher and show greater disparity. In figure 6.3, I illustrate Smith's findings when taking into account only high schools that actually desegregated as part of the court order. Here we see much higher rates, with a suspension rate of 73.7 suspensions per 100 Black students in average daily attendance.[21] In other words, the suspension rates jumped dramatically in the Boston schools that desegregated as part of the initial desegregation plan, with the Black suspension rate more than doubling between 1972–1973 and 1974–1975 in those schools.

Rather than continuing to show all of Smith's analyses—which consistently and clearly document massive jumps in suspensions after desegregation, particularly for Black students and in schools that were directly impacted by phase 1 desegregation—I offer just one more comparison. In subsequent analyses, plaintiffs compared suspension rates between two

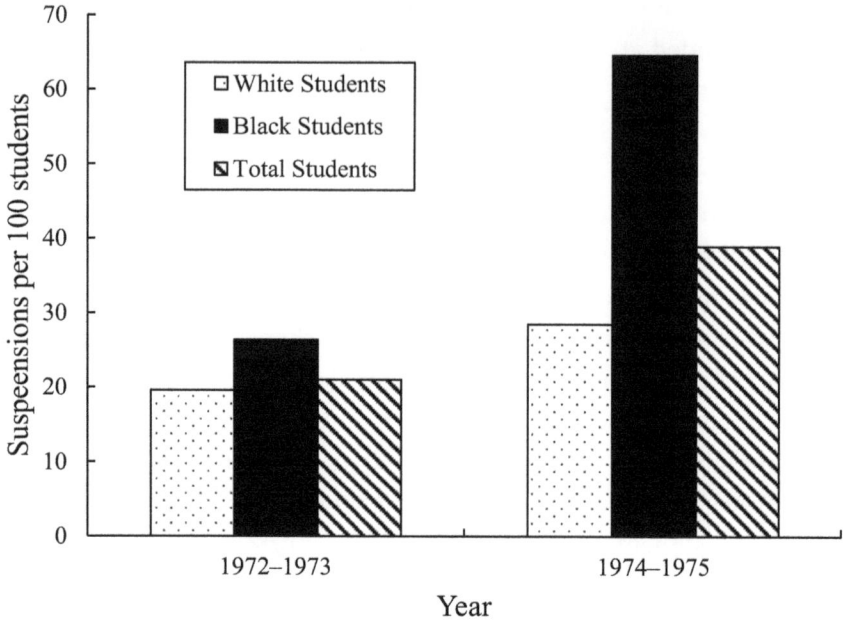

FIGURE 6.2. Suspensions per 100 students in average daily attendance: all Boston high schools. (Author's analysis of data from *Memorandum in Support of Plaintiffs' Motion for Further Relief Concerning Student Discipline*, April 4, 1975, Civil Action No. 72-911-G)

schools at the center of the desegregation controversy: Roxbury High School and South Boston High School. Recall that students were relocated between the two (the low-income Black neighborhood of Roxbury and white Irish enclave of South Boston) and that South Boston was the site of some of the worst violence during this process. In 1974–1975, the suspension rate of Black students at South Boston High School was 215.1 suspensions per 100 students in average daily attendance, while the suspension rate of Black students at Roxbury High School was 8.0 per 100 students. These students came from the same neighborhoods; some lived on blocks chosen for reassignment, and others did not. They were selected for reassignment randomly, based on geocode, not because of any student characteristics; this process provided a "quasi-experimental design" for making comparisons, which allows us an excellent opportunity to better understand any causal effect of desegregation. There is no reason to expect that the Black students from Roxbury who stayed at Roxbury High School were different in behavior, family income, school achievement, or other relevant characteristics than those who were reassigned to South Boston High School. If those factors are similar, which is very likely to be the case, since they were randomly selected, then any difference in suspension we observe is due to school reassignment, not student characteristics. The data tell us that the ridiculous gap in Black students' suspension rates between the schools (215.1 compared to 8.0, and no, I did not forget to add a digit to the latter number) is a product of schools' actions following desegregation, not student characteristics.[22] Figure 6.4 provides a visual reference point for the enormous disparity in Black students' treatment across these two schools.

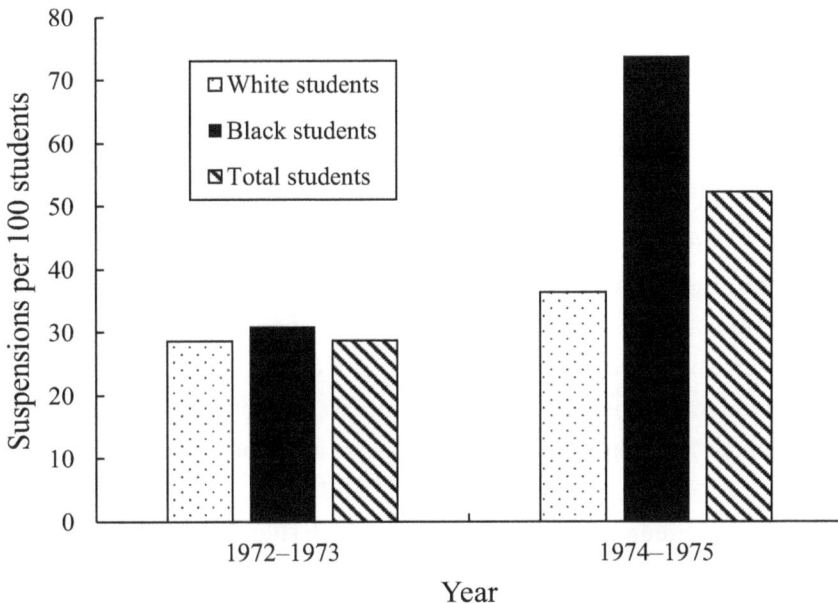

FIGURE 6.3. Suspensions per 100 students in average daily attendance: desegregation-impacted high schools. (Author's analysis of data from *Memorandum in Support of Plaintiffs' Motion for Further Relief Concerning Student Discipline*, April 4, 1975, Civil Action No. 72-911-G)

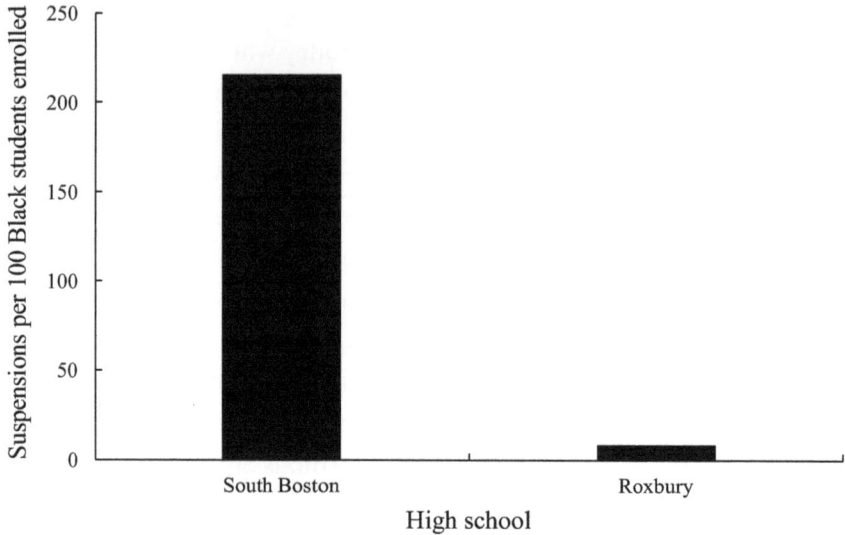

FIGURE 6.4. Comparing suspension rates of Black students in South Boston and Roxbury high schools, 1974–1975. (Author's analysis of data from *Plaintiffs' Proposed Findings of Fact and Conclusions of Law*, Civil Action No. 72-911-G, June 22, 1976, 7)

Student and Staff Testimonials

Plaintiffs included several sworn affidavits from students and school staff that describe what occurred in Boston schools after desegregation to support their argument. These testimonials illustrate the use of racially biased punishment in newly desegregated schools, in which Black students were suspended for trivial misbehavior or no misbehavior, whereas white students' racist epithets and hate-based harassment were largely overlooked. The following are summaries of a few of these testimonials:

- Donna Harding, a Black student at Hyde Park High School, was helping with a school bake sale when she was told that her brother had been sent home from school. She went to a pay phone to inform her mother, since she was afraid for her brother's safety outside of school alone (he would have had to walk past ongoing, sometimes violent, anti-desegregation protesters). The headmaster told her to get off the phone, but she

completed her call. She was later informed that she was suspended for
five days and was not allowed to make up work missed during the suspension. Two weeks later, she was informed that she was again suspended
for accumulating demerits, despite having never been told that she was
given demerits. She later discovered that the demerits were given to her
by a teacher because she was in the hall as "the period bell was about to
ring" and for failing to identify herself to that teacher (despite having
identified herself when requested).[23]

- Bonnie Reynolds, a Black student at South Boston High School, was in the
hallway with several of her friends, who are Black as well. A white student
blocked their way and refused to let them pass. One of Bonnie's friends
fought with the girl. Bonnie tried to pull them apart and was grabbed by
a state trooper who threw her against the wall, held her there, and said,
"Fuck you, N***er." She and her friends filled out reports and then were
sent home. When she returned to school, she was sent home but still not
informed if she had been suspended. She missed six school days before she
was allowed to return but was never officially suspended.[24]

- Harvey Ellison was a Black student at South Boston High School. He was
walking to class when three white boys began pushing him. He fell down,
and his coat was ripped. He claimed to have not fought back or even
raised his hands. A teacher was there in the hallway the whole time. State
troopers came and grabbed him, and while they held him, the white boys
continued to hit and kick him. They carried him to the school holding
room, where police officer said, "Drop the N***er," and they dropped him
on the ground there. The troopers threatened to break his arms, and then
they tore his coat further. He was suspended for fighting.[25]

- Belinda Shivers, a Black student at South Boston High School and
member of the Black Student Caucus, described several instances she
observed in which Black students were attacked by white students without provocation, white students would use hateful epithets against Black
students, or white students would challenge Black students to fights. In
several of these incidents that she described, the Black students, but not
the white students, were suspended.[26]

- Arthur Alexander, a Black teacher at South Boston High School, discussed his white colleagues' statements and actions related to discipline. On several occasions, they had expressed "open resentment" of Black students, resulting in escalation and school punishment. He described how when conflict occurred, some white teachers saw the Black student as the aggressor and a threat to school order, even if this was untrue. He then described multiple incidents in which Black students were attacked without provocation by white students, only for the Black students to be suspended and/or arrested. The school administration asked him to serve as a guidance counselor for Black students but provided him no office or space for doing so, nor was he assigned any students to counsel.[27]

Commonly repeated themes among the affidavits include reports of the common use of violent racial slurs by white students, privileges given to white students (e.g., freedom to walk in the hallways in groups) but not Black students, and violence at the hands of the police who were stationed in the school following the initial violence at South Boston High to start the school year.[28] They describe how Black students were seen as threats, despite often being the victims of hateful speech, harassment, and violence, and how school administrators suspended Black students, often without any notice, explanation, or discussion.

Albert Holland, the South Boston High School administrator whom I quote at the start of this chapter, spoke to me repeatedly about the high suspension rates among Black students immediately after desegregation. He described how suspension became the default response to the daily chaos and violence at South Boston High School, but one that looked very different for Black students and white students:

Everything was just a reaction. And that reaction was to suspend the students, to get them out of the building and try to deescalate the situation. And it was—it was a poor response on how to deescalate, because for—you know, Black parents weren't going to come back up to South Boston High School because they—they felt like they would be jumped as well. So we had to set up satellite meetings outside South Boston High School to meet with Black parents and students, because South Boston High School wasn't an option for Black parents to come up to there. And we had to have a shuttle van on standby to move students out, while white students just went down the hill, walked home, came back with their parents, and were readmitted. Black students sometimes then didn't get back to school for weeks, weeks at a time because kids were angry, parents were fearful, fearful of the children being hurt. And it was just a bad time. Just a bad time. And Boston Public Schools officials, we weren't prepared. I was new to the school district and didn't fully understand everything that was going on. And what I saw was just sometimes some real chaotic situations with kids being suspended, left and right, with little regard to how things happened. And so those initial years were, I would say, very chaotic, very unfair, and there was very little of any type of trying to restore—restorative justice, as we use it now, or bringing the parties together to remediate what took place. So, those initial years at South Boston High School, I think that we were just doing wholesale suspensions, and for the most part Black students were victims. And—and that became a pattern. And I think from that pattern, I think people, and maybe rightly so, maybe people weren't prepared, they weren't trained.

As he describes, South Boston High School suspended en masse rather than trying to resolve conflict, and these suspensions were primarily experienced by Black students. Even when white students were removed from school, they were immediately readmitted; but Black students, whose parents were afraid or unable to escort their children back to school, stayed out of school for longer periods of time.

Explaining High Suspension Rates

The plaintiffs in *Morgan v. Hennigan* were very clear in their explanation of Black students' high rates of suspensions. They argued that removal of

Black students was the schools' way of resisting court-ordered desegregation. To support their argument, they submitted affidavits of scholars familiar with the problem. One that is particularly compelling was provided by Ronald R. Edmonds, the director of the Center for Urban Studies at the Harvard Graduate School of Education and a member of the Citywide Coordinating Council that was appointed to help monitor implementation of the *Morgan* remedy. He stated that he was aware of disparities in suspensions of Black and white students and said, "It is my professional opinion that the root cause of such disparities is the disbelief in, and disrespect for, the findings of Judge Garrity as to the history of racial discrimination in the Boston public schools, that this disbelief and disrespect pervade the entire structure of the Boston public schools, under the active leadership of the Boston School Committee, and are reinforced by those aspects of the wider Boston community with whom members of the Boston public schools identify." He continues to state that the climate within the school system "does not reward fairmindedness to black students. A teacher or administrator might very seriously jeopardize opportunities for career advancement, simply by appearing to be 'too fair' to black students."[29]

The Black educators I spoke to did not tell me about such a concern for career advancement, though they did note problems with the working climate in recently desegregated schools. Barbara Fields, a teacher in Boston and mother of children in Boston public schools during desegregation, discussed with me her experiences during the transition to desegregation. She described how she, like many other qualified Black teachers, was placed in her first permanent teaching position when the court order required that the schools place the Black teachers who had been waiting for teaching assignments. Her new principal assumed that she was an administrative staff member, not a teacher, when he first saw her in the school building just prior to the 1974 school year, the first under desegregation. She told me, "The principal was not pleased to see me there, assumed that I was not there to teach." As Fields described, the initial reaction to Black teachers was sometimes hostile, particularly because Black teachers were seen as taking the positions of the white teachers reassigned away from those schools. She stated,

> So even with the teachers, the teachers were upset because of the court order as it relates to where you could be assigned to a school. . . . [Judge Garrity] was forcing the hiring of Black teachers, some of whom had been on the list to be hired for a while, but the district never hired them. I happened to be one of the first group of folks who were ordered by the court to be appointed permanently by the school department because we were sitting on the list, but we didn't have a job. And so the order also required that the schools be desegregated by staff. So it meant some white teachers who had been in the school for some years had to move so that Black teachers could be assigned to integrate the staff. And so people felt that was a real violation. . . . So all of a sudden, you know, the word was, "Well, you have to move because you have to make room for a Black teacher." Folks didn't . . . appreciate that. So I just mentioned that to say that the teachers also had very strong feelings about what this order meant to them personally. And so who did you take it out on? You take it out on those who, you know, the judge is saying you have to hire, and those students who were there, and, you know, the issues around discipline and how that's, you know, how that kind of happens.

The hiring of Black teachers provoked hostility from many of the white teachers, who took out their frustration on Black students in the form of discipline.

Different Behaviors?

The defendants in *Morgan*, the Boston school system, disagreed that suspensions were the result of resistance to desegregation, of course. In their rebuttal to the plaintiffs' motion, after disputing some of the data points and comparisons to other states, they argued that the statistical evidence produced by Smith showed evidence of disparities but did not find that racism or resistance to desegregation were the causes of these disparities. In other words, they suggested that Black students might be suspended more after desegregation and more than white students, but this was because of their behaviors, not school actions or any racial bias.[30] Five years later, in March 1979, the Faculty Senate of Charlestown High School offered a clear illustration of this justification; it was a response to a 1979 memorandum from the Boston Community District Advisory Council for District VII Boston Schools that expressed concerns about high suspension rates for Black students in Charlestown High School. The Faculty Senate's response stated, "[The Advisory Council's memorandum] also states that the suspension rate for blacks is higher than that of whites. It may also be higher for boys than for girls and it may also be higher for people over 5'2" than for people under that height. People who misbehave are suspended. That is our policy. If a larger number of blacks are being suspended it is because a larger number of blacks are misbehaving."[31]

By all accounts, the levels of school conflict and disorder certainly did rise—*a lot*—after desegregation, particularly in neighborhoods like South Boston that were most resistant to desegregation. But justifying the much-higher rates of suspensions for Black than white students asks us to assume that Black students who won an enormous legal victory, not the white students whose side lost in court and who were forced to open up their schools against their will, were overwhelmingly the aggressors in it. It asks us to see the white students whose parents and elected representatives fought for segregation as the victims in this conflict and to ignore all descriptions of the violent racism directed at Black students who entered these previously white spaces. It seems a logical assumption only for those who hold the racist belief that Black students are naturally predisposed to worse behavior than white students.

In fact, the claim that the growth in suspensions was the result of a fair response to Black students' behaviors is undermined by the data on suspensions, since Black and white students tended to be suspended for different reasons. In a February 1975 memo written for the plaintiffs' legal team by Paul Smith, the plaintiffs' expert witness, he addresses this very issue. Analyzing the first few months of data during the initial desegregation, he found that slightly more white students than Black students were suspended for several objectively defined behaviors: cutting class, tardiness, smoking, truancy, and vandalism. But Black students were far more likely to be suspended for more subjectively perceived misbehaviors: disruptive behavior, defiance, fighting, profanity, and threats/assault, among others. These results show us that when school staff have a more consistent way of measuring misbehavior, they find similar rates of misbehavior among Black and white students, but when the behavior is more subjectively perceived, Black students are judged more harshly. The Charlestown High School Faculty Senate's claim that its policy is that "people who misbehave are suspended" glosses over the complexity and subjectivity in deciding what behaviors should be seen as misbehavior and are worthy of suspension and how race shapes this decision-making process. The racial disparity in suspensions that first year of desegregation was the result of teachers' and administrators' perceptions and actions, not different rates of student behaviors. Interpreting the analyses, Smith wrote, "The pattern that is apparent to me is that the 'black crimes' are those which are perceived by frightened white teachers and administrators. . . . Black kids are clearly frightening to the teachers and principals, and that fear is the heart of the disproportionality."[32]

In June 1975, School Committee chairman John J. McDonough was quoted in a *Boston Globe* article describing the plaintiffs' motion challenging school punishments. He blamed the high rates of suspensions on desegregation itself—not schools' resistance to it—and is quoted saying, "The suspension rate is a barometer of how well the (desegregation) plan is working." Yet the article ends with comments by McDonough that illustrate the role of racial bias as a cause of the suspension disparity: "McDonough conceded that a lack of understanding of black students by white teachers could be partially responsible for the disparity. 'It's much easier to handle your own race than get into a confrontation with students of another race,' he said."[33] While denying that the suspensions were based on racial bias, he admitted that they were partially due to, well, racial bias; these were not his words, but white teachers' difficulty and apprehension in interacting with Black students are due to racialized perceptions and experiences, which is an example of implicit racial bias at the very least.

Barbara Fields also discussed this important topic with me. When explaining to me why Black students were suspended from newly desegregated schools in such high numbers, she described how white teachers had a racially biased view of them and responded differently to them than they would to white students, often provoking confrontations with Black students. She said,

> I think the image that teachers had of Black students, based on their lack of having dealt with Black students before—this was something new for a lot of our teachers as well. . . . I think the—the manner in which they saw them or misinterpreted their actions was done in a stereotypical negative way. And therefore, they would—one thing the court reports talked about was the confrontational manner in which the teachers would approach Black students. . . . Seeing teachers when I was in the classroom approach a student in a certain way, . . . I knew what the reaction would be because it wasn't done in a, let's say, concerned, nurturing way. You know, "Really disappointed in your behavior. I expect better from you than that." You know, not approached in that way but more approached in the way of saying, "the student is bad." Not necessarily [that the] behavior is bad, but the messaging that the student would receive would be that "you are bad." Which—which leads to a confrontation. Because the student feels that he or she, you know, is being, let's say I'll use the word put down, because if you do it in front of the whole class, then the child has to—doesn't have to—but the child will defend his or her reputation, and so you get that kind of a reaction.

White teachers were not used to subtle differences in Black and white students' behaviors. But rather than taking the time to get to know them or trying to understand how frightening it must have been to be a Black student in a newly desegregated school, they responded punitively. They misinterpreted benign behaviors as malicious and responded with hostility. They were unprepared.

Local Tradition?

As I discussed in chapter 5, some commentators explained the resistance to desegregation in the years leading up to the *Morgan* decision as motivated by an appeal to tradition and local community control of schools. These themes are often used to explain the chaos that broke loose in September 1974 as well, with suggestions that much of the protest was rooted in parents' fears that their children would be sent to inferior schools.[34] Not only does such an explanation forgive violent racism, but it also ignores the deeper source of the fears that underlay these concerns. Consider, for example, the following comments of Stephen R. Bing, a lawyer and the executive director of the Massachusetts Advocacy Center:

> I will never forget the first time I went to South Boston High School, after desegregation. The headmaster was still Bill Reid, but they called him Doc Reid. I sat down with him. It was after a suspension hearing, and I said, "Tell me something about this school." He'd been headmaster seventeen years. Prior to desegregation, his formal enrollment in the building was seventeen hundred kids. As a result of court-ordered enrollment, it was reduced to eight hundred. It was still crowded. South Boston High School had not sent a kid to college in fifteen years. Not one. And that's sort of the dirty trick that was played on Roxbury. Roxbury High School, qualitatively compared to South Boston High, was far better. But it's true. And now that school's closed down.[35]

Before desegregation, South Boston High School was an overcrowded school with a poor academic track record. The anger at Black students entering South Boston High School was not about quality of education, since the quality of education at South Boston High School was dismal before desegregation. Instead, the anger was about race and being forced to admit Black students into previously all-white spaces or send white students into previously all-Black spaces.

Albert Holland offered a similar description of the segregationists who protested the court order in the name of "defending their community." It was not about local tradition; it was anger at students who did not belong there coming into "their" schools. He told me, "It was just a very tough time where you could see the anger on people's faces, especially in the white community. They were angry. In the Black community, they wanted better education. In the white community, they felt that Black kids were coming to invade their community, to take over their community, and they weren't going to have it. And you could see the viciousness and anger that that was there."

In Dentler and Scott's analysis of the aftermath of the *Morgan* decision, they argue that concerns about preserving "neighborhood schools" and preventing "busing" are red herrings, fictions that offer a veneer to cover the real reasons for their anger: "The Boston case was never about *busing*. Busing, like the neighborhood school, was an invention of antidesegregationsts. Just as the myth of neighborhood schools gave its believers something 'neutral' to support, so busing gave them something 'neutral' to oppose. But over 30,000 out of an alleged 90,000 students had been taking buses, subways, and taxis from home to public schools in Boston for many years prior to 1974. What is more, all parties to the case, and every individual member of the school committee, agreed that transportation by buses was necessary if system-wide desegregation were to be achieved."[36]

As each of these sources illustrates, the chaos, anger, and school suspensions that came with desegregation were about race and resistance to desegregation, not fair or neutral responses to what was indeed a difficult situation for all involved.

Monty Neill Interviews

While researching what happened after Boston desegregated, I found a series of archived interviews with individuals involved in Boston's desegregation effort.[37] They were conducted by D. Monty Neill, a graduate student at Harvard's Graduate School of Education working on his dissertation. The interviews took place in 1986, with the audio recordings archived and available online through the University of Massachusetts Amherst Libraries' special collections. Neill's dissertation was focused on the Black community's efforts to improve schools in the decade after desegregation, not on school punishment or the consequences of resistance to desegregation. Most of what was discussed pertains to the complex political struggles that shaped the Boston schools and is not very relevant to my work. But some of his interviews highlighted important material by offering those who observed desegregation and its aftermath firsthand the chance to comment on the struggles they observed. These interviews highlighted the role of racial bias in suspension, with some directly stating that the suspension of Black students was due to schools' and communities' resistance to desegregating the schools.

Stephen Bing, the attorney and executive director of the Massachusetts Advocacy Center whom I quoted earlier, told Neill directly that racial discrimination was the cause of the rise in suspensions for Black students and that it was sufficiently clear that the judge understood this to be the cause. He claimed that at one point, Judge Garrity "found as a matter of fact that there was discrimination": "That order was never reduced to writing so you could never find it, but I was in the courtroom when he found it." This discrimination took the form of punishment for what were ostensibly race-neutral behaviors:

> I'll give you an example of things that were suspendable offenses that on their face were racially neutral but weren't, particularly in the first years of desegregation. One was failure to identify yourself. Now, most

school administrators would say, "Well, of course a kid should say who he is and what class he's in and all that." But you have to ask, When is the question asked? Why is it asked? And to whom is it asked? And, in those early years, they were only asking Black kids because they didn't know them. . . . These kids were new to these buildings. But there were elements of harassment, and a lot of the kids resented it. And unlike what you might have heard or read, an overwhelming number of suspensions in the system even to this day are not for incidents of violence. They are incidents of not conforming behavior to sort of institutional rules. Failure to identify yourself, insubordination, truancy—overwhelming number of suspensions were in that category. Not fighting, not bringing drugs to school, not bringing guns to school.[38]

In his interview, Bing provides a clear illustration of color-blind racism, which is exactly what a structural race perspective would predict.

In Albert Holland's interview with Neill, he also offered direct statements about school staff members' desire to remove Black students. Holland was the South Boston High School administrator whom I quoted at the beginning of this chapter. To Neill, he stated, "We found that staff people didn't want the Black kids there. Feelings were very strong about busing, school desegregation. Most of the staff resented the whole desegregation process. They felt that they were being the victims."[39] As a result, he talked about how staff would punish Black students for the disorder that occurred in school, even though it typically occurred because white students attacked Black students.

In another interview, School Committee member Jean McGuire described how Black students who went to school in white neighborhoods were seen as "interlopers." I was shocked to hear McGuire use the same exact term that Gloria Grantham used to describe how Black students were seen in newly desegregated Delaware schools (chapter 4). McGuire continued to describe her observations of teachers who saw Black students in a negative light, as if they did not belong in their schools, and responded punitively to their perceived misbehaviors. Another school committee member, Juanita Wade, also spoke about teachers' hostility toward and fear of students of color and how it resulted in biased interpretations of these students' behaviors.[40]

Tom Atkins, the head of the Boston NAACP during desegregation, offered an interesting perspective on the ripple effects of school desegregation. He told Neill that after the schools desegregated, the NAACP began to receive more complaints from Boston residents about discrimination in a variety of fields:

> The impact of [school desegregation] was to, in effect, rip the lid off the kind of simmering latent racism that had in the past only periodically toppled over and become visible. Blacks in Boston knew that—that racism was there, and many had felt the sting of it. Many felt its physical sting as they had been caught by themselves in areas where, quote, Blacks weren't supposed to be. We knew about it. . . . Anyway, when the [desegregation court] orders came out, [and] it became clear that there were going to be Blacks in every school in the city, it opened up a floodgate of racially discriminatory behavior across the board in housing, in employment, in public [inaudible], in public transit.[41]

He described how the NAACP recruited law student interns to help with the flood of cases, including the cases of students who were now being arrested at school.

Several of Neill's respondents discussed discrimination in school suspension as well as the overall resistance to desegregation. These interviews clearly support my explanation of the increased suspension rates after desegregation, by showing that several people on the ground during desegregation observed how resistance to desegregation and racial bias shaped students' treatment, including suspension rates.

It is worth noting that this outcome was expected by some people. Stephen Bing discussed in his interview the fact that he and others at the Massachusetts Advocacy Center were concerned about the potential for students to be suspended en masse after desegregation, since this was what the Robert F. Kennedy Memorial had found in jurisdictions across the South.[42] He told Neill that despite being prepared for this to occur, the number of suspensions was more than they had expected (or feared). The Boston Freedom House also saw the potential for schools to respond to desegregation by suspending Black students. In a February 1975 letter to Judge Garrity that weighed in on a School Committee plan for phase 2 desegregation (one that was not adopted), the president and codirectors of the Freedom House stated, "We have also asked the Court to require procedures designed to prevent a variety of abuses that often attend desegregation. The procedures include: certification for, and placement in, special education classes; affirmative action; suspension and expulsion; multi-racial advisory bodies; police behavior on school grounds during school hours; . . . [and others]."[43] Schools' resistance to desegregation and its effect on punishment was predicted and observed firsthand.

Other Indicators of the Rise in Suspensions

In chapter 5, I discussed the relative absence of discussions of school suspensions in the Boston news media, school superintendent reports, and other sources. This changed quickly, with desegregation; by the mid-1970s, suspension was a topic that was frequently reported and discussed.

In contrast to the Boston Public Schools superintendent's reports from as late as 1972–1973 that did not comment on or report about any school discipline, the 1975–1976 annual report includes a table reporting the numbers of students suspended from school. The school system's attention to school discipline is visible in other ways as well, such as distribution of its Code of Discipline. In the Boston City Archives, I found School Committee orders for the printing of copies of its Code of Discipline: in 1970, 10,000 copies were ordered to be printed; in 1975, 120,000 copies were ordered. The superintendent and School Committee began prioritizing discipline only after desegregation went into effect.

The Boston school system's new focus on school punishment resulted in documented new school practices in the 1970s, following desegregation. One was the creation of the Boston Public Schools Department of Safety Services, which was formed in the late 1970s.[44] Another was the first use of in-school suspension. In a 1978 memorandum, the acting chief of school safety services described the recently adopted in-school suspension programs in three high schools and one middle school and whether it was a program worth adopting more broadly in Boston.[45]

Even discussions of violence changed after desegregation to focus on suspensions as a typical response. Compare, for example, two reports on violence in Boston public schools, one in 1971 and the other in 1983. The 1971 report was written by a commission for the School Committee.[46] It focused on issues such as the need for administrators to make policies clear and for teachers to engage students, effective communication, supports for students with disabilities, the need for student input into school governance, and so on. Recommendations focused on improving school governance, communication, teaching, student supports, and other inclusive practices. The only reference to suspension was the recommendation that principals should have the right to insist that "the school disrupter be referred to the School Committee for exclusion or expulsion from the school after due process of censure, warnings, hearings, and an exhaustive effort to retain him in school."[47] In other words, suspensions were seen as necessary in only rare circumstances that needed to be approved by the Boston School Committee. In today's schools, suspensions are so common that schools often employ one or even multiple administrators who deal solely with school discipline and assign suspensions; but in Boston in 1971, just before desegregation, they were so rare that the Boston School Committee had time to review each referral for suspension.

The 1983 report looks very different. It was written by Daryl Hellman, a professor of economics at Northeastern University, and submitted to the Boston Safe Schools Commission.[48] It focuses extensively on school suspensions, such that the section "Comparison of Incident and Suspension Data" is section two out of five. In it, the author finds that suspensions are used frequently and that "there is no apparent correspondence, at the School District level, between incidents and suspensions."[49] Overall, the author finds that there are four times more suspensions than incidents of student misbehavior in 1982–1983. Even when restricting the analysis to "suspendable offenses" or even just to physical assault and possession of a dangerous weapon, there are still many more suspensions for these incidents than there are incidents themselves.[50] In other words, suspensions were routinely given, even in absence of incidents that were supposed to result in suspension by rule. Between 1971 (three years prior to desegregation) and 1983 (eight years after it), suspension went from an afterthought that, if necessary, should be in the hands of the School Committee to a practice that is more common than suspendable incidents.

Finally, I return to my discussion in chapter 5 of suspension being mentioned in *Boston Globe* articles. As in Delaware, there was a noticeable spike in articles discussing suspension after desegregation began in 1974. It should hardly be surprising that problems of desegregation were frequently covered, since the violent reception of Black students was a prominent national news story. But it is meaningful that stories specifically about suspension were increasingly common within this coverage, offering yet another observation to support the conclusion that suspensions rose dramatically as Boston schools desegregated.

Conclusion

School desegregation was fiercely resisted in Boston. But the violent protests by segregationists were not the only consequence. School suspensions increased dramatically right after Boston schools desegregated as well. As Albert Holland, who had a front-row seat to the chaos of South Boston High School during desegregation, told me, the schools just were not prepared for desegregation. The resistance to desegregation was a serious problem for schools, since it manifested in violence inside and outside the schools. Without having planned adequately and devised a solution or plan for maintaining order, the schools resorted to suspensions. And they did so in ways that pushed the burden even further onto the Black students, not the white students yelling racial epithets.

The available evidence on Boston's experience with desegregation tells this story clearly. Plaintiffs in the desegregation case returned to court months after phase 1 of desegregation began, to initiate discussions about suspension; statistical analyses document the spike in suspension, most notably for Black students in schools affected by desegregation; sworn affidavits by students and staff who witnessed or experienced racist school punishments document these practices; school reformers and community leaders attested to the use of school punishment as a way to resist desegregation; School Committee records indicate that suspension first became an issue of concern after 1974; and news media reporting on suspension increased after desegregation.

My analysis of Boston before and after desegregation mirrors the Delaware case in important ways. Boston was much more visible in the national media because it was Boston, not New Castle County, Delaware, but also because of the scope of protest, racism, and violence on display. And yet these two independent sites demonstrated a remarkably similar pattern whereby suspension became a prominent problem only after desegregation. The consistency of the experiences of Boston and New Castle County help contextualize and explain my quantitative finding (chapter 2) that resistance to desegregation shapes school punishment across the US, not just in the South or the "border South."

Boston's experience with desegregation also mirrors what we should expect, based on a structural race perspective. The Boston School Committee perpetuated a racially hierarchical school system until it was forced by court order to restructure the public schools. But instead of accepting progress toward equity, the School Committee and citizens fiercely resisted, causing new problems for the Black students whom the court sought to help. Once in formerly all-white schools, Black students were suspended in great numbers and disproportionately for subjectively perceived infractions. As a structural race perspective tells us, this is a common pattern because it reflects the racial hierarchy embedded in all social institutions, so that reforms intended to enhance equity typically only restructure how racial oppression is experienced, rather than eliminate it.

To be clear, I am not arguing that students were never suspended in Boston (or Delaware) before desegregation. My analyses of Boston suspensions shown in figures 6.2 and 6.3 indicate that they were, just far less frequently than immediately after September 1974. I could find no archived records of suspensions in Boston before 1970, so it is impossible to know just how frequently students were suspended in these years before desegregation. The reports of suspension's rise following desegregation in southern schools in the late 1960s and early 1970s (see chapter 1) show that suspension had become a known practice among schools by then, one that was probably copied by other jurisdictions. Some students were clearly suspended in each of my two case-study sites before court-ordered desegregation in the 1970s, just far fewer than immediately afterward. Suspension changed from a somewhat rare occurrence to a normative response, particularly for Black students who were unwanted—seen as "interlopers"—in previously white spaces.

Conclusion

What Is Past Isn't Past

In September 2023, I presented the results of this research to the University of Delaware Lifelong Learning Institute's Current Issues class. The class has no assignments or exams and is open to local residents aged fifty to ninety years old who wish to meet to engage about current issues. I have presented different research projects to this class a few times before over the years, and I love visiting there. It is always a full house of about eighty attentive students in person (more before COVID-19), with more attending via Zoom, many of whom ask amazingly insightful questions. I particularly appreciate the fact that many of them are retired educators who let me know after I present how well (or otherwise) I did. After my recent presentation, one student from the class emailed me:

> Hi Aaron,
> I found your class very interesting. I do agree with the concept of White privilege. However I'm not sure the constant discussing of this concept is helpful. There is no changing history. What is past is past. I believe EEO was probably the best we could do. I believe that the discussions on how blacks have been disadvantaged, need to change to contain more thoughts on how to move forward and how the black community needs to step up. The opportunities are there. The discussions need to focus on how these communities can access these opportunities. You have to realize that every movement that supposedly is created to help stop discrimination, is causing more racism. By saying whites are privileged, do you not realize the affect that has on those "whites" that were not so privileged? By creating a movement called "black lives matter," do you

not realize how that affected whites. I'm not saying that injustices don't exist. I'm saying stop the names and focus on the issues. When we give statistics about how unfair blacks are treated, I do believe we leave out how much of this treatment is a result of their behavior. Their neighborhoods are crime ridden and unsafe to live in so it follows they will have a lot more police interactions and more arrests. I know whites are treated differently. I'm just not sure giving people, any people, a [*sic*] excuse for their failures, is ever helpful.

The student continued with two illustrations, one of which led them to claim, "Programs to help such as welfare, seem to create an attitude of I'm entitled." The other was critical of affirmative action in college admissions.

In this email, the class member acknowledged white privilege—despite the fact that I do not believe I mentioned that term once during my presentation—but then suggested that we should move on from discussing historical racial injustice because "what is past is past"—I disagree. My hope is that with this book, I can do a better job than I apparently did during my presentation at demonstrating how the past is still very relevant today, since past racial injustice left a major imprint on current school practice, and how important it is to understand the ways that past racial injustice continue to affect contemporary life.

This student is certainly not alone in wanting to avoid discussion of past racial injustice. In some states, such as Florida, as well as in the federal government during the Trump administration, we have seen a more extreme form of this resistance to discussing past racial injustice, typically expressed as anger toward CRT. In September 2020, Office of Management and Budget (OMB) Director Russell Vought distributed a memo that, on behalf of then-President Trump, prohibited federal agencies from any professional training activities relating to CRT. The memo states that such trainings "not only run counter to the fundamental beliefs for which our Nation has stood since its inception, but they also engender division and resentment within the Federal workforce."[1] Following Trump's lead, in the following year, states and cities across the US debated CRT, and some passed laws prohibiting the teaching of it in school.[2] A primary concern was that CRT would teach children that they, their families, their communities, or their country are evil and/or that they would be taught to feel guilty for past events that are not their fault.

It is difficult for me to think of a more misleading argument. Whether the focus is on structural theories of racial inequality writ large, discussions of historical racial injustice, or CRT in particular, these ideas are not "anti-American," and they do not encourage students to feel guilty or engender resentment. Anyone with a basic understanding of the central ideas of CRT would know that these claims are a harmful distortion. CRT recognizes that (1) from the nation's first moments, it was marked by racial oppression, and (2) a racial hierarchy has been embedded in social institutions since. One cannot rationally argue against the first point, given the history of slavery, racial oppression in non-slaveholding states, Jim Crow laws, and so on. The second point simply argues that the menace of racial oppression has not gone away—it remains, even if it is sometimes hidden. This point might be more difficult to accept by those who argue that racism is only a problem of the past, but the evidence of racism's enduring effect is overwhelming. As just a single example, how else could one explain the fact that the average white family in the US had $184,000 in wealth in 2019, compared to $38,000 for Black families?[3] This is the result of the passing on of intergenerational wealth, the denial of equal educational and employment opportunities, residential segregation, variation in communities in which people are raised, and other related problems, each of which is the result of historical racial inequities.[4] The only other possible explanation is that the gap is due to innate racial differences, an explicitly racist assumption that is debunked by any scientific inquiry and that I hope few people would make. The point is not to induce guilt or resentment; the point is to better understand historical and structural causes of contemporary inequality.

In addition to being ignorant about what structural race theories actually state, bans of CRT or other structural race theories are harmful. If we cannot talk about race, a history of racial oppression, or current-day forms of racial inequity, then how can we work toward a more racially equitable society? I agree with the sociologists Ruth Thompson-Miller, Joe R. Feagin, and Leslie H. Picca, who state, "To alleviate the contemporary effects on the minds and health of African Americans, the long history of imposed racialized traumas must first be fully acknowledged by both black communities and the larger society."[5] If we turn a blind eye to (or, worse, deny) the facts because of concern that white people might feel guilty, we allow racial inequality to continue and even grow. Another concern about continuing to discuss past racial injustice—the central concern of the student who emailed me about my presentation—is that we obstruct progress by focusing on the past rather than the present or future. This, too, makes no sense, since if we ever want to move forward, we must look carefully at how past forms of racism and racial oppression shape aspects of contemporary life that are taken for granted and insufficiently examined. This is what I have tried to do in this book.

It is widely acknowledged that schools across the US use exclusionary punishments like suspensions far too often and in ways that hurt children, schools, and communities. We suspend children rather than investing in, supporting, and enriching them. It makes no rational sense, given how much harm our compulsion to suspend students causes and how little it helps schools. But, if we understand our use of suspension as a practice rooted in resistance to desegregation, as a way of excluding *unwanted* Black students from previously all-white spaces, then it makes more sense. As a structural race perspective instructs us, present circumstances are shaped by historical racial oppression.

Rather than burying our heads in the sand because we are concerned that recognizing a problem might "engender division and resentment," it is important to recognize why we punish students the way we do. We need to understand the historical racial context of the problem of school punishment if we hope to have any chance of doing better for our children. Despite years of efforts to reform school punishment, starting during the Obama administration, schools across the US still rely primarily on school suspension instead of the array of responses that would be much more effective. One reason for the limited success we have had is because we address the symptoms of the disease, trying to limit the use of suspension in certain cases, rather than focusing on better understanding the disease itself.

In the preceding chapters, I have shown the shared history of resistance to desegregation and the rise of suspension, demonstrated that schools in districts with greater resistance to desegregation suspend more children today, and used the cases of Boston and New Castle County, Delaware, to illustrate how school suspensions rose immediately after, and largely in response to, desegregation. Resistance to desegregation might not have been the only influence on school punishment, but the evidence shows that it clearly was an important one. Before concluding, I discuss a few additional topics that help contextualize, clarify, and support my argument.

Seeing the Forest for the Trees

One important issue I need to clarify is that the problems I have focused on throughout this book are *institutional*. We suspend children the way we do because schools as social systems have developed in a particular way over the past seventy years, because school policy constrains the options available to teachers, and because schools establish systems of discipline that teachers must follow. School systems, not teachers, define schools' problems, solutions, and goals, and the specific practice of school suspension has been institutionalized across the US since the 1970s.

It would be foolish to blame individual teachers for the broad racial context of school suspensions. Certainly, some teachers are bad at their jobs, misunderstand the effects of suspending students, and harbor both implicitly and explicitly racist views of students of color; research shows that teachers hold explicit and implicit bias at the same rates as nonteachers.[6] Teachers vary with regard to their classroom management skills and use of harmful punishments, so their individual skill sets and inclinations matter. But I think there is every reason to assume that the vast majority of teachers are well intentioned. Even during desegregation in Boston and New Castle County, Delaware, I believe that most teachers were well intentioned and that their use of suspensions was often (but not always) a response to lack of preparation, misrecognition of students' behaviors and attitudes, and unintended implicit bias. Teachers have extremely difficult jobs, for which they are paid too little and receive too much blame for a host of problems. I do not mean to blame them for the overuse of school suspension as well. Doing so would be missing the forest for the trees—focusing only on individuals who exist within a system that directs them toward certain options.

Instead of blaming teachers, we need to support them more fully. Teachers need to be trained in how to avoid exclusionary punishments, not just warned that they need to avoid suspending students, so that those who currently turn too quickly to harmful punishment might learn more effective strategies. They need more complete training in classroom management skills. And they need to have trained professionals on staff who can help with tutoring, facilitate students' well-being, and offer guidance on how to practice inclusive behavior management. These supports might not be sufficient to offset the inertia of fifty years of institutionalized punishment practices, but they would certainly help teachers to uplift more students without relying on harmful punishments.

Seeing the problems as institutional, not just due to individuals' actions, also helps clarify how prior battles around desegregation relate to today's schools. As I show for Boston and New Castle County, suspensions first became common immediately after desegregation in the 1970s. But the rate of suspensions has changed since then. Nationally, suspension rates increased throughout the 1990s and early 2000s as schools implemented zero-tolerance policies, hired additional police (School Resource Officers), and generally pursued more punitive responses to student behaviors. This growth in school punishment was a by-product of a general anxiety and wave of punitiveness that pervaded the criminal legal system as well.[7] But the form of these punishments—not just how frequently they are given—is important too, and its origin has not been sufficiently explained before. In the preceding chapters, I illustrate how the form of punishment that arose—suspension—fit with the desire to remove unwanted Black students from previously white spaces. This practice became common and, eventually, deeply embedded as part of what schools do. It became institutionalized practice. The school districts I study have changed since the 1970s, particularly Boston, in which the enrollment has changed from 52 percent white in 1974 to 14 percent white in 2017.[8] And yet the practice of suspending students—removing them from school despite all evidence showing this practice to be ineffective at best, harmful at worst—that became common in the 1970s is still a common form of school punishment.

A More Complex Picture

To maintain a consistent focus, I have looked almost entirely at the experience of Black students entering formerly white schools after the *Brown* decision, in which Black students were plaintiffs. This makes sense for a couple of reasons. In 2017–2018, Black students were given one or more suspensions out of school at a higher rate than any other racial or ethnic group.[9] And the *Brown* Court decision was perhaps the best known, most iconic judicial or legal action regarding education of students of color.

But really, the story is broader than this. To best understand how and why we punish as we do, we should also consider experiences of other marginalized groups of students, including how the intersection of different identities can shape school punishment. US history is marked by the oppression and denial of educational opportunities to Latino/a, Native American, Asian American, and Native Hawaiian students as well. Each group experienced a somewhat different history of segregation and incorporation into previously white schools. Native American students, for example, faced brutal educational oppression; public schools, and particularly the "Indian Schools" to which many Native American youth were forcibly sent, were used as tools to exterminate Native American culture through forced assimilation. The Native American community faced obstacles to retaining its culture and identity, not just to receiving equal opportunity to obtain an education.[10] Mexican Americans likewise were denied educational opportunities but in somewhat different ways than Black students. In many jurisdictions, including in early twentieth-century California, Mexican Americans were considered white and included in the growing number of public schools. But in different places and points in time, they were banned from "white" schools. In the case of *Mendez v. Westminster*, a federal court ruled that Mexican American students could not be denied admission to white schools in California.[11] This case was decided in 1947, seven years before *Brown*.[12] The experiences of each of these groups differed, of course, but they share a history of being unwanted in many public schools that were reserved for white students.

The experiences of LGBTQ+ students and students with disabilities certainly are important as well, particularly because they are at high risk of school punishment.[13] Targeting students for punishment because of their gender identity or sexual orientation can strain these youths' connections to their community and feelings of self-worth at a very vulnerable time. It is also important to understand the role of gender in shaping school punishment and the intersection of gender and race, not to mention the intersection of disability and race. Each of these analyses is worthwhile and important, for it can highlight various ways in which school punishment harms children. By focusing on the segregation, desegregation, and punishment specifically of Black students, I do not mean to imply that other groups' histories, sacrifices, or oppression are less important or less damaging to the well-being of youth. Rather, I have focused on the largest, most visible, and most impactful desegregation movement (in response to *Brown*) as a way of understanding how the legacy of white supremacy, broadly speaking, shapes contemporary school punishment and students' lives.

The sociologist Matthew Ward's recent analysis of the legacy of slavery illustrates how the institution of slavery created racist social structures that today affect members of groups whose ancestors were not enslaved. He writes, "Although U.S. Latinos did not experience slavery as Black populations did, the early exclusionary social structures forged under Black chattel bondage may negatively affect a group that has more recently been criminalized and scapegoated. . . . Precisely because early Black disadvantage served as a foundation upon which the United States was built, other racialized ethnic groups may also be trapped in a contemporary morass of systemic discrimination."[14] A similar observation applies to schools. The initial rise in suspension may have been spurred by resistance to Black students entering previously white spaces, but it affected—and continues to affect—youth in other marginalized groups as well.

The story about resistance to desegregation and school punishment is also broader because of how it harms *all* students (and their families, schools, and communities), not just students of color or in other marginalized groups. Indeed, in 2017–2018, 795,000 white students were suspended from US public schools one or more times. Clearly, suspension is not limited only to students of color! While suspensions became common as Black students began enrolling in previously white schools, the practice became institutionalized. Schools mimicked each other and adopted the practice, as described by the theory of neo-institutionalism. Over time, suspension became a taken-for-granted practice and even the primary option available to many teachers or school administrators faced with disruptive students. Once it was so deeply ingrained into school practice as a solution—sometimes the only available solution—to student misbehavior, it became used frequently for white students too. This, of course, follows other illustrations of racialized control, such as the War on Drugs. While prior scholars such as Michelle Alexander and many others have convincingly argued that the War on Drugs is a tool of racial control, many white people are caught in its net as well.

Heather McGhee vividly illustrates this same phenomenon on a larger scale in her recent book *The Sum of Us*. She shows how racial hostilities and the policies they influence hurt people of color as well as most white people. Often, this occurs because of a false sense of competition—what she refers to as a "zero-sum paradigm"—in which white Americans believe that any economic, political, or legal gain among other racial/ethnic groups means a corresponding loss for them. As a result, people "resist policies that could benefit *them*, just because they might also benefit people of color."[15] Her analysis demonstrates that white and Black Americans, and those of other races/ethnicities as well, are all harmed by contemporary racism. This is clear with regard to school suspensions too, given how all students are at risk of suspension and occasionally suffer its harms, even if Black students experience it more than any other group.

The Problem of a Deficit Perspective

Another limitation to my analyses is that I have written what the sociologist Mary Patillo calls a "deficit perspective" of the lives of Black people.[16] Patillo describes how most social science research on Black people focuses on the harms they have experienced due to racial oppression, and as a result, it reproduces the stigma placed on Black people, adding to the barrage of negative information about them. In a brilliant essay, she calls for more scholarship that instead uses a "Black Advantage Vision" to focus on the strength and resilience of Black individuals and communities and ways that Black people outperform white people in society.

Over the course of my research on school punishment before and after desegregation, I certainly found evidence that fits within a Black Advantage Vision, often by learning about the strength and resilience of educators who worked in segregated Black schools. Black educators who worked in Delaware, for example, spoke of what was lost when schools desegregated. Segregated Black schools in New Castle County might have been underfunded, but they were communities in which children were cared for. Gloria Grantham, the parent, educator, and school administrator whose work and comments I analyze in chapters 3 and 4, discussed the supportive community at the middle school where she taught before desegregation in New Castle County: "At Burnett, we had children from one of the lowest socioeconomic areas of the city of Wilmington, which was Riverside at the time. And, but our kids were wonderful. Our teachers were wonderful, and the atmosphere was absolutely amazing. It was such a relaxed atmosphere, and it was such camaraderie. And there was a lot of love. There were white teachers at Burnett and Black teachers, and we were a family. There was nothing wrong with Wilmington schools—everything wrong with Wilmington schools happened after desegregation." Later in our discussion, she described her perceptions upon leaving her job at an almost entirely white private school and going to this middle school with almost all Black students: "I'll tell you, I felt like I landed, and haven't I? The care that the Black and white teachers gave our kids was amazing. We were like a family." Grantham described how, despite many students in her classes and a lack of funding overall, she and other teachers found the resources that they needed to teach effectively. At times, this meant reaching out to community organizations, such as when she contacted the "Black DuPonters Association" (a group of Black scientists who worked at the nearby DuPont chemical company); about eight members of this association came to her school to help mentor her students as they worked on their science projects. She described students who continued on to graduate school, medical school, and wonderful careers.

Bebe Coker, the social justice leader and parent whose comments informed my analyses of Delaware schools before and after desegregation, offered a similar view of the resilience of Black educators and students before desegregation. She described to me how schools hosting Black students were underfunded, with lower-quality or fewer educational resources, but still wonderful places for learning:

> Of course, the books and that kind of thing. And the things that we didn't have. It might be that your school didn't have a movie screen, you know what I mean? Things like that. And I didn't notice all of that. [Colleague of hers] could tell you the same thing. I didn't notice all that stuff until we started talking about desegregation of schools. I really didn't. And I tell you probably, in all honesty, if you look, the reason we didn't pay attention is because, for whatever reason, Blacks have managed beyond all reason. When something is taken away or reduced in quality of whatever, Blacks have always found a way to do what they have to do, to learn to be, to work, to own a home, to rear our children, and that kind of thing. So you don't just sit back worrying about what it is that the white community didn't give us.

Coker continued to describe how she and some other civil rights leaders in Wilmington had opposed the desegregation plan that took effect. She and colleagues had wanted better funding for their children's schools but did not believe that putting Black children on buses to go to mostly white suburban schools was the best way to accomplish this. Grantham's and Coker's observations mirror both historical and contemporary research on the Black community's resilience in the face of discrimination, in and outside schools.[17]

Granted, my narrative fits within a deficit perspective, focusing on the harms done to Black children because of resistance to school desegregation and their multigenerational repercussions. I present this argument because I believe it is important to understand why we punish children the way we do today and how our practices are informed by historical racism. Hopefully, my analyses result in clearer understandings of these problems, not stigma for Black children. Certainly I do not see the problems I discuss as the fault of the Black students (or other students) who are punished but instead as the errors of the adults who kick them out of schools.

Doing Better

The practice of suspending children did not become common because it was fair or effective—we know that it is neither. It is important to point out that this insight (i.e., that suspending students is ineffective, unfair, and harmful) is hardly new. In each of my two research sites, I found evidence that student advocates and educators understood the harms of exclusionary punishment and benefits of alternative strategies decades ago.

In Boston, for example, the Massachusetts Advocacy Council and Mayor's Office of Human Rights wrote the following in a January 1975 memo to area (community school district) superintendents within the Boston school district. It began by stating, "Pursuant to our earlier conversation, we would like to set out for your response some changes in school discipline practices in the Boston schools. These changes, if adopted, should result not only in greater fairness to all students, but also in a more efficient, less hostile and explosive operation of the schools." It continued,

> Suspension, if used at all, should be used *only* as a *last resort* and then only for *dangerous* and *violent behavior*. Certain behavior or actions by students, while deviating from exemplary behavior, are not sufficiently serious to call for major disciplinary action. . . . [After discussing common minor misbehaviors:] What characterizes these actions is that all should be dealt with on an individualized basis with resort to counselling and discussion. None of them warrant the termination of the educational process. Discipline is invoked to reinforce the process and should be corrective rather than retributive. Measures should be designed to address the cause of the problem rather than to simply ameliorate or eliminate the active symptoms.[18]

Over the next several pages, this memo then details appropriate steps to take in response to student disruption or misbehavior. These steps mirror contemporary recommendations of "best practices," like restorative practices, which seek to support students in an effort to help them solve problems and improve behavior. The document is progressive by today's standards, with regard to proposing evidence-based responses as a replacement for harmful exclusionary discipline. It is not alone. Other documents from decades ago also showed that advocates recognized that school suspension was not an effective response to students, both because it excluded children from school and also because many students saw it as a day off; they advocated for positive corrections rather than exclusionary punishment.[19]

In New Castle County, I found similar examples of concern about exclusionary punishment and preference for what would today be an evidence-based response to student misbehavior. One illustration of this, which I discuss in chapter 3, is in the minutes of an October 9, 1969, meeting among secondary school principals. Though the school district is not identified, I found these minutes in the Delaware State Archives in a box holding records of the state's northernmost district, Brandywine, which was later a part of the New Castle County School District. The first issue discussed was discipline, with the following recorded: "We need to provide another program and facility for unmotivated and aggressive youngsters. (A quote was read from Allen Rusten's letter of September 23 regarding isolation of disruptive students). Although a positive approach must be taken, the principals felt that a stigma would be attached to a program of separatism."[20] In other words, in 1969, secondary school principals in New Castle County recognized the need for a positive approach for discipline that avoided the stigma imposed by school suspensions.

In each site, there is evidence that at the moment in time before suspensions grew in number, we knew better than to engage in such practice. Suspension did not become a common school punishment because the evidence at the time supported its use. Educators knew better but turned to exclusionary punishment anyway. It was not based on advice that came from the best evidence available at the time but then later shown to be problematic. Here I am thinking of mistakes like pediatricians' advice of putting infants to sleep on their stomachs—years before the medical community realized that this increased the chances of sudden infant death syndrome (SIDS). Instead, the evidence suggests that suspension fit the segregationist impulse to remove Black students seen as "interlopers" in previously segregated white spaces. It does not help the school or the student, but it does remove an unwanted child from the school.

Evidence that we have known better is also important because it offers additional context for thinking about how to improve school disciplinary practice. It shows that although we have learned a great deal about effective school disciplinary practices in the past fifty years and still have much to learn, educators and child advocates understood what general form effective practice should take fifty years ago. Despite a wealth of evidence reinforcing what these advocates knew half a century ago, we still overuse exclusionary punishments rather than following this model. Given this, why should we expect that we can reform school discipline to be more effective, fair, and helpful to students?

When I give presentations or talk with journalists about school punishment, I am typically critical of how we punish students in contemporary schools. I am almost always asked about what policies or practices would work better. It is a perfectly reasonable question, and yet it is a frustrating one because we have known for over fifty years what we should do differently but fail to do it. Schools across the US might recognize that suspension is not an effective response and still use it consistently. Rather than asking what we should do differently, the better question is, How do we implement what we know to be a better response? It is not enough to know that there are better strategies we could implement, such as teaching social-emotional learning, positive behavioral interventions and supports (PBIS), or restorative justice; these are insufficient as long as they must compete with the taken-for-granted solution of suspension that is most readily available to many schools.

A structural race perspective helps to explain how and why we have consistently failed to implement best practices over the past fifty years. If we see school suspension as part of a racialized social system, as an illustration that often-subtle racial inequities are deeply embedded in how institutions like schools work, then our failure to do better makes more sense. Even when schools sincerely intend to do better and turn to restorative justice, PBIS, and other strategies, these practices tend to fall short because they are no match for institutionalized, deeply embedded logics about students and responses to student behaviors. The education scholars Hannah Carson Baggett and Carey E. Andrzejewski argue that these progressive, evidence-based strategies fail to combat institutionalized racism's effect on school practices because they either focus on the need for students to change or fail to confront how institutionalized racism shapes school policy. These practices do not force educators to confront taken-for-granted assumptions about students, their behavior, and effective responses. Baggett and Andrzejewski write, "Without examining systems of race, racism, and power and reimagining possibilities to connect and build relationships with students and families, reform efforts will be unable to remedy discriminatory discipline."[21]

I began this conclusion by sharing a conversation that illustrates how even those who agree that our past is marked by systemic racism can resist such a discussion of race, racism, and power in schools. How, then, do we advance this discussion in ways that are inclusive and productive, that allow us to move forward rather than alienating those who feel defensive? Certainly, an important step has to occur in schools. It would be helpful to educate teachers in the history of systemic racial inequality of education but in a way that focuses on future actions and rewards learning rather than induces guilt. Incentives for teachers who adapt their teaching strategies to resist systemic inequality would help this effort. It is also crucial to work with school administrators at the district (i.e., superintendents) and school levels (principals and assistant principals). School leadership matters, and leaders who encourage a critical view of exclusionary school punishment can help move the needle.

Despite the fact that we have known better for decades, there is always hope that schools can improve their disciplinary practices to be more inclusive and supportive of students, rather than relying on exclusionary punishments like suspensions.

Because I have taken a broad, structural approach to viewing the problem of school discipline—seeing it as a legacy of long-standing racial resentment and resistance to desegregation—it seems fitting to think about broad, structural paths forward as well. The most obvious path is to change school funding formulas in order to better and more equitably fund public schools. As long as teachers are overwhelmed and have insufficient time to build rapport with students or interact with them in ways that build them up rather than remove them from class, we will not make much headway in implementing evidence-based disciplinary practices. It takes money to make teachers' jobs easier, so that they have smaller classes, teachers' aides, and certified counselors or psychologists to help address students' needs. This means not only that we need to hire more certified staff but also that we need to increase average salaries in order to attract more people toward careers in education and school counseling and to retain them.

We also need to think beyond schools. The root of the problem of school discipline is the racial inequity that is deeply embedded in social institutions. Further, the harms inflicted on youth through school suspension have lifelong, intergenerational consequences. Because reparations to Black Americans have potential to address both deeply embedded inequality and its intergenerational harms, they offer an opportunity to right some of these wrongs. In different forms and (typically limited) amounts, reparations have been paid to members of other racial and ethnic groups who have been wronged by states or the federal government, including Native Americans and Japanese Americans.[22] Reparations for Black Americans was briefly attempted immediately after the Civil War, when General William Sherman signed Field Order 15, granting each Black family forty acres of land and a mule. This ended when President Abraham Lincoln was assassinated and President Andrew Johnson reversed Field Order 15, returning this land back to former slave owners.[23]

Recently, a movement to establish reparations for Black Americans has gained momentum. US House Bill HR40, which would establish a federal commission to study the legacy of slavery and draft proposals to address its harms, including reparations, has been introduced at every congressional session since 1989 but never reached a committee vote—until 2021.[24] In 2023, it was reintroduced in the House with more cosponsors than ever before, along with a companion bill, S40, in the US Senate. The city of Evanston, Illinois, passed the nation's first reparations law for Black Americans in 2019, seeking to distribute $10 million to Black residents.[25] Harvard University and Georgetown University have each dedicated $100 million to begin to atone for their early reliance on enslaved people. Virginia passed a reparations bill in 2021 that focuses on five state universities, each of which was founded with the help of enslaved people.[26] And, in June 2023, the state of California's reparations task force presented its recommendations to the state legislature in a one-thousand-page report that called for a host of recommendations for addressing historical oppression of Black residents.

The California task force made many recommendations for ways to reduce the state's racial wealth and opportunity gaps. Doing so would help to restore some of what has been lost throughout generations of Black Californians who have been denied an equal education, in part through school punishment. By reducing systemic inequality, it would also undermine the basis of disparities in exclusionary school punishment and therefore probably reduce its use. The task force provided several recommendations that pertain directly to educational equity. Among others, these include the following:

- Increase Funding to Schools to Address Racial Disparities
- Implement Systematic Review of School Discipline Data
- Adopt Mandatory Curriculum for Teacher Credentialing and Trainings for School Personnel and Grants for Teachers

- Employ Proven Strategies to Recruit African American Teachers
- Require that Curriculum at All Levels Be Inclusive and Free of Bias
- Adopt a K–12 Black Studies Curriculum
- Reduce Racial Disparities in the STEM Fields for African American Students
- Fund Free Tuition to California Public Colleges and Universities
- Eliminate Standardized Testing for Admission to Graduate Programs in the University of California and California State University Systems.
- Identify and Eliminate Racial Bias and Discrimination in Statewide K–12 Proficiency Assessments.[27]

These recommendations seek to support Black students by better funding the schools they attend, diversifying the teacher force, creating culturally inclusive curricular programming, and funding Black students' efforts to pursue higher education. The task force also encourages review of disciplinary records.

If the state were able to acknowledge and rectify racial injustices by providing equal educational opportunities for Black students, including schools in which Black students were seen as children to be cared for rather than problems to be managed, then high rates of suspensions and racial disparities in school punishment might become a thing of the past. The education scholar Subini Ancy Annamma describes the change that could occur by training teachers in historical racism and contemporary systemic inequality: "When teachers have a true sense of the systemic inequities their students face and their own evolving dispositions, they may be more likely to develop an ethic of caring. This authentic ethic of caring would replace the disposition of suspicion and be rooted in sustained, reciprocal relationships between students and teachers; one where teachers are invested in their students' lives and students therefore become invested in the institution of schooling."[28]

I realize that reparations are a tall order. Even in California, a majority of the public opposes the effort, according to a recent poll.[29] Were the state or nation to wish to engage in reparations, a host of difficult—but not insurmountable—logistical issues would arise. Agreeing on boundaries of who is eligible, what evidence they need to show eligibility, and how to distribute cash or other benefits that promise to help multiple generations are each daunting tasks. And then there is the question of how it would be financed; certainly our federal government, which is not required to have a balanced budget, *could* finance reparations if the will was there, but that seems unlikely. But if we could find solutions to these challenges and states or the federal government could use reparations to repair and restore some of the damage done by historical racial oppression and multigenerational harms of denial of educational opportunity, then this effort might erode the basis on which the problem of school punishment rests.

The stakes are high. Maintaining a racially hierarchical educational system, in which Black youth receive an inferior education marked by excessive school punishment, perpetuates racial inequality in opportunities and life outcomes that reverberates across generations. It is also fundamentally undemocratic, since it results in the hoarding of opportunity for white youth rather than providing equal opportunities to all children. Indeed, the ways we punish children in schools give lie to the notion that schools are a meritocracy, in which the brightest, most promising young people can fairly earn the credentials to succeed in life.

Thanks to the efforts of many groups, we have seen progress in dismantling harmful school punishment practices in recent years. The numbers of students suspended have gone down in recent years, from a high of 3.4 million youth (estimated) in 2009–2010 to 2.6 million in 2017–2018.[30] The Obama administration's guidance to reduce the use of suspension, particularly for youth of color, drew attention to the problems of exclusionary school punishment, which certainly helped.[31] Several civil rights, racial justice, and childhood advocacy organizations have been lobbying for years to dismantle the "school-to-prison pipeline" by reducing our reliance on suspension; these organizations include the ACLU, Advancement Project, American Bar Association,

NAACP, UCLA Civil Rights Project, and many others. Even more encouraging is the fact that students themselves have effectively organized to advocate for fairer, more transparent, and more productive school practices. In *Willful Defiance*, Mark Warren describes the social movement, with students (and parents) leading the way in many areas, to reform school punishment.[32] This movement demonstrates the resilience of youth whom schools too often silence and marginalize and gains power from the fact that these youths' voices are amplified. As Warren describes, it has resulted in several successful efforts to reduce exclusionary punishment and replace it with restorative practices in jurisdictions such as Denver, Colorado; Oakland, California; and others.

These successes are very encouraging and leave me optimistic that a change is gonna come. Now seems like good timing for broad agreement that we need to keep children in schools. One would hope that more privileged families who recently suffered from school closures during the COVID-19 pandemic would be empathetic to how other students are affected by being excluded from school. But it is important to still keep in mind the obstacles we face in creating real, lasting change on this front. Changing school policy is insufficient, because harmful school punishments have such a deep foundation. They are rooted in the broader system of racial inequality and cannot be dismantled simply by creating new policies that are written in a school code of conduct but not fully implemented or by telling schools to change what they do without altering the basis of how educators perceive and interact with children. True change takes commitment to really doing things differently than we are used to, and it takes critical introspection of why we do what we do.

Resistance to Desegregation and Contemporary Racism

The final point I wish to make is to highlight the continuing importance of racism in the US today. In both Boston and New Castle County, there was fierce resistance to school desegregation. While New Castle County did not see the level of violence that marred Boston's experience, in each case desegregation elicited a great deal of anger, particularly from white parents whose children were impacted. Sometimes the racism behind these protests was clear and explicit, such as when protesters yelled racial epithets and threw rocks and bricks at buses bringing Black students to school in South Boston. But often the protests were not directly about race—instead parents voiced their anger at "busing," being forced by a federal judge to change the school system, fear of violence that awaited their children at their newly assigned schools, and so on. Much of the resistance to desegregation was framed as the desire to protect; white parents sought to protect their own children's opportunities, local community control of schools, and existing traditions. White parents were concerned about how this large social change, whereby people of color would be given greater opportunities, might impact their children.

These concerns echo today's call to "make America great again." The slogan is an appeal to tradition, but it is also a call to voters—primarily white, straight voters—who are concerned that recent social change prioritizes the needs of *other* people (people of color, the LGBTQ+ community, and other historically marginalized groups), causing their status to decline.[33] The fears underlying resistance to desegregation in the 1960s and 1970s overlap considerably with the fears behind the desire to make America "great" again. In each era, white Americans expressed their anger at progressive social change that sought to empower marginalized groups and offer members of these groups greater chances to gain education, wealth, and status. Donald Trump did not create these fears in his first run for president, but he astutely recognized them and spoke to them in powerful ways. Further, when asked what time period he was referring to as "great," he pointed to the late 1940s and the 1950s.[34] I do not know that he intentionally chose the period just before civil-rights-era victories as a way to signal that he was referring to a segregated, Jim Crow nation, but it seems likely that it was intended or at least interpreted that way by many people.

To illustrate the comparison between then and now, consider the following message, from a flier that was included in the archived materials on desegregation in Boston at the University of Massachusetts Boston Library:

TO ALL THE WHITE KIDS IN ALL THE SOUTHIE SCHOOLS

DO YOU KNOW THAT THE BLACKS IN YOUR SCHOOL HAVE EVERY MOVE THAT HAPPENS PLANNED FAR AHEAD OF TIME? DID YOU KNOW THAT THE LIST OF DEMANDS BY THE BLACKS IN SOUTHIE HIGH WERE ACTUALLY WRITTEN WEEKS AHEAD OF TIME? . . .

IF YOU THINK ITS JUST BUSING YOUR WRONG ITS TOTAL TAKE OVER AND YOUR JUST SITTING ON YOUR ASS LETTING THEM. THEY ARE WALKING ALL OVER YOU AND WHAT HAVE YOU DONE TO STOP THEM. WAKE UP AND START FIGHTING FOR YOUR SCHOOL AND TOWN. ITS TIME YOU BECAME THE AGGRESSORS. INSTEAD OF THE BLACKS. . . . YOU HAVE JUST AS MANY RIGHTS AS ANY BLACK. . . .

This handwritten flier is a call to action based on the idea that Black students have been shrewdly maneuvering to take over South Boston High School. When I came across it, it struck me how similar it is to the contemporary "great replacement theory," a white nationalist conspiracy theory that was espoused by white supremacist marchers in Charlottesville, Virginia, in 2017 and by a mass murderer in Buffalo in 2022.[35] Great replacement theory suggests that immigrants and people of color are threatening to replace whites in the US, eroding the power of white Americans by diluting their numbers. According to a *New York Times* analysis, former Fox News host Tucker Carlson promoted either the theory or the ideas behind it in over four hundred episodes of his show.[36] This idea of a decline in whites' power and privilege because of an influx of people of color is precisely what many people in Boston were afraid of during desegregation, as illustrated by the flier.

This fear that motivated resistance to desegregation, as well as the great replacement theory and the desire to "make America great again," is an illustration of the "zero-sum paradigm."[37] Since the 1600s, Americans have been taught to view the relative status of racial groups as a competition, where gains by one group mean losses by another. It is clear that many white families in Boston and New Castle County were afraid of desegregation—that the potential gains by Black students would mean losses for their own children—just as it is clear now that many white citizens are afraid that demographic, political, and legal gains of historically disenfranchised or underrepresented groups amount to losses for themselves.

My point is that contemporary racism, marked by the desire to turn back the clock on civil rights and other victories for historically disadvantaged groups, is an echo of the racism that provoked whites' resistance to desegregation fifty years ago. By highlighting the legacy of resistance to racial desegregation of schools, we can not only understand how and why we punish students the way we do but also better understand contemporary racial oppression and inequity.

ACKNOWLEDGMENTS

Writing a book is an act of hubris and privilege, possible only because so many people have been so generous with their time, insights, and emotional support. I want to thank all of them and express the hope that the outcome is worthy of their trust and generosity. In this book, I write about other people's experiences: Black children who were unwanted in historically segregated schools, the white segregationists who resisted court-ordered desegregation, and the young people who continue to suffer from the legacy of this resistance to desegregation. I have tried to do my best to listen to, understand, and faithfully report their experiences and am thankful for the opportunity to do so.

I was fortunate to meet and learn from several individuals who participated in the historical events I describe in this book. In Boston, I had wonderful conversations with Jay Blitzman, J. Larry Brown, Barbara Fields, Lewis Finfer, Liza Hirsch, Albert Holland, Thomas Mela, and Paul Weckstein. In Delaware, I had the pleasure of talking to Bebe Coker, Gloria Grantham, Jeffrey Raffel, and Jea Street. While I am grateful to each of them for sharing their time, insights, and personal experiences, I want to take a moment to thank Gloria Grantham and Thomas Mela in particular. Each of these amazing individuals went above and beyond in sharing their time to help me fully understand the history I was wrestling with and to introduce me to others who were helpful as well. I am so grateful for their warmth, encouragement, and guidance.

I appreciate the assistance from the staff at the University of Delaware Library's special collections, the Delaware State Archives, the Boston City Archives, the University of Massachusetts Boston special collections, and the National Archives. Alison Wessel, staff member at the

University of Delaware Library and liaison to my department, has always been an amazing support to all of my library inquiries. And I particularly appreciate my sister-in-law and brother-in-law, Marisa Bourgoin and John LeGloahec, archivists extraordinaire, who helped me along the way as I sought to navigate the world of archival research.

I am a member of several networks of smart, critical, knowledgeable scholars who were willing to guide my analyses and my thinking about the problems I discuss in this book. Some of them pointed me toward legal cases or data sources, others read portions of the book, and others engaged with me about critical ideas in it. Thank you to Shakti Belway, F. Chris Curran, Barry Feld, Ben Fisher, Shannon Griffin, Paul Hirschfield, Simone Ispa-Landa, Kayla Jenkins, Matt Kautz, Anthony Peguero, Ranita Ray, Deuel Ross, Russell Skiba, Anuja Thatte, and Kathryn Wiley. The reviewers who helped me work with the first draft of this book—Amy Best, Matt Cregor, Anne Gregory, Ed Morris, and Geoff Ward—were absolutely tremendous, offering thorough and honest feedback that helped me strengthen the work. I also appreciate the responses to and comments on my initial presentations of the ideas I write here at the Improving Data for School Discipline Research Conference, the Rutgers Sociology Department, the Delaware Leadership Institute, and the UD Osher Lifelong Learning Institute.

It is much easier to engage in a multiyear project with institutional support, and my colleagues in my department at the University of Delaware have always made me feel like I am on the right track. I thank them all and particularly Joel Best, Sal D'Antonio, Mieke Eeckhaut, Aaron Fichtelberg, Ben Fleury-Steiner, Felicia Henry, Jim Highberger, Cresean Hughes, Yasser Payne, and Eric Rise, with whom I discussed various parts of this book in one way or another.

Ilene Kalish at NYU Press is more of a collaborator than an editor. As always, she was instrumental in shaping and fine-tuning this book, resulting in a book that is clearer and more compelling than it otherwise would be. I am happy to work with her on this project and hope to continue the collaboration. I am also grateful for all of the help from

Priyanka Ray, Alexia Traganas, Andrew Katz, and others at NYU Press whose efforts have improved this work.

Finally, I want to thank my family. My wife, Elena, does so many things to help me that I'd be a fool to try to list them here, though I want to highlight her patience in allowing me to think out loud (OK, yell and curse, often), particularly while sharing an office post-COVID, and in giving me the space to talk endlessly about the injustices of school punishment. I know I can be a bore—thank you for looking the other way so often. My kids, Sarah and Alexis, are central to everything I do—not just how I spend my time but in shaping my appreciation of how important it is that children are supported and treated fairly. There's nothing like parenthood to highlight your inadequacies as a human being; my journey with them leads me to be thankful for all that we have (despite my flaws) and angry that other children and families aren't able to share the good fortune. My father, Herb, has always been a model of how to approach life and work with a sense of integrity, honesty, and compassion. My mother-in-law, Mary, passed away as I was finishing this book (in December 2023). I don't think there was anyone more eager to talk with me about what I was studying; I appreciate those conversations now, with such fond memories. Lastly, I want to thank my mother, Leona, in whose memory this book is dedicated. She was a unique soul who saw the world just a bit different than anyone else and who taught me to ask questions (I hope the right ones) and listen carefully to the answers. Oh yeah, and my brother—he's cool, too.

Thank you all.

Methods and Detailed Quantitative Results

Archival Sources and Process

Chapters 3 through 6 are based on case studies of desegregation in New Castle County, Delaware, and Boston, Massachusetts. I relied on a variety of sources of information about each of these sites.

New Castle County, Delaware

In April 2021, I made multiple visits to the Delaware State Archives in Dover, Delaware. To prepare for these visits, I used the archive's online search engine to find any collections that referred to school discipline, suspension, or school segregation/desegregation. This led me to several boxes of files in the State Reports Collection, the Governors Papers Database, and Annual Reports for State Agencies. I also searched through several sets of records for the state Department of Education held at the State Archives, including general records, records for the Christina School District, records of State Board of Education meeting minutes, Delaware State Parent Advisory Council files, and the department's general administrative records.

The University of Delaware holds two special collections in its library that were very helpful as well: the Desegregation of Delaware Collection and the papers of Littleton Mitchell. I spent time in the special collections of the University of Delaware Library in August and September 2021 accessing these records. There I found detailed records of the state's experience with desegregation, including details on the court case that resulted in desegregation, *Evans v. Buchanan*; reports on communication between the state and public groups about desegregation; news reports of desegregation; external studies of the desegregation process; and sources on other areas' experiences with desegregation.

I then reached out to several individuals who had been involved in Delaware's desegregation efforts in the 1970s and met with them via videoconference (Zoom) to discuss their experiences and perceptions of that time. These discussions helped to flesh out my understanding of that era and explain much of what I gleaned from the archived records. I am very thankful to Bebe Coker, Gloria Grantham, Jeffrey Raffel, and Jea Street for sharing their memories and insights with me. Before quoting each of them, I contacted them to confirm that the statements I had recorded accurately reflect what they intended to say and made revisions where they requested.

Finally, I also reviewed all news articles from the *News Journal* on school suspensions. Using the newspapers.com database, I searched for articles published 1940–1985. My search terms included "school suspension" or "suspended from school."

Boston, Massachusetts

To learn about Boston's experience with desegregation, I first visited the Boston City Archives in March 2022. There I searched through boxes of records for the city's Department of Implementation, Department of Statistics, and Citywide Parents Council. I also found records on Boston's desegregation court case, *Morgan et al. v. Hennigan et al.* (later renamed *Morgan v. Kerrigan*), as well as Mayor Kevin White's files and files for the School Committee secretary.

I found a trove of helpful records at the University of Massachusetts Boston in its library's special collections. UMass Boston holds the archives of the Massachusetts Advocacy Center, as well as a detailed set of records (eighty boxes) on the *Morgan v. Hennigan* case and the personal records of Judge Garrity, who presided over the case.

Two online university library collections were helpful as well. Northeastern University's library has a digital collection, "The Boston Public Schools Desegregation Collection."[1] Here I was able to find multiple reports and studies about desegregation in Boston. The second was the series of audio files available online through the University of Massachusetts Amherst Libraries' special collections. I discuss these files in chapter 6; they consist of interviews performed by D. Monty Neill in 1986 with civic leaders who were active at that time in the continuing effort to advocate for students of color in Boston public schools.[2]

As in Delaware, I was very fortunate to be able to speak to several individuals who were active participants in Boston's experience with desegregation. Thomas Mela, the former senior director of the Massachusetts Advocates for Children, and Liza Hirsch, who was the Massachusetts Advocates for Children's senior attorney, were my first point of contact in Boston, in June 2021. They helped advise me in my search for information, and Mela connected me to several individuals who helped supplement the information I learned from the archives I had studied. I spoke, again via videoconference (Zoom), with Barbara Fields, Albert Holland, Jay Blitzman, and Paul Weckstein, each of whom was wonderfully helpful. Here, as well, I contacted each individual whom I quote in the preceding chapters and revised the statements that I quoted per their request.

Finally, I also reviewed all news articles from the *Boston Globe* on school suspensions. Using the newspapers.com database, I searched for articles published 1940–1985. My search terms included "school suspension" or "suspended from school."

Chapter 2 Quantitative Analyses

In chapter 2, Felicia Henry and I describe the results of statistical analyses that show the link between resistance to desegregation and contemporary school punishment. Here I provide additional detail on the data we used, our analyses, and the results we obtained. A prior version of these analyses, in which we used older data on student suspensions but otherwise mirrored the analyses in chapter 2, appeared in the *Journal of Research in Crime and Delinquency*.[3] Much of the following discussion of data and methods can be found there, as well as additional details.

Data Sources

Our analyses in chapter 2 rely on data from three sources. Data on public schools and school districts come from the federal Department of Education's Office of Civil Rights (OCR) 2017–2018 Data Collection. The OCR data include information on enrollments, expenditures, punishments assigned (suspensions, days missed due to suspensions), and student misbehavior. We supplement these data with data from the US Census on the racial/ethnic composition of communities represented by these school districts; these data are available from the National Center for Education Statistics in files that allow them to be linked to school districts.

Our measure of historical resistance to school desegregation over time comes from the American Communities Project at Brown University. The project assembled an amazing data set on desegregation court cases and HEW (the federal department formerly known as Health, Education, and Welfare) actions over a fifty-year span. It includes a list of 3,340 cases from 1952 to 2002, linked to school districts.[4] The data set includes all cases and HEW actions specifically related to school desegregation that the American Communities Project researchers were able to locate, at all court levels.[5]

Together, these data allow us to consider how resistance to desegregation over time relates to school-level rates of suspension, including both the risk of suspension among students and days of school missed by students due to school punishment, while controlling for several school-level and school-district-level characteristics. Our combined data set includes information on the universe of public schools that report (as required by law) their 2017–2018 data to the OCR, some of which were involved with desegregation court cases or HEW Actions. Our final sample includes 95,260 schools, clustered within 16,831 school districts. All states plus Washington, DC, are included.

Variables

The OCR provides data on punishments separately by student race/ethnicity. We use these data, and the OCR data on school enrollments by race/ethnicity, to calculate the percentage of Black students and of white students suspended in each school and the days of school missed by Black and by white students due to suspension, per one hundred students in the school population. Because each of these outcomes is positively skewed, we use the natural log of each punishment rate in our regression models.[6] Table A.1 shows summary statistics of all variables we use in the following analyses.

Our primary independent variable is the measure of court cases or HEW actions (hereafter, desegregation court cases). The data on desegregation court cases include information on up to nine desegregation cases per school district. We collapsed these data into a district-level variable that indicates the number of desegregation court cases in which each school district was involved. About two-thirds (67.8 percent) of districts had no cases, and 16.0 percent were involved in one case. Because of the rarity of districts having many cases, we recoded this variable into an ordinal scale (no cases, one case, two or more cases). This recoded variable counts only cases that were successful, which we define as not dismissed within five years of initiation. In one set of models, instead of the number of court cases, we instead consider the timing of court cases (or of the first court case, if there are more than one). For these analyses, we group cases into the following year ranges: 1950s, 1960–1964, 1965–1969, 1970–1974, 1975–1979, and 1980s and 1990s.

Table A.2 offers some context for understanding what school districts were involved in court cases. It shows contemporary (2017–2018) school racial/ethnic compositions—the mean percentages of schools' student

TABLE A.1. Description of Sample and Summary Statistics

	%	Mean	Std. dev.
No. of court cases			
None	67.81		
One	15.97		
Two or more	16.22		
First desegregation case (among n = 27,478 with 1+ cases)			
1950s	7.36		
1960–1964	13.52		
1965–1969	22.18		
1970–1974	31.67		
1975–1979	17.18		
1980s and 1990s	8.09		
% suspended: overall (ln)		1.22	1.01
% suspended: Black students (ln)		1.29	1.37
% suspended: white students (ln)		1.03	1.00
Days missed: overall (ln)		1.95	1.54
Days missed: Black students (ln)		1.90	1.99
Days missed: white students (ln)		1.63	1.53
School-level variables			
Enrollment (ln)		5.89	1.05
Proportion white students		0.52	0.33
Expenditures (ln)		8.66	1.07
Violence (ln)		1.23	1.48
Support staff (ln)		0.32	0.32
Preschool	31.84		
Second grade	54.25		
Eighth grade	30.79		
Eleventh grade	25.24		
Special education school	2.28		
Charter school	6.86		
Magnet school	4.32		

	%	Mean	Std. dev.
District-level variables			
% Hispanic residents		15.80	19.98
D dissimilarity index		0.31	0.29
Region			
Northeast	15.87		
Midwest	26.02		
West	23.40		
South	34.71		

TABLE A.2. Average Racial Composition of Schools by Number of Court Cases

No. of court cases	% Black students	% Hispanic students	% white students
None	8.54	22.08	58.98
One	22.85	22.75	45.50
Two or more	34.95	28.85	28.06

bodies that are Black, Hispanic, or white—for schools in districts that had zero, one, or two or more court cases. It shows that court cases were more common in districts whose schools educate larger percentages of students of color, and particularly Black students, today. On average, schools in districts with no court cases have student bodies that are 8.5 percent Black, 22.1 percent Hispanic, and 59.0 percent white; but schools in districts with two or more court cases have, on average, student bodies that are 35.0 percent Black, 28.9 percent Hispanic, and 28.1 percent white.

Most of our other independent variables (i.e., control variables) come from the OCR database. To control for the type of school and age ranges served, we include variables indicating whether or not the school is a charter school, a magnet school, or a school specializing in special education. We also include variables indicating whether the school serves preschoolers, second graders, eighth graders, and eleventh graders; because some schools have a wide span of grades, these variables are not mutually exclusive. To control for the size of a school, we include the natural log of each school's enrollment. Because schools with better funding and more supports may have more opportunity to avoid exclusionary punishments by providing inclusive, restorative responses, we include measures of each. Our measure of funding is the natural log of expenditures per student (dollars spent divided by 2017–2018 total enrollment), and our measure of supports is calculated as the natural log of the number of support staff (including counselors, psychologists, and social workers) per one hundred students enrolled. We control for the natural log of the number of students (per one hundred enrolled) who are retained (i.e., not promoted to the next grade) that year, in order to control for any potential confounding effect of students' academic success and failure. We include the proportion of each school's enrollment that is white students.[7] Finally, in order to consider how resistance to desegregation relates to school punishments above and beyond actual student misbehavior, we control for the natural log of the number of violent crimes reported for each school in 2017–2018. The list of violent crimes that schools report include rape, sexual assault, robbery with a weapon/without a weapon/with an explosive device, attack with a weapon/without a weapon/with an explosive device, threats with a weapon/without a weapon/with an explosive device, and possession of a weapon.

We also control for two school-district-level variables. One, a D index of dissimilarity, measures intradistrict segregation of Black and white students, based on enrollment data in the OCR data.[8] Our second district-level variable is the percentage of the residents within the district catchment area who are identified by the US Census as Hispanic in 2016.[9] Finally, to control for regional variation in punishment norms, we created a variable to represent region of the US. We used US Census categories of Northeast, South, Midwest, and West.[10]

Analyses

Preliminary work with our data showed some problematic (outlier) values that needed to be cleaned. These include values over 100 percent of the student body, or of Black students, suspended; we presume that these values are due to inputting or reporting errors but cannot verify if this is correct. For both variables, these excessive values showed two clusters: some were slightly over 100 percent, while others were far greater than 100 percent (sometimes over 1,000 percent). We recoded those within a standard deviation over 100 percent to equal 100 percent and removed higher values as missing. A small number of schools reported very high numbers of support staff (over one hundred staff per school); we removed these values as missing as well. Three schools each reported over one thousand cases of threat with a weapon; we removed these outliers as missing. Finally, several schools reported implausible expenditures per student; we capped this value at $250,000 per student and removed the remaining values as missing.

Because we analyze outcomes among schools nested within school districts, we use multilevel models. More specifically, we run a series of random-intercept models using the "mixed" regression command in Stata, with school district as our clustering variable. We regress punishment rates on the number of desegregation court cases and other school-level and district-level variables, while including fixed effects of region of the US.[11] For models predicting racial-group-specific outcomes (such as percentage of Black or of white students suspended), we exclude schools that report no students of that racial group attending their school. Because some schools are excluded in this way, there is some variation in the numbers of cases included in each analysis. Diagnostic tests revealed that between- and within-group effects of most of our school-level (level 1) variables significantly differ. We accommodate this by including the group mean of each level 1 variable (for between-group effect estimates) as well as the group mean-centered version of each level 1 variable (for within-group effect estimates) in all models.

Our analyses thus consider how historical battles over desegregation relate to contemporary school punishments across the US. We understand desegregation court cases and HEW actions to be important indicators of resistance to desegregation: they mark sites chosen by HEW and other civil rights advocates as battlegrounds where the fight over school desegregation needed to be taken to court.

Results

In chapter 2, we show the predicted rates of suspension and days missed due to suspension for Black students and, as a comparison, for white students. To calculate these predictions, we use the Stata "predict" command following our multivariate analyses. Here we provide the full regression model results on which these predictions are based. Table A.3 shows the regression of Black suspension rates and days missed due to suspension by Black students in 2017–2018 on our independent variables. Table A.4 is similar, but instead of using an overall variable for number of desegregation court cases, it uses a series of variables for the timing of court cases. Finally, table A.5 shows our regression of suspension rate and rate of days missed due to suspension for white students in 2017–2018.

Older OCR Data

After discussing our analyses of the relationship between desegregation court cases and contemporary suspensions in chapter 2, we then turn to a descriptive analysis of suspension rates over time. This analysis, shown in figure 2.6, is based on assembling older data on suspension rates from the OCR. These older OCR data are no longer available on the OCR website, but they are archived at the National Archives (#1436514).

TABLE A.3. Mixed-Effects Regression of Punishment for Black Students on Number of Court Cases, School-Level Variables, and District-Level Variables

	% Black students suspended	Days missed per 100 Black students
Number of desegregation cases	0.152***	0.215***
District-level variables		
% Hispanic residents	−0.017***	−0.025***
D dissimilarity index	−0.227***	−0.344***
School-level variables: between effects		
Enrollment (ln)	0.296***	0.448***
Proportion white students	−1.592***	−2.351***
Expenditures (ln)	−0.021*	−0.021
Violence (ln)	0.178***	0.279***
Support staff (ln)	0.191***	0.305***
Preschool	−0.096**	−0.149**
Second grade	−0.126**	−0.211**
Eighth grade	−0.051	−0.090
Eleventh grade	0.0934*	0.182**
Retentions (ln)	0.276***	0.422***
Special education school	0.085	0.023
Charter school	0.469***	0.552**
Magnet school	−0.046	−0.043
School-level variables: within effects		
Enrollment (ln)	0.201***	0.311***
Proportion white students	−1.120***	−1.629***
Expenditures (ln)	0.055***	0.074***
Violence (ln)	0.270***	0.407***
Support staff (ln)	0.421***	0.653***
Preschool	−0.105***	−0.137***
Second grade	−0.418***	−0.658***
Eighth grade	0.245***	0.362***
Eleventh grade	0.096***	0.227***
Retentions (ln)	0.083***	0.148***
Special education school	−0.157***	−0.333***
Charter school	−0.059*	−0.111**
Magnet school	−0.155***	−0.187***
Region (contrast: Northeast)		
Midwest	0.104***	0.128***
West	−0.173***	−0.263***
South	0.056*	0.080*
N	75225	75410

* p < .05; ** p < .01; *** p < .001

TABLE A.4. Mixed-Effects Regression of Punishment for Black Students on Timing of First Court Case, School-Level Variables, and District-Level Variables

	% Black students suspended	Days missed per 100 Black students
First desegregation case (contrast: no cases)		
1950s	0.276**	0.437***
1960–1964	0.218***	0.192*
1965–1969	0.318***	0.450***
1970–1974	0.245***	0.419***
1975–1979	0.300***	0.462***
1980s and 1990s	−0.044	−0.043
District-level variables		
% Hispanic residents	−0.017***	−0.025***
D dissimilarity index	−0.223***	−0.337***
School-level variables: between effects		
Enrollment (ln)	0.300***	0.454***
Proportion white students	−1.558***	−2.299***
Expenditures (ln)	−0.021*	−0.020
Violence (ln)	0.176***	0.275***
Support staff (ln)	0.181***	0.287***
Preschool	−0.103**	−0.159**
Second grade	−0.124**	−0.213**
Eighth grade	−0.044	−0.075
Eleventh grade	0.098*	0.192**
Retentions (ln)	0.276***	0.420***
Special education school	0.070	−0.002
Charter school	0.443***	0.508**
Magnet school	−0.054	−0.065
School-level variables: within effects		
Enrollment (ln)	0.201***	0.310***
Proportion white students	−1.120***	−1.629***
Expenditures (ln)	0.055***	0.073***
Violence (ln)	0.270***	0.407***
Support staff (ln)	0.421***	0.652***
Preschool	−0.104***	−0.136***
Second grade	−0.419***	−0.659***

	% Black students suspended	Days missed per 100 Black students
Eighth grade	0.245***	0.362***
Eleventh grade	0.096***	0.227***
Retentions (ln)	0.083***	0.147***
Special education school	−0.156***	−0.333***
Charter school	−0.059*	−0.111**
Magnet school	−0.155***	−0.188***
Region (contrast: Northeast)		
Midwest	0.110***	0.132***
West	−0.167***	−0.253***
South	0.051	0.075
N	75225	75410

* p < .05; ** p < .01; *** p < .001

TABLE A.5. Mixed-Effects Regression of Punishment for White Students on Number of Court Cases, School-Level Variables, and District-Level Variables

	% white students suspended	Days missed per 100 white students
Number desegregation cases	0.063***	0.066***
District-level variables		
% Hispanic residents	−0.005***	−0.008***
D dissimilarity index	−0.026	−0.058
School-level variables: between effects		
Enrollment (ln)	0.110***	0.241***
Proportion white students	−0.064*	0.112*
Expenditures (ln)	−0.011	−0.016
Violence (ln)	0.175***	0.295***
Support staff (ln)	0.075**	0.074
Preschool	−0.036	−0.072*
Second grade	−0.303***	−0.522***
Eighth grade	0.151***	0.236***
Eleventh grade	0.265***	0.417***
Retentions (ln)	0.278***	0.463***
Special education school	−0.073	−0.163

(*continued*)

TABLE A.5. (*cont.*)

	% white students suspended	Days missed per 100 white students
Charter school	0.060	0.012
Magnet school	−0.137	−0.226*
School-level variables: within effects		
Enrollment (ln)	0.045***	0.144***
Proportion white students	−0.698***	−0.769***
Expenditures (ln)	0.068***	0.098***
Violence (ln)	0.210***	0.328***
Support staff (ln)	0.307***	0.479***
Preschool	−0.102***	−0.144***
Second grade	−0.314***	−0.553***
Eighth grade	0.261***	0.410***
Eleventh grade	0.162***	0.343***
Retentions (ln)	0.057***	0.087***
Special education school	−0.130***	−0.303***
Charter school	−0.154***	−0.242***
Magnet school	−0.145***	−0.196***
Region (contrast: Northeast)		
Midwest	0.108***	0.127***
West	0.188***	0.234***
South	0.088***	0.083**
N	83365	83469

* p < .05; ** p < .01; *** p < .001

NOTES

INTRODUCTION

1 I repeat the incident as close as I recall, though I have filled in details that extend the narrative (in a way that is consistent with my understanding of the story) and assigned pseudonyms.

2 Throughout this book, I follow recent convention by capitalizing "Black" but not "white." Organizations such as the Associated Press follow this convention because white people have less shared history and culture and do not have a shared experience of discrimination due to skin color. See David Bauder (2020) "AP Says It Will Capitalize Black but Not White." AP, July 20, 2020, https://apnews.com.

3 Charles Bell (2021) *Suspended: Punishment, Violence, and the Failure of School Safety*. Baltimore: Johns Hopkins University Press; Matthew Kautz (2023) "From Segregation to Suspension: The Solidification of the Contemporary School-Prison Nexus in Boston, 1963–1985." *Journal of Urban History* 49(5): 1049–1070, https://doi.org/10.1177/00961442221142059.

4 Thank you to R. Bradley Snyder for summarizing the problem in this helpful way (during personal correspondence in 2023).

5 Data available at Civil Rights Data Collection, Office for Civil Rights (n.d.) "2017–18 State and National Tables." https://ocrdata.ed.gov (accessed 9/18/2021).

6 Wade C. Jacobsen, Garret T. Payce, and Nayan G. Ramirez (2019) "Punishment and Inequality at an Early Age: Exclusionary Discipline in Elementary School." *Social Forces* 97(3): 973–998.

7 Kristen Harper, Renee Ryberg, and Deborah Temkin (2018) "Schools Report Fewer Out-of-School Suspensions, but Gaps by Race and Disability Persist." *Child Trends*, December 17, 2018, www.childtrends.org; Mark R. Warren (2022) *Willful Defiance: The Movement to Dismantle the School-to-Prison Pipeline*. New York: Oxford University Press.

8 Sheryl A. Hemphill, Aneta Kotevski, Todd I. Herrenkohl, Rachel Smith, John W. Toumbourou, and Richard F. Catalano (2013) "Predictors of Teen Non-violent Antisocial Behaviour." *Australian Journal of Psychology* 65: 236–249, https://doi.org/10.1111/ajpy.12026; Jacobsen et al. (2019); Stephanie A. Wiley, Lee Ann Slocum, Jennifer O'Neill, and Finn-Age Esbensen (2020) "Beyond the Breakfast Club: Variability in the Effects of Suspensions by School Context." *Youth & Society* 52(7): 1259–1284.

9 Greg Chen (2008) "Communities, Students, Schools, and School Crime: A Confirmatory Study of Crime in U.S. High Schools." *Urban Education* 43(3): 301–318, https://doi.org/10.1177/0042085907311791; see C. Bell (2021).

10 See Damien M. Sojoyner (2016) *First Strike: Educational Enclosures in Black Los Angeles*. Minneapolis: University of Minnesota Press.

11 Anthony A. Peguero, Zahra Shekarkhar, Ann Marie Popp, and Dixie J. Koo (2015) "Punishing the Children of Immigrants: Race, Ethnicity, Generational Status, Student Misbehavior and School Discipline." *Journal of Immigrant & Refugee Studies* 13: 200–220. E.g., John M. Wallace Jr., Sara Goodkind, Cynthia M. Wallace, and Jerald G. Bachman (2008) "Racial, Ethnic, and Gender Differences in School Discipline among U.S. High School Students: 1991–2005." *Negro Educational Review* 59: 47–62.

12 Hilary Burdge, Zami T. Hyemingway, and Adela C. Licona (2014) *Gender Nonconforming Youth: Discipline Disparities, School Push-Out, and the School-to-Prison Pipeline*. San Francisco: Gay-Straight Alliance Network, and Tucson: Crossroads Collaborative at the University of Arizona; Daniel J. Losen and Jonathan Gillespie (2012) *Opportunities Suspended: The Disparate Impact of Disciplinary Exclusion from School*. Los Angeles: Civil Rights Project at UCLA; Hanno Petras, Katherine E. Masyn, Jacquelyn A. Buckley, Nicholas S. Ialongo, and Sheppard Kellam (2011) "Who Is Most at Risk for School Removal? A Multilevel Discrete-Time Survival Analysis of Individual- and Context-Level Influences." *Journal of Educational Psychology* 103(1): 223–237.

13 Kimberlé Williams Crenshaw, Pricilla Ocen, and Jyoti Nanda (2015) *Black Girls Matter: Pushed Out, Overpoliced and Underprotected*. New York: African American Policy Forum; Monique W. Morris (2016) *Pushout: The Criminalization of Black Girls in Schools*. New York: New Press.

14 Jacobsen et al. (2019); Michael Rocque (2010) "Office Discipline and Student Behavior: Does Race Matter?" *American Journal of Education* 116: 557–581; Michael Rocque and Raymond Paternoster (2011) "Understanding the Antecedents of the 'School-to-Jail' Link: The Relationship between Race and School Discipline." *Journal of Criminal Law & Criminology* 101: 633–666; Russell J. Skiba, Choong-Geun Chung, Megan Trachok, Timberly L. Baker, Adam Sheya, and Robin L. Hughes (2014) "Parsing Disciplinary Disproportionality: Contributions of Infraction, Student and School Characteristics to Out-of-School Suspension and Expulsion." *American Educational Research Journal* 51: 640–670.

15 John Paul Wright, Mark Alden Morgan, Michelle A. Coyne, Kevin M. Beaver, and J. C. Barnes (2014) "Prior Problem Behavior Accounts for the Racial Gap in School Suspensions." *Journal of Criminal Justice* 42: 257–266.

16 US Federal Commission on School Safety (2018) *Final Report of the Federal Commission on School Safety*. Washington, DC: US Department of Education.

17 Francis L. Huang (2020) "Prior Problem Behaviors Do Not Account for the Racial Suspension Gap." *Educational Researcher* 49(7): 493–502.

18 Aaron Kupchik (2016) *The Real School Safety Problem: The Long-Term Consequences of Harsh School Punishment*. Oakland: University of California Press.

19 Brea L. Perry and Edward W. Morris (2014) "Suspending Progress: Collateral Consequences of Exclusionary Punishment in Public Schools." *American*

Sociological Review 79: 1067–1087; Francis A. Pearman II, F. Chris Curran, Benjamin Fisher, and Joseph Gardella (2019) "Are Achievement Gaps Related to Discipline Gaps? Evidence from National Data." *AERA Open* 5: 1–18; Kupchik (2016); Thomas J. Mowen, John J. Brent, and John H. Boman IV (2020) "The Effect of School Discipline on Offending across Time." *Justice Quarterly* 37: 739–760; Wiley et al. (2020).

20 Allison A. Payne and Kelly Welch (2015) "Restorative Justice in Schools: The Influence of Race on Restorative Discipline." *Youth & Society* 47: 539–564; David M. Ramey (2015) "The Social Structure of Criminalized and Medicalized School Discipline." *Sociology of Education* 88: 181–201; Kelly Welch and Allison A. Payne (2010) "Racial Threat and Punitive School Discipline." *Social Problems* 57: 25–48.

21 Jason A. Okonofua and Jennifer L. Eberhardt (2015) "Two Strikes: Race and the Disciplining of Young Students." *Psychological Science* 26: 617–624.

22 Hubert M. Blalock Jr. (1967) *Towards a Theory of Minority Group Relations*. New York: Capricorn Books.

23 Payne and Welch (2015); Welch and Payne (2010); Kelly Welch and Allison Ann Payne (2012) "Exclusionary School Punishment: The Effect of Racial Threat on Expulsion and Suspension." *Youth Violence and Juvenile Justice* 10: 155–171.

24 Katherine Irwin, Kay S. Varela, and Anthony Peguero (2022) "Punishment and Racial Segregation of Schools: Against Racial Threat and toward a Racial Control Perspective." *Critical Criminology* 30: 1075–1090.

25 Jonathan Simon (2007) *Governing through Crime: How the War on Crime Transformed American Democracy and Created a Culture of Fear*. New York: Oxford University Press.

26 Aaron Kupchik (2010) *Homeroom Security: School Discipline in an Age of Fear*. New York: NYU Press.

27 See David Garland (2001) *The Culture of Control: Crime and Social Order in Contemporary Society*. Chicago: University of Chicago Press; Philip Goodman, Joshua Page, and Michelle Phelps (2017) *Breaking the Pendulum: The Long Struggle over Criminal Justice*. New York: Oxford University Press; Marie Gottschalk (2015) *Caught: The Prison State and the Lockdown of American Politics*. Princeton, NJ: Princeton University Press; Heather Schoenfeld (2018) *Building the Prison State: Race and the Politics of Mass Incarceration*. Chicago: University of Chicago Press.

28 See also Michael Rocque and Quincy Snellings (2018) "The New Disciplinology: Research, Theory, and Remaining Puzzles on the School-to-Prison Pipeline." *Journal of Criminal Justice* 59: 3–11.

29 Freeden Blume Oeur (2018) *Black Boys Apart: Racial Uplift and Respectability in All-Male Public Schools*. Minneapolis: University of Minnesota Press.

30 Paul Hirschfield is particularly persuasive on this point; Paul Hirschfield (2008) "Preparing for Prison? The Criminalization of School Discipline in the USA." *Theoretical Criminology* 12: 79–101; see also Aaron Kupchik and Torin Monahan

(2006) "The New American School: Preparation for Post-Industrial Discipline." *British Journal of Sociology of Education* 27: 617–631.

31 Kupchik (2016).

32 Campbell F. Scribner and Bryan R. Warnick (2021) *Spare the Rod: Punishment and the Moral Community of Schools.* Chicago: University of Chicago Press. Rather than using Scribner and Warnick's distinction, I refer to exclusionary punishments like suspension as punishment, not discipline. I do so to distinguish between these school actions, which attempt to punish (often without any reformative or rehabilitative effort) from a version of "discipline" discussed by Foucault that teaches subjects self-discipline. See Michel Foucault (trans. Alan Sheridan) (1977) *Discipline and Punish: The Birth of the Prison.* New York: Vintage Books.

33 See also Judith Kafka (2011) *The History of "Zero Tolerance" in American Public Schooling.* New York: Palgrave Macmillan.

34 Russell J. Skiba, Edward Fergus, and Anne Gregory (2022) "The New Jim Crow in School: Exclusionary Discipline and Structural Racism." In Edward J. Sabornie and Dorothy L. Espelage (eds.) *Handbook of Classroom Management (3rd ed.).* New York: Routledge, 213.

35 Eduardo Bonilla-Silva (1997) "Rethinking Racism: Towards a Structural Interpretation." *American Sociological Review* 62(3): 465–480; Eduardo Bonilla-Silva (2015) "More than Prejudice: Restatement, Reflections, and New Directions in Critical Race Theory." *Sociology of Race and Ethnicity* 1(1): 73–87; Eduardo Bonilla-Silva (2017) *Racism without Racists: Color-Blind Racism and the Persistence of Racial Inequality in America (5th ed.).* Lanham, MD: Rowman and Littlefield. See also Joe R. Feagin (2010) *Racist America: Roots, Current Realities, and Future Reparation.* New York: Routledge; Michael Omi and Howard Winant (2014) *Racial Formation in the United States (3rd ed.)* New York: Routledge.

36 Lauren Camera (2021) "What Is Critical Race Theory and Why Are People So Upset about It?" *US News and World Report,* June 1, 2021, www.usnews.com.

37 Richard Delgado and Jean Stefancic (2013) *Critical Race Theory: The Cutting Edge (3rd ed.)* Philadelphia: Temple University Press; Derrick A. Bell Jr. (1976) "Serving Two Masters: Integration Ideals and Client Interests in School Desegregation Litigation." *Yale Law Journal* 85: 470–516; Derrick Bell (1992) *Faces at the Bottom of the Well: The Permanence of Racism.* New York: Basic Books.

38 E.g., Amanda E. Lewis and John B. Diamond (2015) *Despite the Best Intentions: How Racial Inequality Thrives in Good Schools.* New York: Oxford University Press.

39 Robert Starobin (1974) *Blacks in Bondage: Letters of American Slaves.* New York: Viewpoints.

40 Grey Gundaker (2007) "Hidden Education among African Americans during Slavery." *Teachers College Record* 109: 1591–1612.

41 W. E. B. DuBois (2007) *The Souls of Black Folk*. New York: Oxford University Press (originally published 1903); W. E. B. DuBois (1973) *The Philadelphia Negro*. Millwood, NY: Kraus-Thomson (originally published 1899). For an excellent discussion of how schools have historically been used to restrict Black cultural autonomy and maintain white power, see Sojoyner (2016).

42 Russell Skiba and Ashley White (2022) "Ever Since Little Rock: The History of Disciplinary Disparities in America's Schools." In Nicholas Gage, Luke J. Rapa, Denise K. Whitford, and Antonis Katsiyannis (eds.) *Disproportionality and Social Justice in Education*. Cham, Switzerland: Springer, 3–33.

43 Kenneth J. Meier, Joseph Stewart Jr., and Robert E. England (1989) *Race, Class, and Education: The Politics of Second-Generation Discrimination*. Madison: University of Wisconsin Press.

44 See Stephanie (2020) "Striking down 'Freedom of Choice' Plans for School Desegregation: Green v. New Kent County." *Education Updates*, National Archives, March 11, 2020, https://education.blogs.archives.gov.

45 Ansley T. Erickson (2016) *Making the Unequal Metropolis: School Desegregation and Its Limits*. Chicago: University of Chicago Press; Matthew F. Delmont (2016a) *Why Busing Failed: Race, Media, and the National Resistance to School Desegregation*. Oakland: University of California Press.

46 Gary Orfield and Erica Frankenberg, with Jongyeon Ee and John Kuscera (2014) *Brown at 60: Great Progress, a Long Retreat and an Uncertain Future*. Los Angeles: University of California Los Angeles Civil Rights Project.

47 Jonathan Kozol (2005) *The Shame of the Nation: The Restoration of Apartheid Schooling in America*. New York: Three Rivers Press; see also Erickson (2016).

48 E.g., Kozol (2005); Meier et al. (1989); Jeannie Oakes (2005) *Keeping Track: How Schools Structure Inequality (2nd ed.)*. New Haven, CT: Yale University Press.

49 Sarah D. Sparks (2020) "Hidden Segregation within Schools Is Tracked in New Study." *Education Week*, February 2020, www.edweek.org.

50 Throughout this book, I focus mainly on out-of-school suspensions. Not only are they the most common exclusionary punishment, but they best illustrate the problem of students being removed because they are seen as a nuisance or are unwanted. While in-school suspension is important as well, data on it often are less available, and its use varies considerably; in-school suspension can be used in an inclusive way, if it is used as brief "cooling off" periods in which students are actually educated, though prior research suggests that this is typically not the case (e.g., Kupchik [2010]). Expulsions, the other form of exclusionary punishment, are rare events, making them more difficult to study.

51 Stevenson said this during an October 2014 episode of *The Daily Show* with Jon Stewart. See Kay Campbell (2014) "'Slavery Didn't End; It Evolved,' Brian Stevenson of Equal Justice Initiative Tells 'Daily Show' Host Jon Stewart." *Al.com*, October 17, 2014, www.al.com.

52 Scribner and Warnick (2021).

53 See Barry C. Feld (2017) *The Evolution of the Juvenile Court: Race, Politics, and the Criminalizing of Juvenile Justice.* New York: NYU Press; Kafka (2011).

54 Simon (2007).

55 Kupchik (2010).

56 Irby J. Decoteau (2014) "Revealing Racial Purity Ideology: Fear of Black-White Intimacy as a Framework for Understanding School Discipline in Post-*Brown* Schools." *Educational Administration Quarterly* 50: 783–795.

57 Michelle Alexander (2010) *The New Jim Crow.* New York: New Press.

58 For an explicit discussion of how school punishment mirrors the process Alexander describes as "the New Jim Crow," see Warren (2022).

59 Bonilla-Silva (2015), 75.

60 Bonilla-Silva (2017); Feagin (2010); Omi and Winant (2014).

61 Victor Ray (2019) "A Theory of Racialized Organizations." *American Sociological Review* 84(1): 26–53, 34 (citations omitted).

62 Lewis and Diamond (2015).

63 Jessica L. Dunning-Lozano (2018) "School Discipline, Race, and the Discursive Construction of the 'Deficient' Student." *Sociological Spectrum* 38: 326–345, 328.

64 Indeed, some critical scholars go further to suggest that schools are founded on anti-Blackness. See Savannah Shange (2019) *Progressive Dystopia: Abolition, Antiblackness, and Schooling in San Francisco.* Durham, NC: Duke University Press; Sojoyner (2016).

65 Margaret K. Nelson (2010) *Parenting Out of Control: Anxious Parents in Uncertain Times.* New York: NYU Press.

66 Kupchik (2010).

67 Meier et al. (1989).

68 Meier et al. (1989), 30.

69 Meier et al. (1989), 56.

70 Alexander (2010), 254.

71 Ashley T. Rubin (2019) "Punishment's Legal Templates: A Theory of Formal Penal Change." *Law & Society Review* 53: 518–553.

72 John W. Meyer and Brian Rowan (1977) "Institutionalized Organizations: Formal Structure as Myth and Ceremony." *American Journal of Sociology* 83(1): 340–363; John W. Meyer (1977) "The Effects of Education as an Institution." *American Journal of Sociology* 83(1): 55–77; Richard Arum (2000) "Schools and Communities: Ecological and Institutional Dimensions." *Annual Revie of Sociology* 26: 395–418.

73 Meyer and Rowan (1977), 340–341.

74 Paul J. DiMaggio and Walter W. Powell (1983) "The Iron Cage Revisited: Institutional Isomorphism and Collective Rationality in Organizational Fields." *American Sociological Review* 48(2): 147–160.

75 Charles Tilly (1998) *Durable Inequality.* Berkeley: University of California Press.

76 Tilly (1998), 7–8.

77 Heather McGhee (2021) *The Sum of Us: What Racism Costs Everyone and How We Can Prosper Together*. New York: One World.

78 D. Bell (1976), 488; italics added.

79 Derrick A. Bell (1980) "*Brown v. Board of Education* and the Interest-Convergence Dilemma." *Harvard Law Review* 95: 518–533.

80 Khalil Gibran Muhammad (2011) *Condemnation of Blackness: Race, Crime, and the Making of Modern Urban America*. Cambridge, MA: Harvard University Press.

81 E.g., Georg Rusche and Otto Kirchheimer (2017) *Punishment and Social Structure*. New York: Routledge (originally published 1939); Dario Melossi and Massimo Pavarini (2018) *The Prison and the Factory: Origins of the Penitentiary System (40th anniversary ed.)*. London: Palgrave Macmillan; David Garland (1990) *Punishment and Modern Society: A Study in Social Theory*. Chicago: University of Chicago Press.

82 See Gottschalk (2015); Goodman et al. (2017); Schoenfeld (2018).

83 David Leeming (2015) *James Baldwin: A Biography*. New York: Simon and Schuster, 368.

84 See also McGhee (2021).

CHAPTER 1. "THEY JUST WANT THE BLACKS OUT OF SCHOOL"

1 To watch video of the encounter see theGrio (2013) "A Confrontation for Integration at the University of Alabama." YouTube, February 26, 2013, https://youtu.be/4WbLGlIzW88.

2 Warren Breed (1962) "Group Structure and Resistance to Desegregation in the Deep South." *Social Problems* 10: 84–94; Jeremy R. Porter, Frank M. Howell, and Lynn M. Hempel (2014) "Old Times Are Not Forgotten: The Institutionalization of Segregationist Academies in the American South." *Social Problems* 61: 576–601; Sojoyner (2016).

3 Muhammad (2011).

4 Brown v. Board of Education of Topeka, 347 U.S. 483, 495 (1954).

5 Brown v. Board of Education of Topeka, 349 U.S. 294 (1955).

6 See National Park Service (n.d.) "The Little Rock Nine." www.nps.gov (accessed January 31, 2022).

7 See Debra Michals (2015) "Ruby Bridges (1954–)." National Women's History Museum, www.womenshistory.org.

8 Christopher Bonastia (2012) *Southern Stalemate: Five Years without Public Education in Prince Edward County, Virginia*. Chicago: University of Chicago Press; Neil R. McMillen (1971) "Organized Resistance to School Desegregation in Tennessee." *Tennessee Historical Quarterly* 30: 315–328.

9 *Congressional Record*, 84th Cong., 2nd sess., Vol. 102, part 4, 4460 (March 12, 1956).

10 Bonastia (2012).

11 Bonastia (2012).

12 See Irwin et al. (2022).

13 E.g., Wright et al. (2014).

14 Kautz (2023).

15 Kenneth T. Andrews (2002) "Movement-Countermovement Dynamics and the Emergence of New Institutions: The Case of 'White Flight' Schools in Mississippi." *Social Forces* 80(3): 911–936.

16 Mark Golub (2013) "Remembering Massive Resistance to School Desegregation." *Law and History Review* 31: 491–530; Harrell R. Rodgers Jr. and Charles S. Bullock III (1972) "School Desegregation: A Policy Analysis." *Journal of Black Studies* 2: 409–437.

17 Leon Jones (1978) "School Desegregation in Retrospect and Prospect." *Journal of Negro Education* 47(1): 46–57.

18 US Commission on Civil Rights (1967) *Southern School Desegregation, 1966–67.* Washington, DC: US Government Printing Office. Cited in Jones (1978), 50.

19 Porter et al. (2014).

20 Erickson (2016).

21 Christopher Bonastia (2022) *The Battle Nearer to Home: The Persistence of School Segregation in New York City.* Stanford, CA: Stanford University Press.

22 Bonastia (2022).

23 Erickson (2016); see also Delmont (2016a).

24 To re-create this graph, I used the data in table 14 of Gary Orfield and Chungmei Lee (2007) *Historic Reversals, Accelerating Resegregation, and the Need for New Integration Strategies.* Los Angeles: UCLA Civil Rights Project, 33; and added my estimate of the 2010 data points based on figure 2 of Gary Orfield and Erica Frankenberg (2014) "Increasingly Segregated and Unequal Schools as Courts Reverse Policy." *Educational Administration Quarterly* 50(5): 718–734, 729.

25 Orfield and Frankenberg (2014); Orfield et al. (2014).

26 US Government Accountability Office (2022) *K–12 Education: Student Population Has Significantly Diversified, but Many Schools Remain Divided along Racial, Ethnic, and Economic Lines.* GAO-22-104737. Washington, DC: US GAO. Note that a "predominantly same-race/ethnicity" school is one in which 75 percent or more of the students are of a single race/ethnicity, and an "almost exclusive same-race/ethnicity" school is one in which 90 percent or more of the students are of a single race/ethnicity.

27 Rucker C. Johnson with Alexander Nazaryan (2019) *Children of the Dream: Why School Integration Works.* New York: Basic Books. See also Thurston Domina, Deven Carlson, James Carter III, Matthew Lenard, Andrew McEachin, and Rachel Perera (2021) "The Kids on the Bus: The Academic Consequences of Diversity-Driven School Reassignments." *Journal of Policy Analysis and Management* 40: 1197–1229.

28 Southern Regional Council and the Robert F. Kennedy Memorial (1973) *The Student Pushout: Victim of Continued Resistance to Desegregation*. Atlanta: Southern Regional Council, and Washington, DC: Robert F. Kennedy Memorial, v.

29 Southern Regional Council and the Robert F. Kennedy Memorial (1973), vii–viii.

30 Southern Regional Council and the Robert F. Kennedy Memorial (1973), 14.

31 Southern Regional Council and the Robert F. Kennedy Memorial (1973), 15.

32 Southern Regional Council and the Robert F. Kennedy Memorial (1973), 2.

33 Southern Regional Council and the Robert F. Kennedy Memorial (1973), 18; see also Susan C. Kaeser (1979) "Suspensions in School Discipline." *Education and Urban Society* 11: 465–484.

34 Ann A. Ferguson (2000) *Bad Boys: Public Schools and the Making of Black Masculinity*. Ann Arbor: University of Michigan Press; Simone Ispa-Landa (2013) "Gender, Race, and Justifications for Group Exclusion: Urban Black Students Bussed to Affluent Suburban Schools." *Sociology of Education* 86(3): 218–233; Edward W. Morris (2007) "'Ladies' or 'Loudies'? Perceptions and Experiences of Black Girls in Classrooms." *Youth & Society* 38: 490–515; Okonofua and Eberhardt (2015); Jayanti Owens (2022) "Double Jeopardy: Teacher Biases, Racialized Organizations, and the Production of Racial/Ethnic Disparities in School Discipline." *American Sociological Review* 87(6): 1007–1048.

35 Southern Regional Council and the Robert F. Kennedy Memorial (1973), 65.

36 Nancy L. Arnez (1978) "Implementation of Desegregation as a Discriminatory Process." *Journal of Negro Education* 47(1): 28–45, 34.

37 Arnez (1978), 35.

38 Arnez (1978), 34–35.

39 Clarence H. Thornton and William T. Trent (1988) "School Desegregation and Suspension in East Baton Rouge Parish: A Preliminary Report." *Journal of Negro Education* 57(4): 482–501.

40 See Nicolaus Mills (1975) "Public Schools and the New Segregation Struggle." *Equal Opportunity Review*, August 1975.

41 For an excellent review of research demonstrating the rise in suspensions and racial disparities in suspension after desegregation, see Skiba and White (2022).

42 Charles S. Bullock III and Joseph Stewart Jr. (1978) "Second-Generation Discrimination in American Schools." *Policy Studies Journal* 7 (Winter): 219–224; Kaeser (1979).

43 Hawkins et al. v. Coleman et al., 376 F. Supp. 1330 (N.D. Tex. 1974).

44 *Hawkins*, 376 F. Supp. at 1337.

45 *Hawkins*, 376 F. Supp. at 1333.

46 *Hawkins*, 376 F. Supp. at 1336.

47 Joe Larkin (1979) "School Desegregation and Student Suspension: A Look at One School System." *Education and Urban Society* 11(4): 485–495.

48 Children's Defense Fund (1975) *School Suspensions: Are They Helping Children?* Cambridge, MA: Children's Defense Fund, 12.

49 Children's Defense Fund (1975), 14.

50 National Public Radio (1974) "Options on Education, September 9, 1974." Transcript available through ERIC education database, #ED096373, 3.

51 National Public Radio (1974), 2.

52 Rocque and Paternoster (2011); Welch and Payne (2012).

53 Tamela NcNulty Eitle and David James Eitle (2004) "Inequality, Segregation, and the Overrepresentation of African Americans in School Suspensions." *Sociological Perspectives* 47(3): 269–287.

54 Kendralin J. Freeman and Christina R. Steidl (2016) "Distribution, Composition and Exclusion: How School Segregation Impacts Racist Disciplinary Patterns." *Race and Social Problems* 8: 171–185. In another study, however, these results are complicated, if not questioned. K. Jurée Capers finds that while school racial segregation on its own does not significantly predict disproportionate punishment, it does interact with teacher race to do so. See K. Jurée Capers (2019) "The Role of Desegregation and Teachers of Color in Discipline Disproportionality." *Urban Review* 51: 789–815.

55 To be clear, I do not mean to suggest that schools should seek greater levels of segregation in order to reduce punishment disparities, since replacing one harmful problem with another does not benefit students.

56 Lionel R. Olsen (1957) "Effective Discipline Practices of Secondary School Administrators." *American School Board Journal*, 134, as cited in Charles E. Harwood (1969) "Suspension: A Valid Disciplinary Tool?" *Clearing House* 44(1): 29–32.

57 Kristen L. Allman and John R. Slate (2011) "School Discipline in Public Education: A Brief Review of Current Practices." Connexions Project, module m38415, 2; Avarita L. Hanson (2005) "Have Zero Tolerance School Discipline Policies Turned into a Nightmare? The American Dream's Promise of Equal Educational Opportunity Grounded in *Brown v. Board of Education.*" *University of California Davis Journal of Juvenile Law & Policy* 9(2): 289–380; Kafka (2011).

58 Hanson (2005), 299.

59 Scribner and Warnick (2021).

60 A. Troy Adams (2000) "The Status of School Discipline and Violence." *Annals of the American Academy of Political and Social Science*, 567: 140–156, 144.

61 Elizabeth T. Gershoff and Sarah A. Font (2016) "Corporal Punishment in U.S. Public Schools: Prevalence, Disparities in Use, and Status in State and Federal Policy." *Social Policy Report* 30: 1–37.

62 Ted Glackman, Roy Martin, Irwin Hyman, Eileen McDowell, Valerie Berv, and Phil Spino (1978) "Corporal Punishment, School Suspension, and the Civil Rights of Students: An Analysis of Office for Civil Rights School Surveys." *Inequality in Education* 23: 61–65, 64.

63 Benjamin Spock (1946) *The Common Sense Book of Baby and Child Care*. New York: Duell, Sloan and Pearce.

64 See Feagin (2010); Ruth Thompson-Miller, Joe R. Feagin, and Leslie H. Picca (2015) *Jim Crow's Legacy: The Lasting Impact of Segregation*. Lanham, MD: Rowman and Littlefield.

65 See Aaron Kupchik (2014) "The School-to-Prison Pipeline: Rhetoric and Reality." In Franklin E. Zimring and David S. Tanenhaus (eds.) *Choosing the Future for American Juvenile Justice*. New York: NYU Press, 94–119; Erica R. Meiners, *Right to Be Hostile: Schools, Prisons, and the Making of Public Enemies*. New York: Routledge; Catherine Y. Kim, Daniel J. Losen, and Damon T. Hewitt (2010) *The School-to-Prison Pipeline: Structuring Legal Reform*. New York: NYU Press; Kupchik (2016); United States v. City of Meridian et al. (4:12 cv168-HTW-LRA), complaint filed October 24, 2012.

66 Megan Andrew and Mary Kate Blake (2023) "The Long Arm of Early Exclusionary School Discipline? A Multi-Model Analysis." *Youth & Society* 55(2): 238–258, https://doi.org/10.1177/0044118X211042643; Robert Balfanz, vaughan byrnes, and Joanna Fox (2014) "Sent Home and Put Off-Track: The Antecedents, Disproportionalities, and Consequences of Being Suspended in the Ninth Grade." *Journal of Applied Research on Children: Informing Policy for Children at Risk* 5(2): article 13.

67 Brianna L. Kennedy-Lewis and Amy S. Murphy (2016) "Listening to 'Frequent Flyers': What Persistently Disciplined Students Have to Say about Being Labeled as 'Bad.'" *Teachers College Record* 118: 1–40; Carla Shedd (2015) *Unequal City: Race, Schools, and Perceptions of Injustice*. New York: Russell Sage Foundation.

68 Paul Hemez, John J. Brent, and Thomas J. Mowen (2020) "Exploring the School-to-Prison Pipeline: How School Suspensions Influence Incarceration during Young Adulthood." *Youth Violence and Juvenile Justice* 18(3): 235–255; Joel Mittleman (2018) "A Downward Spiral? Childhood Suspension and the Path to Juvenile Arrest." *Sociology of Education* 91(3): 183–204; Thomas Mowen and John Brent (2016) "School Discipline as a Turning Point: The Cumulative Effect of Suspension on Arrest." *Journal of Research in Crime and Delinquency* 53(5): 628–653; Abigail Novak (2018) "The Association between Experiences of Exclusionary Discipline and Justice System Contact: A Systematic Review." *Aggression and Violent Behavior* 40: 73–82; Wiley et al. (2020).

69 Yolanda Anyon, Duan Zhang, and Cynthia Hazel (2016) "Race, Exclusionary Discipline, and Connectedness to Adults in Secondary Schools." *American Journal of Community Psychology* 57: 342–352; Mara Eyllon, Carmel Salhi, John L. Griffith, and Alisa K. Lincoln (2022) "Exclusionary School Discipline Policies and Mental Health in a National Sample of Adolescents without Histories of Suspension or Expulsion." *Youth & Society* 54(1): 84–103.

70 Perry and Morris (2014).

71 Aaron Kupchik, James Highberger, and George Bear (2022) "Identifying the Helpfulness of School Climate: Skipping School, Cheating on Tests, and Elements of School Climate." *Psychology in the Schools* 59(8): 1538–1555.

72 Kupchik (2016), chapter 4.

73 Aaron Kupchik and Thomas Catlaw (2015) "Discipline and Participation: The Long-Term Effects of Suspension and School Security on the Political and Civic Engagement of Youth." *Youth and Society* 47: 95–124; see also Sarah K. Bruch and Joe Soss (2018) "Schooling as a Formative Political Experience: Authority Relations and the Education of Citizens." *Perspectives on Politics* 16(1): 36–57.

74 Warren (2022), 238.

75 Feagin (2010).

76 See Annette Lareau (2011) *Unequal Childhoods: Class, Race and Family Life (2nd ed.).* Berkeley: University of California Press.

CHAPTER 2. THE LEGACY OF RACIAL INJUSTICE

1 Children's Defense Fund (1975), 2.

2 Hannah Carson Baggett and Carey E. Andrzejewski (2021) *The Grammar of School Discipline: Removal, Resistance, and Reform in Alabama Schools.* New York: Lexington Books, 71–72; I have paraphrased based on Baggett and Andrzejweski's description of the incident they observed.

3 EdBuild (2019) *Nonwhite School Districts Get $23 Billion Less than White Districts Despite Serving the Same Number of Students.* https://edbuild.org.

4 Christopher Ingraham (2021) "Homes in Poor Neighborhoods Are Taxed at Roughly Twice the Rate of Those in Rich Areas, Study Shows." *Washington Post,* March 12, 2021, www.washingtonpost.com.

5 See Neil Bhutta, Andrew C. Chang, Lisa J. Dettling, and Joanne W. Hsu, with assistance from Julia Hewitt (2020) "FEDS Notes: Disparities in Wealth by Race and Ethnicity in the 2019 Survey of Consumer Finances." Board of Governors of the Federal Reserve System, September 28, 2020, www.federalreserve.gov; Melvin L. Oliver and Thomas M. Shapiro (1995) *Black Wealth / White Wealth: A New Perspective on Racial Inequality.* New York: Routledge.

6 See Kozol (2005).

7 Geoff Ward, Nick Petersen, Aaron Kupchik, and James Pratt (2021) "Historic Lynching and Corporal Punishment in Contemporary Southern Schools." *Social Problems* 68: 41–62.

8 The D dissimilarity index measures the intradistrict segregation of Black and white students, based on enrollment data in the OCR data set. The D index is used in prior research to consider separation of students by race, e.g., John R. Logan, Wewei Zhang, and Deirdre Oakley (2017) "Court Orders, White Flight, and School District Segregation." *Social Forces* 95(3): 1049–1075. It ranges from 0 to 1 and indicates the proportion of students who would need to move

schools in order to achieve the level of balance between Black and white students that exists within the district.

9 Interestingly, we found that our D dissimilarity index was negative and statistically significant. This tells us that schools in districts with greater levels of intradistrict racial segregation suspend fewer Black students. We interpret this finding as consistent with prior work on contemporary segregation and school punishment, which finds that schools with more *integration* suspend fewer students. See Eitle and Eitle (2004). We list the full model results in the appendix.

10 Mark J. Chin (2024) "JUE Insights: Desegregated but Still Separated? The Impact of School Integration on Student Suspensions and Special Education Classification." *Journal of Urban Economics* 141: article 103389.

11 Chin (2024).

12 For a review, see Kupchik (2016).

13 Irwin et al. (2022), 1082.

14 E.g., Kupchik (2010); Simon (2007).

15 Simon (2007).

16 Kupchik (2010).

17 Skiba and White (2022).

18 Meyer and Rowan (1977).

19 DiMaggio and Powell (1983).

20 Tilly (1998).

CHAPTER 3. SEPARATE AND UNEQUAL

1 Quoted in Brett Gadsden (2013) *Between North and South: Delaware, Desegregation, and the Myth of American Sectionalism.* Philadelphia: University of Pennsylvania Press, 71–72.

2 Yasser A. Payne, Brooklynn K. Hitchens, and Darryl L. Chambers (2023) *Murder Town USA: Homicide, Structural Violence, and Activism in Wilmington.* New Brunswick, NJ: Rutgers University Press.

3 Hagley Museum and Library (n.d.-a) *A Separate Place: The Schools P. S. du Pont Built,* www.hagley.org (accessed 7/21/2023).

4 Robert L. Hayman (2009) "A History of Race in Delaware 1639–1950." In Robert L. Hayman Jr. and Leland Ware (eds.) *Choosing Equality: Essays and Narratives on the Desegregation Experience.* University Park: Pennsylvania State University Press, 21–73.

5 Gadsden (2013).

6 For a detailed history of Delaware's inconsistent record of racial oppression laws through 1950, see Hayman (2009).

7 Delaware.gov (2020) "Whipping Post to Be Removed from Public Display." June 30, 2020, https://news.delaware.gov.

8 See in particular, Gadsden (2013); Hayman and Ware (2009).

9 Hayman (2009), 54.

10 Hayman (2009).

11 "Primitive Delaware: State of the Whipping Post and 'Bound Children,' Awakened Now, Is Fightin Hard for Decent Schools." *New York Times Magazine*, November 30, 1919, 2.

12 Leland Ware (2009) "Educational Equity and *Brown v. Board of Education*: Fifty Years of School Desegregation in Delaware," in Hayman and Ware (2009), 119.

13 It is worth noting that the du Pont family has had an enormous legacy in the state. As far as I can tell as a New Castle County, Delaware, resident, most of our (excellent) state parks as well as several mansion museums are either former du Pont estates or gifted by a du Pont. It is also difficult to identify schools with only a single word (your child could go to A. I. du Pont Middle School, A. I. du Pont High School, P. S. du Pont Middle School, or H. B. du Pont Middle School, for example).

14 Hayman (2009), 61.

15 National Park Service (n.d.) "(H)our History Lesson: Pierre Samuel Du Pont's Delaware Experiment." www.nps.gov (accessed 7/20/2023); Hagley Museum and Library (n.d.-a); Hayman (2009), 61.

16 Hayman and Ware (2009).

17 Hagley Museum and Library (n.d.-a).

18 Hagley Museum and Library (n.d.-b) "A Separate Place: The Schools P.S. du Pont Built." YouTube, December 19, 2011, https://youtu.be/t1OO3i6UQEw; Gadsden (2013), 72.

19 Littleton Mitchell (2009) "Delaware Voices: Littleton Mitchell," in Hayman and Ware (2009), 163.

20 Mitchell (2009), 162.

21 Redding was admitted to the Delaware bar in 1929. See *News Journal* (1929) "Negro Is Admitted to Delaware Bar: L. L. Redding First of His Race to Practice Law in This State." March 22, 1929.

22 Hayman (2009), 59.

23 Courtesy of Delaware Public Archives.

24 See, for example, the 1956 "Southern Manifesto" signed by southern congressional delegates.

25 June Shagaloff (1955) "Desegregation of Public Schools in Delaware." *Journal of Negro Education* 24(3): 188–204.

26 Shagaloff (1955), 191.

27 Delaware has three counties. New Castle County, which I focus on, is in the north of the state and includes the urban area of Wilmington and its suburban ring. The two more southern counties have smaller populations and, other than the capital city of Dover, are more rural. Milford is on the border between the two more southern counties, Kent and Sussex.

28 Hagley Museum and Library (n.d.-b).

29 Gadsden (2013).

30 Shagaloff (1955), 193.

31 Gadsden (2013), 106.

32 The booklet, titled *Wilmington High School*, has a cover letter dated March 14, 1965, and appears to be written for a visiting committee. Found in DE State Archives.

33 For an excellent, detailed review of how residential segregation was a product of government policy, see Richard Rothstein (2017) *The Color of Law: A Forgotten History of How Our Government Segregated America*. New York: Liveright. See also Ta-Nehisi Coates (2014) "The Case for Reparations." *The Atlantic*, June 2014, www.theatlantic.com; Erickson (2016).

34 To learn more about Coker's lifelong activism, see Beth Miller (2021) "A Champion of Education and Racial Justice." *UD Daily*, April 23, 2021, www.udel.edu.

35 Wilmington High School (1965) *Wilmington High School*. Booklet, March 14, 1965, 4.

36 Jeffrey A. Raffel (1980) *The Politics of School Desegregation: The Metropolitan Remedy in Delaware*. Philadelphia: Temple University Press.

37 Folder 27, box 3, Littleton Mitchell Papers Special Collection, University of Delaware Library (accessed 8/18/2021).

38 Other than racial slurs and substituting italics for underlining, I have tried to reproduce the handwritten reports as accurately as possible.

39 James Baldwin (February–March 1965) *Integrated Education*, 9, quoted in Delmont (2016a), 6.

40 Rothstein (2017). For an analysis of contemporary housing discrimination, see Eva Rosen, Philip M. E. Garboden, and Jennifer E. Cossyleon (2021) "Racial Discrimination in Housing: How Landlords Use Algorithms and Home Visits to Screen Tenants." *American Sociological Review* 86: 787–822.

41 Raffel (1980).

42 This, for example, was suggested by Jeffrey Raffel, political scientist at the University of Delaware who advocated for more transparency and collection and reporting of school performance measures in the early 1970s (personal correspondence, December 2022).

43 Samuel Bowles and Herbert Gintis (1976) *Schooling in Capitalist America: Educational Reform and the Contradictions of Economic Life*. New York: Routledge and Kegan Paul; David B. Tyack (1974) *The One Best System: A History of American Urban Education*. Cambridge, MA: Harvard University Press.

44 Box 8005-007-2998, Delaware State Archives.

45 Kafka (2011).

46 C. L. Cleveland to Secondary Principals (1975) memo, January 26, 1975. Box 8182-000-012, Delaware State Archives.

47 "Proposed Program for School Aides (Monitors) for the Secondary Schools of Wilmington, Delaware" (1968) presented to Governor Charles L. Terry Jr., Mayor John E. Babriarz, and the Wilmington Board of Education, October 8, 1968. Box 8182-000-012, Delaware State Archives.

48 See Benjamin Fleury-Steiner (2012) *Disposable Heroes: The Betrayal of African American Veterans*. Lanham, MD: Rowman and Littlefield.

49 "Proposed Program for School Aides (Monitors)" (1968), 3.

50 "Proposed Program for School Aides (Monitors)" (1968), 3.

51 Joseph R. Biden (1973) "The Role of Educators in Solving the Drug Abuse Problem." *Congressional Record*, 93rd Cong. 2nd sess., Vol. 119, part 16, 19776–19779 (June 15, 1973).

52 See Kupchik (2010).

53 It was not until 1975–1976 that the Office for Civil Rights requested that all schools receiving federal funding maintain counts of numbers of students disciplined by race/ethnicity, sex, and school attended; see Acting Director Martin H. Gerry, Department of Health, Education, and Welfare (1975) *Memorandum for Chief State School Officers*. August 1975. University of Massachusetts Boston Archives.

54 E.g., Bowles and Gintis (1976).

CHAPTER 4. AN ISSUE ON DAY ONE

1 Rothstein (2017).

2 For an excellent summary of *Evans v. Buchanan*, see Dorothy R. Marengo (1978) *History of Evans v. Buchanan*. Sane of Delaware, January 11, 1978. "Desegregation of Delaware" collection, University of Delaware Archives.

3 Raffel (1980).

4 See Jeffrey A. Raffel (1975) *Analysis of Alternative Desegregation Plans and Reports of Meetings and Conferences*. Delaware Committee on the School Decision, June 13, 1975. Desegregation in Delaware Collection, Special Collections, University of Delaware Library.

5 Gloria Grantham (2019) "New Castle County School District." PowerPoint presentation for Colonial School District, July 16, 2019 (provided by the author); Jeffrey Raffel, personal correspondence, December 2022.

6 For an in-depth analysis of public opinion, see Raffel (1980).

7 Raffel (1980).

8 *Congressional Record*, 93rd Cong., 2nd sess., Vol. 120, No. 175, 39904 (December 14, 1974).

9 Johnson (2019).

10 Raffel (1980).

11 These concerns are enumerated in a letter from Robert B. Moore, chairman of the Delaware Committee on the School Decision, to Governor Tribbitt, February 10, 1975, in the Desegregation in Delaware Collection at the University of Delaware Library. See also the Delaware Committee on the School Decision's June 13, 1975, report *Analysis of Alternative Desegregation Plans and Reports of Meetings and Conferences*, in Desegregation in Delaware Collection, Special Collections, University of Delaware Library.

12   Gloria Grantham, Albert Miller, and Claire Fitzpatrick (1979) *An Interim Report of the Special Student Concerns Project: New Castle County Delaware.* Dover: Delaware Department of Community Affairs and Economic Development (report provided by author). See also Jane L. Dilley, chair of Delaware State Human Relations Commission (n.d.) *Desegregation: A Human Relations Commission Dilemma.* Desegregation in Delaware Collection, Special Collections, University of Delaware Library. As Grantham et al. (1979) report, these specialists were assigned to schools in teams of two, typically one male and one female and one white person and one person of color. They worked to facilitate desegregation, counsel students, and perform other tasks to enhance student life.

13   Department of Public Instruction (1978) *A Plan for the Reorganization and Desegregation of Designated School Districts in New Castle County, Delaware: A Four District Reorganization Plan,* Document No. 95-01/78/02/29, prepared for the State Board of Education, 33. Desegregation in Delaware Collection, Special Collections, University of Delaware Library.

14   Grantham et al. (1979), 52.

15   Grantham et al. (1979).

16   Grantham et al. (1979), 151.

17   Project Confidence Group (1980) *Final Report.* March 27, 1980. Delaware State Archives.

18   Project Confidence Group (1980), 13.

19   Charles M. Achilles, Esther Campbell, Charles Faires, Cynthia Jackson, and Oneida Martin (1982) *A Study of Issues Related to Discipline, Grouping and Tracking, and Special Education in New Castle County, Delaware, Desegregation Area: Volume I, General Issues and Introduction Discipline Study.* Dover: Delaware Department of Public Instruction, x. Delaware State Archives.

20   Achilles et al. (1982), 10.

21   *News Journal* (1978) "Deseg School Study Subject: Discipline against Minorities." June 29, 1978, 4.

22   Steve Goldberg (1980) "Schools Still Lack Uniform Discipline System." *Sunday News Journal,* March 16, 1980, A1, A5.

23   Coalition to Save Our Children v. State Board of Education, 901 F. Supp. 784 (1995).

24   Gary Orfield (2014) Foreword. In Arielle Niemeyer with Jennifer Ayscue, John Kuscera, Gary Orfield, and Genevieve Siegel-Hawley, *The Courts, the Legislature, and Delaware's Resegregation: A Report on School Segregation in Delaware 1989–2010.* Los Angeles: Civil Rights Project at UCLA, 7.

25   E.g., D. Bell (1980); Lewis and Diamond (2015).

26   Lewis and Diamond (2015).

27   Skiba and White (2022).

28   Goldberg (1980), A5.

29 Charles Bell (2020) "'Maybe If They Let Us Tell the Story I Wouldn't Have Been Suspended': Understanding Black Students' and Parents' Perceptions of School Discipline." *Children and Youth Services Review* 110: 1–11; Prudence L. Carter (2005) *Keepin' It Real: School Success beyond Black and White*. New York: Oxford University Press; Ferguson (2001); Ed Morris (2005) "'Tuck in That Shirt!': Race, Class, Gender, and Discipline in an Urban School." *Sociological Perspectives* 48: 25–48; Morris (2016); Victor M. Rios (2017) *Human Targets: Schools, Police, and the Criminalization of Latino Youth*. Chicago: University of Chicago Press.

30 California Legislative Information: Bill Information (n.d.) "SB-419 Pupil Discipline: Suspensions: Willful Defiance (2019–2020)." https://leginfo.legislature. ca.gov (accessed 8/31/2021).

31 Grantham et al. (1979), 52.

32 E.g., Alexander (2010).

33 Raffel (1980), 28.

34 Raffel (1980), 28.

35 This is discussed in the Hagley Museum and Library documentary *A Separate Place*. Importantly, evidence from other jurisdictions, particularly in the South and border South, shows that Black teachers were often a casualty of desegregation; once schools desegregated, many lost their jobs. See Deirdre Oakley, Jacob Stowell, and John R. Logan (2009) "The Impact of Desegregation on Black Teachers in the Metropolis, 1970–2000." *Ethnic and Racial Studies* 39: 1576–1598.

36 In my archival research, I saw no recognition of the irony that equity concerns resulted in a six-week teachers' strike only when the equity concern was of suburban (mostly white) teachers receiving less pay.

37 Raffel (1980).

38 Ray (2019), 40 (citations omitted).

39 Grantham et al. (1979), 89.

40 Simon (2007).

41 William Julius Wilson (1993) *The Truly Disadvantaged: The Inner City, the Underclass, and Public Policy*. Chicago: University of Chicago Press.

42 As Skiba and White (2022) note, since the 1970s, many people, especially school administrators, have responded to noted increases in Black students' suspension rates after desegregation by claiming that students are "suspended based on their actions and behaviors, not on the color of their skin" (13).

43 Raffel (1980), 22–23.

44 Raffel, personal correspondence, December 27, 2022.

45 Raffel, personal correspondence, August 11, 2021. Skiba and White (2022) note that a similar explanation has been offered by others as well.

46 Raffel, personal correspondence, December 27, 2022; see Grantham et al. (1979).

47 Coalition to Save Our Children v. State Bd. of Educ., 901 F. Supp. 784 (D. Del. 1995), items 274a–g.

48 E.g. Jacobsen et al. (2019); Rocque (2010); Rocque and Paternoster (2011); Skiba et al. (2014).

49 I was debating between this analogy and suggesting that (imagine your parent's voice when reading this) just because other school districts jump off bridges doesn't mean the New Castle County school district should jump off a bridge too.

50 Campbell (2014).

CHAPTER 5. THE CRADLE OF LIBERTY?

1 For details of the event, see National Constitution Center (2019) "On This Day in 1856: Violence on the U.S. Senate Floor." May 22, 2019, https://constitutioncenter. org; and US Senate (n.d.) "The Caning of Senator Charles Sumner." www.senate. gov (accessed 7/27/2022).

2 Zebulon Vance Miletsky (2017) "Before Busing: Boston's Long Movement for Civil Rights and the Legacy of Jim Crow in the 'Cradle of Liberty.'" *Journal of Urban History* 43: 204–217.

3 Miletsky (2017), 205.

4 Ronald P. Formisano (2004) *Boston against Busing: Race, Class, and Ethnicity in the 1960s and 1970s.* Chapel Hill: University of North Carolina Press, 12–13. Originally published 1991. I grew up in one of those suburban areas in the 1970s and 1980s. Go Natick, "Home of Champions"!

5 See Rothstein (2017).

6 Formisano (2004), 14.

7 Matthew Delmont (2016b) "The Lasting Legacy of the Busing Crisis." *The Atlantic*, March 29, 2016, 7; note that "imbalance" was defined as a school's student population consisting of more than 50 percent of a single racial/ethnic group.

8 Formisano (2004), 34.

9 Robert A. Dentler and Marvin B. Scott (1981) *Schools on Trial: An Inside Account of the Boston Desegregation Case.* Boston: Abt Books, 4–5.

10 Delmont (2016a).

11 Delmont (2016a), 3.

12 Paul Parks, Member Education Committee, Boston Branch NAACP (1963) "A Statement on the Education of Negro Children in the Boston Public Schools." May 22, 1963. Accessed from Northeastern University's library online collection.

13 PBS (2023) *Busing Battleground. American Experience.* Batson makes this statement at approximately seventeen minutes into the documentary.

14 Dentler and Scott (1981), 5.

15 Jonathan Kozol (1995) *Death at an Early Age: The Destruction of the Hearts and Minds of Negro Children in the Boston Public Schools.* New York: Plume. Originally published 1967.

16 E.g., Eesha Penharkar (2021) "He Taught about White Privilege and Got Fired. Now He's Fighting to Get His Job Back." *Education Week*, September 13, 2021, 3.

17 Kozol (1995) describes how the same parent was also upset that Kozol discussed the United Nations Human Rights Commission, presumably because the parent mistook the Human Rights Commission for the civil rights movement (195).

18 Delmont (2016a).

19 In the PBS documentary *Busing Battleground*, the civil rights leader Hubert Jones notes the irony that the June 11, 1963, Boston School Committee meeting, in which it refused to acknowledge the NAACP's concerns about de facto school segregation, occurred on the same day as George Wallace's infamous stand at the schoolhouse door and President John F. Kennedy's televised statement condemning school segregation.

20 See Formisano (2004); Delmont (2016a).

21 Russell James Dever (1981) "Equity in Discipline: Boston." EdD dissertation, Boston University School of Education.

22 Dentler and Scott (1981).

23 Formisano (2004) 44.

24 Delmont (2016a), 78.

25 Formisano (2004).

26 Formisano (2004), 46, table 3.1.

27 Dever (1981), 140–141.

28 Kozol (1995), 51.

29 Kozol (1995), 51.

30 Formisano (2004), 49.

31 Meeting of School Committee with Representatives of the Department of Health, Education, and Welfare (HEW) (1965). 15 Beacon Street, Boston, June 25, 1965, 12:15 p.m. Boston City Archives, 3–4.

32 Meeting of School Committee with Representatives of HEW (1965), 8–9.

33 Meeting of School Committee with Representatives of HEW (1965), 3.

34 Bonilla-Silva (2017).

35 Delmont (2016a), 5.

36 Formisano (2004).

37 See also Dentler and Scott (1981); Arthur L. Stinchcombe and D. Garth Taylor (1980) "On Democracy and School Integration." In Walter G. Stephan and Joe R. Feagin (eds.) *School Desegregation: Past, Present and Future*. New York: Plenum.

38 Matthew Kautz (2023) makes this very point when he describes how white politicians in Boston portrayed Black youth as inherently dangerous and criminal in order to justify state power and maintain white privilege in the Boston school system.

39 Kozol (1995), 135; Kozol cites statements printed in the *Boston Globe* on April 15 and 16, 1965, and in the *Boston Herald* on April 16, 1965.

40 Formisano (2004), 119.

41 Delmont (2016a), 172.

42 Boston Public Schools (1958) "Code of Discipline," 4. Boston City Archives.

43 The Massachusetts Supreme Court case *Davis v. City of Boston*, 133 Mass. 103 (1882), suggests the same conclusion. In this case, a student plaintiff challenged his exclusion from school. His exclusion came because he repeatedly refused to submit to corporal punishment, so the school repeatedly sent him home until he would submit to it. The court ruled that the school committee may exclude a child from school and that a parent can challenge this exclusion by petitioning the school committee but that plaintiffs are not entitled to damages when it occurs. See Caselaw Access Project (n.d.) "Davis v. City of Boston, 133 Mass. 103 (1882)." https://cite.case.law (accessed 7/31/2023). In other words, exclusion was possible as early as the 1880s, though corporal punishment was far more common.

44 Kozol (1995), 125.

45 Massachusetts banned the use of corporal punishment in schools soon thereafter. Thomas Mela, personal correspondence, December 2022; see also 193rd General Court of the Commonwealth of Massachusetts (n.d.) "General Laws: Part I, Title XII, Chapter 71, Section 37G." https://malegislature.gov (accessed 12/17/2022).

46 Boston Public Schools (1970) "Code of Discipline," 3. Boston City Archives.

47 Boston Public Library (n.d.) "Boston (City) Department Reports: School Department." https://guides.bpl.org (accessed 12/17/2022).

48 Boston Superintendent of Schools (1971–1972) *Annual Report*, 38. https://archive.org.

49 Kupchik (2010).

50 Using newspapers.com, search terms: ("school suspension" OR "suspended from school" OR ("school" AND "suspensions"))

51 National Association for the Advancement of Colored People (n.d.) home page. https://naacp.org (accessed 7/29/2022).

52 Task Force on Children Out of School (1970) *The Way We Go to School: The Exclusion of Children in Boston*. Boston: Beacon, iii.

53 Task Force on Children Out of School (1970), 5.

54 Task Force on Children Out of School (1970), 13.

55 Task Force on Children Out of School (1970), 44–45.

CHAPTER 6. UNPREPARED

1 Landsmark was on his way to a meeting and was not intending to participate in any protest when he was attacked. He suffered a broken nose but was not harmed more severely. See NPR (2016) "Life after Iconic 1976 Photo: The American Flag's Role in Racial Protest." September 18, 2016, ,www.npr.org.

2 US Commission on Civil Rights (1975) *Desegregating the Boston Public Schools: A Crisis in Civic Responsibility*. Washington, DC: US Commission on Civil Rights.

3 Details of this case and the decision have been reported and analyzed extensively in prior texts. See, e.g., Formisano (2004); Dentler and Scott (1981). My discussion here is not intended to be a full legal analysis but a summary of prior work that

allows me to move forward with my analysis of how resistance to desegregation shaped school punishment.

4 Formisano (2004), 69.

5 Dentler and Scott (1981), 15.

6 Formisano (2004), 70.

7 Dentler and Scott (1981), 21.

8 See Dentler and Scott (1981).

9 Raffel (1980).

10 Formisano (2004), 75; see also US Commission on Civil Rights (1975).

11 Formisano (2004) 77.

12 Megan E. Irons, Shelley Murphy, and Jenna Russell (2014) "History Rolled in on a Yellow School Bus." *Boston Globe*, September 6, 2014.

13 Morgan v. Kerrigan, 1 Cir. 1974, 509 F.2d 580.

14 Civil action No. 72-911-G, filed April 4, 1975.

15 After litigation, Judge Garrity declined to rule on this motion; Paul Weckstein, codirector, Center for Law and Education, personal correspondence, August 2022.

16 *Memorandum in Support of Plaintiffs' Motion for Further Relief Concerning Student Discipline*, April 4, 1975, Civil Action No. 72-911-G, 4.

17 *Memorandum in Support of Plaintiffs' Motion*, 3.

18 The founder and director of the Children's Defense Fund, Marian Wright Edelman, was personally involved in litigating this phase of the *Morgan* case. The Children's Defense Fund had, in 1974, published the influential report *Children Out of School in America* and, in 1975, the report that I discuss in chapter 1, *School Suspensions: Are They Helping Children?*

19 Cited in Kautz (2023), 11.

20 *Memorandum in Support of Plaintiffs' Motion*, table 6, 31.

21 *Memorandum in Support of Plaintiffs' Motion*, table 7, 33.

22 *Plaintiffs' Proposed Findings of Fact and Conclusions of Law*, Civil Action No. 72-911-G, June 22, 1976, 7. Boston City Archives.

23 Affidavit given March 31, 1975. Boston City Archives.

24 Affidavit given March 31, 1975. Boston City Archives.

25 Affidavit given November 14, 1975. University of Massachusetts Boston Archives.

26 Affidavit given November 13, 1975. University of Massachusetts Boston Archives.

27 Affidavit given June 19, 1975. Boston City Archives.

28 For an analysis of the role of Boston police in desegregation, and in particular how they acted in ways that enabled white segregationists' protests and discrimination against Black students, see Kautz (2023).

29 Affidavit given June 23, 1975. Boston City Archives.

30 Kautz (2023).

31 Letter from Faculty Senate of Charlestown High School to co-chairpersons of the CDAC VII (Community District Advisory Council, District VII), March 8, 1979. University of Massachusetts Boston Archives.

32 Memo from Paul Smith to Marian, Tim, Sandy, February 3, 1975, with the subject line "Boston Suspension Issue Data." University of Massachusetts Boston Archives.

33 Walter V. Robinson (1975) "Blacks Get 58% of School Suspensions: State Control Urged to Cut Hub Disparity." *Boston Evening Globe*, June 17, 1975, 3.

34 E.g., Formisano (2004), 129.

35 This quote comes from an interview by D. Monty Neill, which I describe in the following section; D. Monty Neil (1986a) Interview with Stephen R. Bing. University of Massachusetts, Amherst Library. https://credo.library.umass.edu (accessed 8/4/2021).

36 Dentler and Scott (1981), 27 (italics in original); see also Delmont (2016a).

37 I am very grateful to Thomas Mela and Liza Hirsch for pointing me toward this wonderful resource.

38 Neil (1986a).

39 D. Monty Neil (1986b) Interview with Albert Holland. University of Massachusetts, Amherst Library. https://credo.library.umass.edu. (accessed 8/4/2021)

40 D. Monty Neil (1986c) Interview with Jean McGuire. University of Massachusetts, Amherst Library. https://credo.library.umass.edu (accessed 8/4/2021). D. Monty Neil (1986d) Interview with Juanita Wade. University of Massachusetts, Amherst Library. https://credo.library.umass.edu (accessed 8/4/2021).

41 D. Monty Neil (1986e) Interview with Thomas I Atkins. University of Massachusetts, Amherst Library. https://credo.library.umass.edu (accessed 8/4/2021).

42 See chapter 1 for discussion of this report.

43 Letter and report from the Freedom House Institute on Schools and Education, Phase II Study Panel, to Judge Garrity, February 4, 1975. Northeastern University's special collection on Boston Public Schools Desegregation Project (available online).

44 This vague timeline comes from the Boston Public Schools website. Boston Public Schools (n.d.) "Department of Safety Services." www.bostonpublic-schools.org (accessed 8/4/2022); I could find no actual date on any other documentation.

45 Memorandum from James F. Walsh, Acting Chief of School Safety Services, to Superintendent Marion J. Fahey, June 16, 1978. Boston City Archives. Kaeser (1979) likewise mentions in-school suspension as an alternative that is "being developed" in many schools as of 1979.

46 Commission on Violence (1971) *Report on the Boston Public Schools*. Submitted to the Boston School Committee. Boston City Archives.

47 Commission on Violence (1971), 12.

48 Daryl Hellman (1983) *Analysis of Violence in the Boston Public Schools: Incident and Suspension Data*. Submitted to the Safe Schools Commission. Boston City Archives.

49 Hellman (1983), 17.
50 Hellman (1983), 22–24.

CONCLUSION

1 Russell Vought (2020) "Memorandum for the Heads of Executive Departments and Agencies: Training in the Federal Government." Office of Management and Budget, September 4, 2020, www.whitehouse.gov.

2 Char Adams (2021) "How Trump Ignited the Fight over Critical Race Theory in Schools." *NBC News*, May 10, 2021. www.nbcnews.com.

3 US Department of the Treasury (2022) "Racial Differences in Economic Security: The Racial Wealth Gap." September 15, 2022, https://home.treasury.gov.

4 Oliver and Shapiro (1995).

5 Thompson-Miller et al. (2015), 3.

6 Jordan G. Starck, Travis Riddle, Stacey Sinclair, and Natasha Warikoo (2020) "Teachers Are People Too: Examining the Racial Bias of Teachers Compared to Other American Adults." *Educational Research* 49: 273–284.

7 See Kupchik (2010); Simon (2007).

8 Based on annual calculations of enrollments from OCR data.

9 This is based on my calculations from OCR data, using discipline and enrollment data from Civil Rights Data Collection, Office for Civil Rights (n.d.) "2017–18 State and National Tables." https://ocrdata.ed.gov (accessed 1/19/2023).

10 Katie Johnston-Goodstar and Ross VeLure Roholt (2017) "'Our Kids Aren't Dropping Out; They're Being Pushed Out': Native American Students and Racial Microaggressions in Schools." *Journal of Ethnic & Cultural Diversity in Social Work* 26: 30–47; Teresa L. McCarty (2018) "Twelfth Annual 'Brown' Lecture in Educational Research: So That Any Child May Succeed: Indigenous Pathways toward Justice and the Promise of 'Brown'" *Educational Researcher* 47: 271–283.

11 Mendez, et al. v. Westminster School District of Orange County, et al., 64 F. Supp. 544, aff'd, 161 F.2d 774.

12 See Philippa Strum (2010) *Mendez v. Westminster: School Desegregation and Mexican-American Rights*. Lawrence: University Press of Kansas.

13 Burdge et al. (2014).

14 Matthew Ward (2023) "Enduring Consequences of Dehumanizing Institutions: Slavery and Contemporary Minority Social Control in the U.S. Northeast and South." *Social Problems* 70: 575–597.

15 McGhee (2021), xix (italics in original).

16 Mary Patillo (2021) "Black Advantage Vision: Flipping the Script on Racial Inequality Research." *Issues in Race & Society* 10: 5–39.

17 See Payne et al. (2023); Vanessa Siddle Walker (2018) *The Lost Education of Horace Tate: Uncovering the Hidden Heroes Who Fought for Justice in Schools*. New York: New Press.

18 Memo from Massachusetts Advocacy Council and Mayor's Office of Human Rights to Boston area school superintendents, January 1975, 1–2 (emphasis in original). University of Massachusetts Boston Archives.

19 See memo from Donna Crowley to the Community District Advisory Council-VII, February 27, 1979. University of Massachusetts Boston Archives.

20 Minutes of Secondary Principals' Meeting, October 9, 1969, sent from C. L. Cleveland to Secondary Principals. Delaware State Archives.

21 Baggett and Andrzejewski (2021), 140 (chapter written with Nanyamka A. Shukura, Sangah Lee, and Jasmine S. Betties).

22 Rashawn Ray and Andrew Perry (2020) *Why We Need Reparations for Black Americans.* Washington, DC: Brookings Institution.

23 Ray and Perry (2020).

24 Human Rights Watch (2021) "US: Congress Advances Slavery Reparations Bill." April 9, 2021, www.hrw.org.

25 Char Adams (2021) "Evanston Is the First U.S. City to Issue Slavery Reparations. Experts Say It's a Noble Start." *NBC News,* March 26, 2021, www.nbcnews.com.

26 Nkeichi Taifa (2023) *Reparations, in Our Lifetime.* New York: American Civil Liberties Union, www.aclu.org.

27 California Task Force to Study and Develop Reparation Proposals for African Americans (2023) "Policies Addressing Separate and Unequal Education." Chapter 23 of *Final Report.* June 2023. For the full report, see https://oag.ca.gov.

28 Subini Ancy Annamma (2015) "Whiteness as Property: Innocence and Ability in Teacher Education." *Urban Review* 47: 293–316, 310.

29 Wendy Fry, Erica Yee, and Rya Jetha (2023) "California Is the First State to Tackle Reparations for Black Residents. What That Really Means." *CalMatters,* September 12, 2023, https://calmatters.org.

30 For 2009–2010 data see https://ocrdata.ed.gov/estimations/2009-2010; for 2017–2018, see https://ocrdata.ed.gov/estimations/2017-2018

31 See US Department of Education (n.d.) "Joint 'Dear Colleague' Letter." www2.ed.gov (accessed 10/12/2023).

32 Warren (2022).

33 See D. Bell (1992).

34 Gregory Krieg (2016) "Donald Trump Reveals When He Thinks America Was Great." *CNN,* March 28, 2016. www.cnn.com.

35 Dustin Jones (2022) "What Is the 'Great Replacement' and How Is It Tied to the Buffalo Shooting Suspect?" *NPR,* May 16, 2022. www.npr.org.

36 Nicholas Confessore and Karen Yourish (2022) "A Fringe Conspiracy Theory, Fostered Online, Is Refashioned by the G.O.P." *New York Times,* May 15, 2022.

37 McGhee (2021).

APPENDIX

1 Northeastern University (n.d.) "Beyond Busing." https://bpsdesegregation.library. northeastern.edu (accessed 10/12/2023).

2 University of Massachusetts Amherst (n.d.) "D. Monty Neill Collection." http:// scua.library.umass.edu (accessed 10/12/2023)

3 Aaron Kupchik and Felicia A. Henry (2023) "Generations of Criminalization: Resistance to Desegregation and School Punishment." *Journal of Research in Crime and Delinquency* 60: 43–78.

4 The American Communities Project researchers linked to school districts using the 2000 NCES school district codes, with older districts allocated the year 2000 district code.

5 Details on the data set that do not appear on the project website (https://s4.ad. brown.edu/Projects/USSchools/) are based on personal communication with that project principal investigator, John Logan.

6 We take the natural log of the percentage punished +1, in order to avoid missing values for rates of 0.

7 We include the percentage of white students to account for the balance of white students versus all students of color, not just Black students, and to avoid multicollinearity that arises because of the high correlation between percentage of students who are Black.

8 See note 8 in chapter 2.

9 Initially models included a variable for percentage of district residents who identify as Black. We removed this variable because of multicollinearity.

10 US Census Bureau (n.d.) "Census Regions and Divisions of the United States." www2.census.gov (accessed 7/2/2021).

11 In preliminary models, we used three-level models that accounted for grouping within states. But because regional differences are more relevant, conceptually, we replaced this with fixed effects for region of the US. Substantive results are similar with either method.

INDEX

Page numbers in italics indicate Figures, Tables, and Photos.

ABOUT THE AUTHOR

AARON KUPCHIK is Professor of Sociology and Criminal Justice at the University of Delaware. His prior books include *Homeroom Security: School Discipline in an Age of Fear* and *The Real School Safety Problem: The Long-Term Consequences of Harsh School Punishment*. His book *Judging Juveniles: Prosecuting Adolescents in Adult and Juvenile Courts* is the winner of the 2007 American Society of Criminology Michael J. Hindelang Award for the Most Outstanding Contribution to Research in Criminology.

www.ingramcontent.com/pod-product-compliance
Ingram Content Group UK Ltd.
Pitfield, Milton Keynes, MK11 3LW, UK
UKHW031535160225
455130UK00003B/43/J
9781479821143

www.ingramcontent.com/pod-product-compliance
Ingram Content Group UK Ltd.
Pitfield, Milton Keynes, MK11 3LW, UK
UKHW031535160225
455130UK00003B/43/J

9 781479 821143